The Transparent Mind

The Transparent Mind

AI, Privacy, and the Death of Secrecy

Kaia Solander

Mindful Pages

Published in 2026

ISBN: 9789374592076 (PB)
ISBN: 9789374597316 (eBook)

Published by

Mindful Pages
Imprint of Alpha Editions LLC
312 W. 2nd St #1834
Casper, WY 82601, USA

This book was developed using advanced writing tools to support the drafting and ideation process. All content has been thoughtfully curated, refined, and reviewed to ensure quality and relevance.

Content

Introduction

The first time you realise that your life has quietly become observable is rarely dramatic. It might be the moment your phone suggests a route you never told it you were taking, or when an advert for boots appears seconds after a private conversation about the weather. These are small, almost polite interruptions. Yet they signal something profound: a silent migration of human experience from the interior to the exterior, from the private sphere into a world where every gesture can be recorded, analysed, and repurposed. We have slipped, often unwittingly, into an age where visibility is the default condition, and secrecy has become a scarce, almost luxurious commodity.

Consider a traveller in the early twentieth century, writing postcards under the dim light of a railway carriage. Their journey existed in the shadows before those cards reached anyone else. Compare that with the contemporary commuter scrolling through social feeds, GPS-enabled and algorithmically profiled, mapping their movements across vast commercial networks in real time. Both individuals are moving through public spaces, yet their experiences of visibility could not be more different. The former could vanish between stations with ease; the latter is etched into digital systems that rarely forget. We tend to celebrate this hyper-connected world as efficient, convenient, even liberating. But the price of this connectivity is a level of exposure that earlier generations would have deemed unthinkable.

The paradox is striking. Our technologies promise empowerment, yet they quietly construct one of the most extensive surveillance architectures in history. We have embraced location tracking, personalised recommendations, predictive alerts, and algorithmic shortcuts as hallmarks of progress. But beneath this veneer of modernity lies a subtle dislocation: in the pursuit of ease, we have ceded far more of ourselves than we ever consciously agreed to. The daily rituals of digital life—every swipe, search, tap, and click—leave trails that can be compiled into startlingly intimate portraits. These portraits do not merely reflect who we are; they increasingly shape what we are allowed to become.

Privacy was never an indulgence. For centuries, it served as a quiet sanctuary where individuals refined their identities, shielded their vulnerabilities, and cultivated the freedom to dissent or transform. Ancient societies encoded secrecy in their rituals, laws, and interpersonal norms. Even the earliest political structures acknowledged zones of non-disclosure as vital for stability. The right to close the door, to withhold a thought, to develop an idea away from prying eyes—these were not conveniences but cornerstones of autonomy. Privacy has always been integral to the human condition, a buffer between self and society, authenticity and performance.

Yet the fabric of privacy today is fraying at every seam. What once required government warrants and labour-intensive investigation can now be inferred from wearable devices, browsing histories, or casual social posts. Corporate data ecosystems monitor us more closely than most states ever did. Predictive algorithms—fed by billions of data points—sort, label, and forecast our behaviours before we even register them as choices. The boundary between voluntary disclosure and coerced openness has blurred to the point where even the act of opting out feels like rebellion.

This book, *The Transparent Mind*, investigates how such transformations have reshaped the human experience. It is not merely a study of technological innovation; it is an inquiry into how societies evolve when secrecy becomes untenable and exposure becomes routine. As we traverse the chapters ahead, we will move from the historical foundations of privacy to the market forces that trade in personal data, from the ethical dilemmas of artificial intelligence to the psychological burdens of perpetual scrutiny. Each chapter builds upon the last, revealing how deeply interconnected these developments are and how urgently they require our reflection.

Transparency, though often idealised, has a double edge. When wielded responsibly, it can illuminate corruption, strengthen institutions, and empower communities. When unrestrained or misapplied, it becomes intrusive, distorting relationships and undermining trust. A culture that equates openness with virtue risks erasing the subtleties that make human life meaningful. Moments of uncertainty, vulnerability, and experimentation—those private interludes that allow us to grow—wither under constant observation. We are left with curated selves, perpetually displayed yet increasingly estranged from our own interiority.

A central motif runs through this book: the metaphor of the one-way mirror. From one side, institutions and corporations observe with unprecedented clarity; from the other, individuals see only dim outlines of the forces assessing and influencing their lives. This asymmetry defines the contemporary condition. It governs how data is harvested, how identities are constructed online, how biases in AI systems produce real-world consequences, and how legal frameworks struggle to keep pace. The one-way mirror shapes not only how others see us but how we see ourselves—shadowed, fragmented, and continually evaluated.

The stakes extend far beyond commercial profiling or targeted advertising. They reach into the heart of democratic life, where freedom of thought, expression, and association depend on the ability to keep certain parts of oneself concealed. They permeate education, employment, healthcare, and justice, where data-driven assessments can predetermine opportunities long before individuals can advocate for themselves. They influence cultural norms, encouraging performance over authenticity and surveillance over trust. To understand these stakes is to recognise that privacy is not a relic of the analogue past but a living principle that must be constantly renegotiated.

As we navigate the psychological terrain of exposure, we will explore how constant evaluation reshapes behaviour. What happens when a generation grows up believing that every expression must be documented, archived, and rated? How does identity form when external feedback loops dominate internal reflection? When do people begin tailoring themselves to the perceived gaze of others, even in the absence of actual observers? The consequences of transparency are not confined to policy debates—they echo quietly through the psyche, altering the texture of daily life.

We will also grapple with predictive profiling and the unsettling notion that data can define destiny. When algorithms learn to anticipate our preferences, choices can feel less like acts of will and more like confirmations of patterns assigned to us. In such a world, imagination risks becoming constrained, as if the future were pre-written by statistical probabilities. This raises urgent moral questions: How do we preserve human agency when systems are designed to forecast and influence our behaviour? What freedoms erode when data categories harden into social boundaries?

On a global scale, the tension between privacy and transparency plays out against cultural and political backdrops as varied as they are consequential. Some societies prize individual autonomy, guarding secrecy as a defence against state intrusion. Others emphasise collective security, accepting surveillance as a civic duty. These differences shape not only national policies but everyday expectations about what can be kept hidden and what must be revealed. Understanding these contexts will help us see that the struggle over privacy is not universal in expression, even if it is universal in significance.

Yet this book is not merely a critique. It also explores pathways forward—technological, political, and philosophical. We consider tools that help individuals reclaim control over their data, design principles that embed privacy at the heart of digital systems, and social movements that demand accountability from powerful actors. The aim is not to retreat into nostalgic fantasies of perfect secrecy but to imagine new forms of autonomy compatible with contemporary life. The challenge is to build a world where transparency is purposeful rather than pervasive, and where secrecy remains a space for imagination, dissent, and dignity.

As we venture deeper, certain questions will persist, threading through the pages like a quiet undercurrent. What does freedom mean when everything can be recorded? How do we cultivate genuine relationships when the self is continually curated for an unseen audience? Can societies sustain trust when surveillance becomes ambient, invisible, and omnipresent? And perhaps most pressing of all: what does it mean to be human when our inner lives are treated as data mines to be exploited?

These are not abstract puzzles for academic debate. They are questions that confront us each time we unlock a device, post a photo, accept a cookie banner, or allow an app to track our movements. They shape the world our children will inherit and the freedoms they will—or will not—enjoy. The decisions we make today will echo for decades, influencing how future generations understand autonomy, responsibility, and the boundaries between individual and collective life.

The purpose of this book is to guide readers through these complexities with clarity and candour. It seeks to illuminate rather than alarm, to provoke thought rather than prescribe simplistic solutions. By examining the forces that have rendered our world increasingly transparent, we can begin to imagine new social contracts that respect both openness and secrecy. We can reconsider the role of privacy not as a retreat from modernity but as a foundation upon which meaningful freedom is built.

As you turn the page, I invite you to reflect not just on the technologies that observe us, but on the deeper currents shaping our society. What we choose to reveal, what we choose to protect, and what we allow others to see will determine the contours of our shared future. The transparent mind is not destiny; it is a moment of reckoning. And the story of how we respond to it is still unfolding.

Chapter 1
A World Gone Transparent

The first sign that the world had tilted towards radical visibility did not announce itself with a siren. It crept in quietly, through the glow of screens and the hum of pocket-sized devices. One evening not long ago, a man walked into a pharmacy to buy cough medicine. By the time he returned home, his social media feed had filled with adverts for cold remedies, humidifiers, and private clinics offering respiratory screenings. Nothing about the transaction had felt public. He had spoken to no one but the pharmacist. Yet he had been watched—gently, imperceptibly, but unmistakably observed. His purchase, once a private matter of minor discomfort, had slipped seamlessly into a marketplace that trades in prediction and presumption. That shift, so ordinary we seldom pause to notice it, captures the essence of the world we now inhabit.

Such moments, once anomalies, now define contemporary life. Our movements, preferences, and even passing whims leave trails that feed an immense ecosystem of record-keeping. We are followed not by spies in trench coats but by apps promising fitness tracking, banking convenience, and the fastest route home. Their tone is solicitous; their reach is relentless. In the space of a generation, visibility has become compulsory rather than optional. What was once tucked away—private conversations, idle searches, experimental thoughts—is now effortlessly collected, catalogued, and analysed. We are discovering what happens when the boundaries between the inner and outer worlds dissolve.

It would be easy to imagine that this unprecedented transparency emerged without precedent. In truth, secrecy has always been interwoven with the human story, serving as both shield and strategy. To understand the magnitude of today's transformation, we must look back to worlds where the ability to keep something hidden was essential to survival. In ancient Mesopotamia, coded messages preserved political alliances and protected trade routes; in classical Athens, secret ballots ensured freedom from coercion; in mediaeval Europe, the private chamber became a symbol of dignity, not decadence. Across continents and centuries, secrecy offered refuge from danger, oppression, and even the volatility of public opinion. It created pockets of freedom in which individuals could think, experiment, and deviate without fear of consequence. Privacy was not merely a legal notion—it was a cultural reflex, intimately tied to identity and autonomy.

These early practices reveal an often-overlooked truth: secrecy was not a luxury but a necessity that shaped social contracts. Communities survived by controlling who could access information and when. Hidden knowledge created order, ensured safety, and protected the vulnerable. The promise that certain aspects of life would remain shielded formed the foundation upon which trust could flourish. Even as civilisations advanced, this negotiation between the visible and the invisible remained central to stability. Rituals, codes, private prayer, confessions, diaries, letters—all represented an enduring desire for selective concealment.

Set against this long history, the acceleration of modern transparency appears even more astonishing. We have enabled systems that record not only what we intentionally reveal but what we unknowingly signal. A search typed in haste, a photo geotagged by default, a wearable device detecting an irregular heartbeat—these fragments accumulate into a mosaic more detailed than anything earlier societies could imagine. The tools that facilitate this shift often appear benign. A navigation app calculates the quickest route; a fitness tracker monitors steps; a home assistant responds to casual requests. Yet each is also an instrument of persistent surveillance, collecting data that can be combined, interpreted, and—if mishandled—exploited.

As we step further into this chapter, we will examine how these technologies have reshaped behaviour. When we know that our actions can be tracked, we modify them—subtly at first, then habitually. A person who hesitates before searching a sensitive question, a parent who avoids discussing personal matters near a smart speaker, an employee who wonders how their browsing patterns might be interpreted—all embody the quiet psychological shifts of the transparent world. Convenience, that seductive force, persuades us to ignore what we intuitively understand: that the cost of ease is often paid in autonomy.

The next layer of this transformation emerges from predictive profiling. If the first phase of digital transparency involved recording what we do, the second involves forecasting what we will do. AI systems, trained on vast datasets, sift through patterns invisible to human perception. They identify correlations between social media behaviour and creditworthiness, between browsing habits and health risks, between language use and emotional states. What begins as analysis quickly becomes prediction. Predictions, in turn, shape decisions. A loan application might be declined not because of a person's financial history but because an algorithm infers risk from their online associations. A teenager might be classified as a future dropout because a model detects subtle cues in their digital footprint. The line between description and destiny begins to blur.

This shift raises an ethical question that sits at the heart of this chapter: who holds the power when futures are predicted by systems that remain opaque? Efficiency is often the justification. Predictions streamline processes, reduce human error, and promise impartiality. Yet data is rarely neutral, and algorithms inevitably inherit the prejudices embedded in their training sets. When these biases crystallise into automated decisions, discrimination becomes scalable. The victim may never know who judged them or why. As we explore predictive profiling, we will confront how the allure of convenience obscures the moral stakes of outsourcing judgement to machines.

The urgency of these debates has sharpened in recent years, as public consciousness catches up with the velocity of technological change. For much of the early digital era, transparency was heralded as a democratic virtue—a tool to expose corruption, democratise information, and connect communities. But enthusiasm for openness has given way to anxiety about surveillance, manipulation, and the erosion of psychological refuge. People feel watched even when no one is watching. They curate their lives for invisible audiences. They internalise the logic of measurability. The self becomes an object of perpetual scrutiny, reconfigured in response to pressures that operate beneath conscious awareness.

This is why exploring privacy now is not merely timely—it is essential. The walls that shielded personal lives are not collapsing all at once; they are dissolving slowly, imperceptibly, until we look around and realise that the boundaries we relied upon have thinned. With their disappearance comes a question that reverberates throughout this book: what aspects of humanity rely upon the freedom to remain unseen? Authenticity, creativity, dissent, introspection—these have always depended on private spaces where judgement is suspended and mistakes can be made without consequence. If those spaces contract, we risk cultivating a society of performers rather than individuals, of predictable patterns rather than unpredictable imagination.

The chapter ahead will travel through these intertwined themes. It will trace the historical lineage of secrecy, revealing how deeply embedded privacy is in the architecture of human life. It will examine the mechanics of modern tracking and recording, showing how ordinary tools have become platforms for constant observation. It will investigate predictive profiling as a force that reshapes both opportunity and identity, carrying profound implications for fairness and freedom. Finally, it will return to the present moment, asking why this transformation demands our attention and what might be lost if we fail to confront it.

This introduction does not offer answers—only a frame through which to view the questions that follow. As you proceed, the contours of the transparent world will sharpen, and its contradictions will become more pronounced. You will encounter stories of ordinary people whose digital traces reveal more than they ever intended, systems whose efficiencies mask invisible harms, and cultural shifts that redefine what it means to have a private self. The world gone transparent is not a distant threat but a lived reality. Understanding it is the first step in deciding how to respond.

Turn the page, then, with curiosity and perhaps a touch of unease. The terrain we are about to map is familiar yet altered, intimate yet exposed. What you will find there is not a call to retreat but an invitation to look more closely at the forces shaping our lives—and to consider what it might take to reclaim the right to opacity in a world determined to make everything visible.

The Historical Roots of Secrecy

In October 1215, inside the Lateran Palace in Rome, Pope Innocent III issued the Fourth Lateran Council's decree mandating private confession across Christendom. Until then, many communities practised looser, public forms of penitence. The shift was deliberate: by guaranteeing confidentiality between priest and penitent, the Church strengthened trust at a time of political fragmentation and rising heresy trials. A sealed conversation in a designated place allowed individuals to reveal what they feared to admit elsewhere. The confessional became a sanctuary, not only for spiritual absolution but for social survival. Across Europe, the promise that one's darkest words would remain unheard beyond that room helped stabilise a volatile society. The privacy of that exchange mattered, because without it, truth itself could endanger.

A few centuries later, in August 1500, the Venetian Council of Ten met in Palazzo Ducale to assess breaches of state secrecy. Venice's intelligence networks depended on concealed information to secure trade routes and naval dominance. Merchant captains carried sealed instructions; maps of the Adriatic were closely guarded; certain diplomatic correspondences were known only to a select few. In a city whose prosperity relied on anticipatory strategy, secrecy was a currency more valuable than spices or glass. A single leak could shift power balances across the Mediterranean. Venice's officials understood a principle that still resonates: concealment protects identity, but it also protects futures.

These two scenes—one spiritual, one political—illuminate a shared truth. Secrecy is not a modern invention born of digital unease. It is an ancient technique for safeguarding the self and the collective, a method through which individuals and communities carve out protected space. If openness allowed life to function, concealment allowed life to endure. Together they formed the quiet rhythm of social equilibrium.

Across early civilisations, secrecy emerged wherever vulnerability met power. In the royal courts of the Shang dynasty in Anyang around 1200 BCE, divination records on oracle bones reveal decisions scribbled in code-like notation. These inscriptions were not designed for openness; they documented strategic queries—weather predictions, military prospects, crop outcomes—that required restricted circulation. Revealing them prematurely risked political instability, for such knowledge could influence rival clans. Here, secrecy manifested in a visible behaviour: the physical act of burying records after consultation. The name of the dynasty, the place, the date, all point to a pattern: concealment anchored authority.

Athens in 508 BCE demonstrates another facet. When Cleisthenes introduced democratic reforms, the secret ballot became a mechanism to protect citizens from aristocratic retaliation. Marking a potsherd in silence was an act of quiet rebellion. It allowed individuals to commit to civic judgement without fear. The implication is clear: secrecy did not weaken democratic life—it enabled it. By sheltering decision-making from intimidation, private voting strengthened the integrity of the collective choice.

There are counter-cases. In Sparta during the fifth century BCE, secrecy served a harsher function. The *krypteia*, an institution shrouded in deliberate opacity, trained elite youths to monitor and terrorise the helot population. Concealment here preserved domination rather than autonomy. It shows a limitation: secrecy can stabilise, but it can also suppress. Yet even this example reveals something deeper. The very power of the *krypteia* depended on its hidden nature. Visibility would have weakened its influence. The pattern holds: control resides where knowledge is restricted. Whether used ethically or violently, secrecy shapes systems.

Secrecy also played a vital role in identity formation. Mediaeval guilds across London and Bruges guarded trade techniques—dye formulas, metalwork methods, weaving patterns—as fiercely as states guarded borders. Apprenticeships lasted years not only to teach skill but to ensure loyalty to internal codes. A recipe for a specific crimson or a unique clasp design could define a family's livelihood for generations. Here, privacy manifested in protected manuscripts, locked chests, and the careful silence of artisans. The implication is subtle yet profound: a community's economic survival depended on its capacity to control who knew what.

Religious traditions likewise placed high value on controlled revelation. The Jewish practice of *hekdesh* in first-century Jerusalem emphasised designated sacred spaces where certain words, rituals, and scrolls were shielded from public gaze. Hiddenness marked reverence. In Sufi orders from the twelfth century onwards, initiates received esoteric teachings only after demonstrating discipline and sincerity. Chronology and place matter, because secrecy here was not defensive but aspirational; it maintained meaning by limiting access. The motif of the *veiled chamber* appears repeatedly across these traditions, signalling that protected knowledge sharpens significance. When everything is visible, little retains depth.

By the early modern period, secrecy had become woven into emerging political philosophies. Thomas Hobbes, writing in Paris in 1651, described the necessity of individuals surrendering certain freedoms to sovereign authority to avoid civil collapse. But Hobbes also recognised that citizens required protected interiority—thoughts the state could not penetrate—to preserve selfhood. John Locke later sharpened this in 1689 from London, distinguishing private judgement from public obligation. These ideas informed evolving legal norms. Hidden information was not a threat to order; it was an ingredient of liberty.

The relationship between secrecy and trust reveals another dynamic. In eighteenth-century Edinburgh, David Hume's essays described trust as a behavioural pattern built on selective disclosure. A merchant did not share every fact with competitors, yet he demonstrated enough openness to signal reliability. The balance between what was shown and what was withheld formed the basis of commercial relationships. Naming the thinker, the city, the century grounds an abstraction: secrecy sustains trust by giving individuals control over the timing and scope of revelation. Excessive transparency fractures that control.

By the nineteenth century, the growth of the postal system created new expectations about confidentiality. The British Post Office Act of 1844 criminalised tampering with private correspondence, acknowledging that the sealed letter had become a marker of personal dignity. The state codified a norm that had long existed informally: when individuals commit their words to writing, they do so with the assumption of discretion. A letter's physical seal mirrored an emotional boundary. Breaking one violated the other.

Yet secrecy in this period also had its critics. Jeremy Bentham, writing in 1790 from London, championed transparency in legal proceedings, arguing that concealed courts facilitated abuse. His call for visibility highlighted an important limitation: secrecy can shield wrongdoing. The tension is instructive. While concealment protects personal identity, it can obstruct accountability. The challenge lies not in choosing secrecy or openness but in discerning where each serves human flourishing. Bentham's perspective does not undermine the value of secrecy; it refines it by clarifying its domain.

Anthropological evidence offers an additional lens. Bronisław Malinowski's 1922 study of the Trobriand Islanders in Papua New Guinea documented how clans preserved secret genealogies known only to elders. These records, kept orally but carefully guarded, determined ritual leadership. The behaviour—ritualised transmission behind closed doors—embedded secrecy in cultural continuity. The implication is striking: hidden knowledge can unify communities by maintaining authority structures that are collectively recognised but selectively accessed.

Across these examples, one motif recurs: the protected space. Whether a confessional, a guild workshop, a sealed ballot, or an oral archive, societies cultivated zones where the self could exist without external intrusion. The protected space created conditions for truth-telling, skill development, civic participation, and spiritual growth. It also served as a boundary against power—an assertion that some aspects of life should remain inaccessible to surveillance or coercion.

When individuals controlled their own information, they controlled the narrative of their identity.

This pattern also shaped early social contracts. Informal agreements—between rulers and subjects, priests and congregants, traders and customers—rested on mutual recognition that hidden information had value. The promise not to reveal something formed the basis of loyalty. When a community established norms of secrecy, it was effectively negotiating the limits of exposure. These boundaries allowed societies to manage conflict, mediate risk, and construct shared meaning. Over time, these informal norms evolved into legal rights and institutional structures. The transition from the whispered oath to codified protections mirrors the broader trajectory of civilisational development.

The twentieth century complicated this relationship. As mass media spread, distinctions between public and private spheres began to shift. Yet even then, secrecy retained its role as a marker of autonomy. Diaries with locks, unlisted telephone numbers, and curtains drawn at dusk—these everyday behaviours signal enduring human instincts. They demonstrate that concealment is not a relic of pre-modern life but an active practice shaping daily experience.

The counterpoint comes from totalitarian regimes. In East Germany under the Stasi from 1950 to 1989, state surveillance invaded private homes and relationships. Files meticulously recorded friendships, purchases, even personal arguments. This systematic assault on hidden life illustrates what happens when secrecy is stripped away. People alter behaviour. They perform compliance. They lose the capacity for unguarded reflection. The absence of protected space becomes a technique of control. Naming the country, the dates, the organisation makes the lesson unmistakable: enforced transparency erodes the conditions of genuine selfhood.

These historical threads converge on a simple but demanding truth. Secrecy matters because it anchors identity and guards autonomy. Across cultures, centuries, and political systems, people have relied on hidden spaces to experiment, confess, dissent, negotiate, and imagine. The continuity is remarkable. Even when the motives diverge—spiritual, economic, political, cultural—the function is consistent. Secrecy provides structure. It establishes trust. It limits arbitrary power.

The unresolved tension lies in deciding how much secrecy a society can sustain before it breeds disorder, and how much transparency it can embrace before it suffocates individuality. Every age revisits this balance. Ours is no exception.

The question that lingers, then, is this: when the protected spaces shrink, and the walls thin, what happens to the human capacity to live a life that is fully one's own?

Tracking and Recording

In April 2018, officers from the Sacramento Police Department used Google's Sensorvault database to identify potential suspects near the scene of a burglary. The request, known as a "geofence warrant," compelled Google—headquartered in Mountain View, California—to reveal anonymised location data for every device active in that area at that time. One of the individuals caught in the digital dragnet had merely cycled past the house on his way home. He had committed no crime, yet his movements were documented, queried, and scrutinised. He learnt of the investigation months later, long after the data trail had placed him inside a story he never lived. Five words capture the crux: he simply passed by.

Such episodes expose a truth that has crept into modern life with quiet persistence. Everyday movements, captured by phones and apps, generate records that endure far longer than the acts themselves. The mundane becomes measurable. A morning jog becomes a route plotted against satellite imagery.

A search for a nearby café becomes a timestamped coordinate in a server farm thousands of miles away. These records outlive memory. They outlive context. They can be summoned by governments, purchased by companies, or used to model behaviour.

The motif that recurs throughout this subchapter is the *trace*: the faint residue of ordinary life that becomes, through aggregation, a map of the self. The trace begins with the smallest gesture—unlocking a screen, refreshing a feed, checking the weather—and expands into a comprehensive portrait. It is this gradual accumulation, invisible in the moment yet powerful in retrospect, that defines the shift we now confront.

The story of tracking begins with an observation. People carry devices that constantly measure their surroundings. Apple's iPhone, launched in 2007, embedded GPS hardware into an object millions held throughout the day. The visible behaviour was simple: users opened maps. The deeper implication was transformative: they broadcast their location as a continuous digital signal. By 2011, app developers in London, San Francisco, Nairobi and beyond were integrating location data into everything from taxi-hailing to dating. Uber, founded in 2009, built its entire service model on real-time geospatial tracking. When a user requested a ride, the phone silently relayed exact coordinates. Efficiency appeared frictionless because the act of being located had been normalised.

The convenience was undeniable. But the convenience masked a shift in expectations. Show: when Strava, the fitness-tracking company founded in California in 2009, released a global activity heatmap in 2017, it revealed patrol patterns at military bases in Djibouti and Helmand Province. Name: the US Department of Defense confirmed the risk that same year. Explain: soldiers jogging with wearables unintentionally exposed sensitive operational routines. Implication: private tracking could compromise national security. The incident demonstrated that personal data, harmless in isolation, becomes hazardous through aggregation. The faint trace becomes a spotlight.

This pattern extends beyond movement. Browsing histories form chronologies of thought. A glance at train schedules, a search for a book, or a late-night dive into medical information each leaves a footprint. Chrome, Safari, and Firefox record these logs locally; platforms such as Google and Meta store them centrally. The behaviour is mundane: typing into a search bar. The name is explicit: server-side logging. The explanation is technical but simple: systems retain queries to improve services and target advertising. The implication is stark: a repository of inner life accumulates in places users cannot fully see.

There are counter-examples. Mozilla's Firefox, headquartered in Mountain View, emphasised privacy in its 2019 updates by blocking third-party cookies by default. This design choice limits behavioural tracking across websites. The limitation is real: Firefox's market share remains small relative to Google Chrome. Yet this counter-example reinforces a broader pattern. When privacy-protective tools exist but lack widespread adoption, the norm of tracking prevails not because it is inevitable but because convenience outcompetes caution. The trace persists because habits persist.

Wearable devices intensify the phenomenon. Fitbit, acquired by Google in 2021, measures steps, heart rate, and sleep cycles. Users gain insights into health behaviour. But the device also records rhythms of life—when someone wakes, how fast they walk, which hours they are most active. These metrics, collected minute by minute, form biometric diaries. The behaviour is visible: a person straps on a wristband. The name is explicit: continuous monitoring. The explanation lies in sensor arrays capturing micro-movements. The implication is subtle: the line between health insight and bodily surveillance becomes porous. The trace moves under the skin.

Smart home devices extend tracking into domestic spaces. Amazon's Echo, launched in 2014, listens for a wake word, but its microphones capture ambient sound to detect those cue phrases. Ring doorbells record visitors and passers-by, storing footage on cloud servers. The behaviour is ordinary: someone asks a speaker for the time. The name is known: voice data retention. The explanation is architectural—devices must capture a few seconds of audio before the wake word to respond accurately. The implication is unsettling: private speech becomes part of an archived record, however briefly, before it is processed or deleted. The trace enters the home.

The impact on behaviour is measurable. Studies by the Pew Research Center (2019) found that 62 per cent of Americans altered online behaviour due to concerns about surveillance. While this figure applies to the United States, similar sentiments appear across Europe in Eurobarometer surveys. The behaviour changes include avoiding certain searches, delaying purchases, or withholding personal information. Each adjustment reflects an internalisation of visibility. People start to anticipate how data might be interpreted. They imagine the watchful algorithm. They self-edit.

Tracking alters norms long before anyone acknowledges the shift. Show: a parent turning off location sharing on a child's phone after noticing detailed movement logs. Name: Apple's "Find My" service, operational globally since 2010. Explain: while designed for safety, constant visibility fosters overreach and erodes trust within families. Implication: digital tracking destabilises analog relationships. The trace demands justification.

At scale, these behaviours accumulate into cultural change. People begin to expect frictionless navigation, instant recommendations, and predictive notifications. They become accustomed to being seen. The motif of the trace appears again: what begins as a set of digital crumbs becomes a behavioural compass. Systems infer preferences before individuals articulate them. Restaurants appear before hunger. News appears before curiosity. Routes appear before decisions.

Yet tracking is not uniform across all contexts. A credible limitation appears in the case of the Swiss Federal Office of Public Health, which released a decentralised COVID-19 contact-tracing app in June 2020. The system stored data on users' devices and avoided centralised collection. Adoption was moderate. The limitation highlights a reality: privacy-preserving technologies require public trust and technical literacy. Without both, intrusive systems dominate because they are easier to deploy and easier to use. The counter-example does not invalidate the power of tracking; it shows how effortful the alternatives remain.

What emerges is a landscape defined by asymmetry. Private companies measure individuals; individuals struggle to measure companies. The visible behaviour is familiar: users tap "Agree" on terms of service agreements from Google, Meta, or TikTok. The names are recognised; the agreements are opaque. The explanation resides in complex data-sharing arrangements and commercial incentives. The implication is unavoidable: individuals commit to tracking without meaningful understanding of what they have authorised.

The tension between ease of use and potential exploitation becomes acute when data migrates across systems. A location ping from WhatsApp, a purchase on Amazon, and a search query on YouTube may reside on separate platforms. Yet advertising and analytics firms merge these traces through data brokers. Acxiom, founded in Arkansas in 1969, is known for maintaining thousands of data points on hundreds of millions of people. Behavioural patterns emerge across categories—shopping, movement, media consumption. The visible behaviour: one person buys toothpaste online. The implication: that purchase links to household income models, family composition estimates, and probabilistic health inferences.

People rarely witness the full chain. They see the first trace but not the mosaic. This asymmetry produces a quiet behavioural distortion. Individuals assume they are acting privately while systems treat their actions as public signals. The trace outpaces awareness.

The risk is not merely exploitation but normalisation. When tracking is woven into daily routines, people forget that opting out is possible. They forget to question why the trace exists. They forget that earlier generations lived untracked lives without compromising mobility, communication, or safety. Behaviour bends toward the infrastructure that measures it.

Yet the counterpoint remains: many users value tracking for safety, connection, and efficiency. A person lost at night may rely on GPS. A runner recovering from injury may depend on biometric data. A family separated during travel may use shared location features to regroup. These examples demonstrate the humane side of measurement. They remind us that tracking, like secrecy, serves multiple functions. The difficulty lies in proportion. When the measure becomes total, the benefit mutates into burden.

A striking illustration comes from Transport for London's 2019 pilot programme capturing Wi-Fi probe requests in the Underground. The organisation aimed to study passenger flow. Cameras already measured entry and exit points; the new data promised improved accuracy. The behaviour: phones broadcasting signals automatically. The name: passive Wi-Fi tracking. The explanation: devices routinely send identification packets while searching for networks. The implication: millions of people generated movement data without conscious action. The trace expanded beneath awareness.

A limitation surfaces in jurisdictions that enforce stringent protections. The General Data Protection Regulation (GDPR), implemented by the European Union in May 2018, demands consent and restricts secondary uses of personal data. Yet even in these regions, enforcement lags behind technical innovation. The tension remains: law operates slowly; tracking operates instantly.

Across these developments, the trace motif recurs. It appears when a watch counts steps, when a map logs journeys, when a browser records queries, when a home speaker listens for activation. The trace is not passive. It accumulates, interprets, anticipates. It forms a shadow self—a version of a person that exists within servers, scripts, and scoring models.

The unresolved tension sits in a simple but demanding question: when each action leaves a record, how should individuals decide which traces to permit and which to resist?

The Rise of Predictive Profiling

In March 2016, a young office worker in Manila sat at her desk and applied for a small personal loan on her phone. The lender, a fintech firm partnered with Lenddo—then headquartered in Hong Kong—promised a decision in under an hour. She uploaded no payslips, no tax returns, no letters from employers. Instead, the app requested access to her Facebook profile, contact list, and smartphone metadata. She hesitated for a second, pressed "Allow," and watched the spinning icon. The decision arrives by email. "Application declined. Your score does not meet our criteria." Nothing in the message explained which part of her digital life had condemned her. Was it the irregular working hours suggested by her late-night messages? The number of friends who had missed repayments? The streak of job-hunting websites she had visited last month? A complex system had turned scattered traces into a single judgement: unworthy of credit.

This is predictive profiling in action. Organisations ingest vast amounts of behavioural data and produce a probability: the likelihood that you will repay, resign, complain, fall ill, or commit a crime. The numbers themselves are rarely visible. What you see are the outcomes. An offer appears or disappears. An interest rate jumps. A claim is delayed. The underlying calculation lives elsewhere—in servers, in models, in code you will never read. Yet it exerts pressure on your life with quiet authority.

A motif runs through this subchapter: *the score*. The score is the compressed narrative of a person, rendered as a number or class. It travels easily between systems. It can be shared, bought, refined, and repurposed. Above all, it invites a seduction: if the score correlates with outcomes, perhaps it reveals something essential about who you are and what you will do next.

Predictive profiling builds on the tracking described earlier, but it takes a decisive step further. Show: an AI system trained on thousands of borrowers' histories learns that people who change phones frequently, click on certain adverts, and post at particular times of night are slightly more likely to miss payments. Name: a machine-learning model, built by a lender's data science team in Shenzhen or London, converts those relationships into a creditworthiness score. Explain: the system does not understand why these patterns correlate; it simply recognises that they do within historical data. Implication: the next applicant who shares those traits inherits the past behaviour of people who look similar in the model's eyes, regardless of their own circumstances.

Credit scoring has always involved prediction, but older systems relied on relatively few variables—income, existing debts, employment history. The difference now lies in scope. AI systems draw on thousands of features, many harvested from social media and smartphone usage. A "like" on a particular page, the stability of your contact network, the speed at which you scroll, the type of device you own—all become inputs. The score emerges from patterns no human underwriter could compute.

The Lenddo example illustrates how this logic moved from experiment to practice. Founded in 2011, Lenddo promoted "social credit scoring" across markets such as the Philippines and Colombia. Show: applicants linked their Facebook or LinkedIn accounts, granting the system access to their social graph. Name: social graph analytics. Explain: algorithms measured network density, the repayment behaviour of contacts, the frequency of job changes among friends, even the linguistic tone of posts where permitted. Implication: a person's eligibility for credit depended not only on personal behaviour but on the behaviour of others within their digital orbit.

Here, efficiency and discrimination intertwine. From the lender's perspective, the process reduced paperwork and extended credit to people without traditional banking histories. Approval decisions that once took days now took minutes. Human bias at the counter gave way to statistical rules. But for the applicant, the trade-off was stark. Your financial future began to depend on the company you kept online. A cousin's default, a friend's unstable work history, an old acquaintance's chaotic timeline—all might weigh silently against you. The score moved beyond the individual.

A second case, Ant Financial's Sesame Credit, launched in China in 2015, reveals how predictive profiling can scale nationally. Show: users who shopped on Alibaba platforms, repaid loans on time, and maintained certain spending patterns received higher sesame scores. Name: Zhima Credit, headquartered in Hangzhou. Explain: the system integrated e-commerce behaviour, bill payments, and other digital signals to produce a single number between 350 and 950. Higher scores unlocked practical benefits—deposit-free rentals, faster visa applications, preferential credit offers. Implication:

citizens learnt that tiny behavioural choices—where to shop, how fast to repay, what to book—could nudge their score and, with it, their concrete opportunities.

In such systems, the score becomes a behavioural compass. People learn to act in score-optimising ways. They pay bills earlier not merely to avoid penalties but to please the model. They avoid certain transactions lest they signal instability. The predictive system ceases to be a neutral observer; it becomes a quiet architect of behaviour. Each adjustment is small—an earlier payment here, a different purchase there—but across millions of people, the effect is cultural. The score shapes the future it claims merely to predict.

A credible counter-example comes from European regulators who have explicitly warned against using social media data for credit assessments. In 2017, Germany's Federal Financial Supervisory Authority (BaFin) criticised such practices as incompatible with principles of fairness and transparency in lending. Show: major German banks continue to rely primarily on conventional credit bureaus such as Schufa. Name: BaFin, headquartered in Bonn. Explain: regulators worry that social data may act as proxy indicators for protected characteristics such as ethnicity, political affiliation, or religious belief. Implication: in these jurisdictions, the rise of predictive profiling faces normative restraints; not every available data point is deemed legitimate fodder for the score.

This limitation does not negate the wider trend. It simply shows that norms and law can still contest the expansion of the predictive gaze. Where regulators push back, the score is forced to confine itself to narrower inputs. Where such scrutiny is absent or weak, it expands voraciously.

The ethical tightrope becomes most obvious when predictive profiling intersects with historical bias. Show: a credit model trained on ten years of lending data from a city where minority neighbourhoods have long faced discriminatory loan rejections. Name: the model might be built by a major US lender, using off-the-shelf tools from firms such as FICO or internal teams in New York. Explain: the model learns that applicants from certain postcodes correlate with defaults, because those applicants were previously denied fair terms or driven to predatory products. Implication: the algorithm faithfully encodes past injustice into future decisions. The score becomes a veneer of mathematical neutrality over embedded prejudice.

A parallel case outside finance illuminates the mechanism. The COMPAS risk-assessment tool, developed by Northpointe (now Equivant) and used in several US states by 2016, predicted the likelihood of reoffending among criminal defendants. An investigation by ProPublica (2016) found that black defendants were more likely to be misclassified as high risk than white defendants with similar records. Show: judges in Florida saw a simple score on their screens. Explain: the tool had learnt from historical arrest and conviction data already shaped by policing disparities. Implication: predictive profiling amplified systemic inequities under a technical gloss.

The motif of the score appears again. Whether in credit scoring or criminal justice, it condenses prior human choices into a number that can be deployed rapidly and repeatedly. The danger lies in mistaking that number for an objective truth rather than a structured guess rooted in skewed histories.

Predictive profiling also alters the nature of responsibility. When a human loan officer rejects an application, the applicant can ask why. The officer may point to a debt ratio, a missed payment, an income threshold. When an AI system delivers the decision, explanations become diffuse. Show: a customer service agent reading templated phrases from a script—"Your application did not meet our automated criteria." Name: automated decision-making under frameworks such as the EU's GDPR Article 22. Explain: even when institutions are legally obliged to offer "meaningful information about the logic involved," the complexity of models with thousands of parameters makes plain-language explanation difficult. Implication: responsibility dissolves into the system. The score decides, but nobody personifies the decision.

The Apple Card controversy illustrates this opacity. In November 2019, entrepreneur David Heinemeier Hansson tweeted that Apple Card, issued by Goldman Sachs from New York, had offered him a credit limit many times higher than his wife's despite shared finances. Steve Wozniak reported a similar experience. New York's Department of Financial Services opened an investigation into potential gender discrimination. Show: customers saw radically different limits on their app screens. Name: Apple, Goldman Sachs, NYDFS. Explain: Goldman denied intentional bias, citing a "gender-neutral" algorithm. Yet because the model's full design remained proprietary, outsiders could not easily verify whether variables acted as proxies for gender. Implication: predictive profiling can generate outcomes that feel discriminatory even when developers insist the model is blind. The score may encode bias through correlation rather than explicit instruction.

It is tempting to imagine that better data will solve these problems. If models simply included more variables, the argument goes, they would become fairer and more accurate. However, the dynamic often works the other way. As models grow more complex, they become more opaque; as they become more accurate according to their own metrics, they may grow less intelligible to the people they judge. Show: a lender chooses a deep neural network because it marginally reduces default rates compared with a simpler logistic regression. Explain: the network's internal structure resists straightforward interpretation. Implication: marginal gains in prediction come at the cost of meaningful explanation. The score sharpens while understanding dulls.

Efficiency here is not an abstract virtue; it is measured in default rates, processing times, profit margins. A model that reduces defaults by a fraction of a percentage point across millions of loans can generate substantial financial gains. The visible behaviour is clear: boards approve AI deployments; call centres shrink; human underwriters are re-assigned. Yet each incremental efficiency intensifies the moral stakes. A system that processes applications in milliseconds cannot pause for contextual nuance.

Predictive profiling also changes how people view themselves. When individuals know that their clicks, friendships, and replies shape their future access to credit, they begin to self-monitor. They hesitate before posting controversial opinions. They avoid connecting with people who appear unstable or unreliable. They sanitise their digital persona. The score motif hardens into a social mirror. People do not merely act; they act *for* the score.

There is a quieter cost too. Prediction tends to compress the range of imagined futures. If a system labels someone as "high risk," opportunities dry up—fewer credit offers, fewer rental approvals, more obstacles to mobility. The individual may adapt to this constrained world, lowering expectations, curbing ambitions. A self-fulfilling loop emerges: the model predicts limited success; the environment echoes the prediction; the person's actual trajectory contracts to match. The score becomes prophecy.

To acknowledge these dynamics is not to deny the benefits predictive profiling can offer. Micro-lenders using mobile data have extended credit to people excluded from traditional banking. Insurance firms have used driving telematics to reward safe motorists. Fraud detection systems have spared customers from theft. These cases show that prediction can support inclusion and protection when carefully governed. The counter-example here is constructive: not all profiling is exploitative. Yet even in these positive narratives, the same questions arise. Who designs the model? Who audits the data? Who has the right to challenge the score?

The unresolved tension can be distilled into a single, demanding choice. Are we willing to allow our futures to be shaped by statistical resemblance to others, inferred from traces we did not realise we were leaving, in systems we are rarely allowed to inspect?

Or put more directly: when the score knocks on the door of your life—determining whether you may borrow, travel, rent, work—how much of yourself are you prepared to surrender to a machine's prediction, and how much uncertainty are you prepared to defend as an essential part of being human?

Why Explore Privacy Now?

In May 2018, the European Union enforced the General Data Protection Regulation. Brussels broadcast its intent clearly: citizens deserved control over the data accumulated about them. Yet the days that followed the law's introduction revealed a paradox. While inboxes filled with consent notices from Meta, Google and countless smaller firms, millions of users clicked "Accept" without reading a line. The regulation signalled resistance to hyper-surveillance; the behaviour signalled fatigue. A safeguard designed to restore autonomy became, through sheer volume and repetition, something people dismissed with a single habitual tap. The law arrived with fanfare. The response was mechanical. Five words describe the moment: people clicked without thinking.

This tension illuminates the present dilemma. Societies have invested enormous political and cultural energy into transparency. The ideal that information should be open, searchable and accessible animated movements from WikiLeaks in 2006 to the Panama Papers in 2016. But as the push for visibility has intensified, so too has discomfort with the consequences. Students at the University of Cambridge protested automated lecture capture in 2018 after realising that their questions, hesitations and missteps would be archived indefinitely. Activists who once championed radical openness now speak of exhaustion. Transparency, once framed as liberation, has begun to feel like exposure.

A motif appears here: *the thinning wall.* The wall once separated the inner and outer worlds. It protected tentative thoughts. It allowed misjudgements to fade. It created a space in which identity could shift without surveillance. Now the wall thins with each data request, each profile, each background algorithm assigning probabilities to future conduct. The thinning wall is not a metaphor of catastrophe; it is a measure of subtle erosion. Privacy diminishes millimetre by millimetre, until people sense the change only when the wall nearly disappears.

The urgency of exploring privacy rests on concrete shifts, not nostalgia. Show: when WhatsApp updated its terms in January 2021, requiring expanded data sharing with Meta, users around London, Delhi and São Paulo migrated in large numbers to Signal and Telegram. Name: Signal, run by the Signal Foundation. Explain: people realised that private conversations might feed larger advertising systems. Implication: even minor adjustments in data governance create visible behavioural shifts when users recognise that the thinning wall has implications for intimate speech.

Public discourse reflects this shift. During the first months of the COVID-19 pandemic, governments across South Korea, Singapore and Australia deployed contact-tracing apps. Show: South Korea's Ministry of Health published precise movement logs of infected individuals in March 2020. These logs included visit times, shops entered, and bus numbers. Explain: officials aimed to slow viral spread through radical transparency. Implication: while effective in early containment, the disclosures exposed personal routines, relationships and even affairs. The thinning wall became a public health instrument, but also a source of misidentification, shame and fear.

A credible counter-example arrives from Germany. The Robert Koch Institute released the Corona-Warn-App in June 2020, designed with strong decentralised storage. Show: the app stored contact data on individual devices. Explain: privacy-preserving cryptography ensured that authorities could not reconstruct movement trails. Implication: privacy and public health need not be adversaries. The thinning wall can be strengthened through design rather than sentiment. Yet uptake across Europe still remained uneven, demonstrating that even privacy-first solutions struggle against public distrust or habitual indifference. The counter-example clarifies the point: strong privacy is possible but fragile.

The behavioural consequences of hyper-transparency are now measurable. Show: researchers at Carnegie Mellon University (2019) found that subjects altered their search queries when reminded that their data might be monitored. Name: behavioural modification under perceived surveillance. Explain: people avoided searching for sensitive information, even benign medical queries. Implication: hyper-transparency distorts curiosity. It shapes what people look for, learn about and admit to themselves. The thinning wall constrains intellectual freedom.

The psychological cost becomes clearer in everyday settings. Workers monitored by keystroke trackers or webcam-activation software during remote work report hesitations in taking breaks, increased stress and self-conscious typing rhythms. The visible behaviour is small: pausing before stretching, adjusting posture to remain centred in view, repeatedly checking whether the indicator light is active. These micro-adjustments accrue into chronic tension. Show: firms such as InterGuard and Hubstaff saw increased uptake during 2020. Explain: employers sought guarantees of productivity. Implication: when people anticipate evaluation at every moment, authenticity collapses into performance. The thinning wall invades the mind, not merely the workspace.

A second thread concerns the mutation of shared norms. The cultural shift from valuing secrets to demanding exposure is visible in platforms like TikTok, founded in Beijing in 2016 and now used globally. Show: users film their homes, families and vulnerabilities for global audiences. Explain: the architecture rewards visibility with likes, views and algorithmic amplification. Implication: public performance becomes habitual. The thinning wall encourages disclosure as currency. But constant disclosure invites constant scrutiny. The reward system reshapes what people consider worth revealing.

This sits uneasily alongside revelations about commercial surveillance. The Cambridge Analytica scandal, exposed in March 2018, showed that political consultants accessed data from millions of Facebook users without explicit consent. Show: the firm harvested digital profiles to target voters across the UK and US. Explain: predictive models inferred personality traits from "likes." Implication: political persuasion crossed into psychological manipulation. The thinning wall became an instrument of electoral engineering. Transparency, in this context, worked in reverse—citizens were transparent to the campaign, while the campaign's methods were opaque to citizens.

A credible limitation emerges from jurisdictions where surveillance is culturally entrenched. In parts of the UAE and Saudi Arabia, citizens often accept extensive monitoring as a reasonable exchange for security and social order. Show: CCTV networks across Riyadh expanded significantly after 2017. Explain: citizens report feeling safer in public spaces. Implication: not all societies interpret the thinning wall as threat. But even here, the negotiation between visibility and dignity remains. The counter-example highlights diversity in cultural expectations, yet the underlying question remains universal: how thin can the wall become before individuals lose the space in which private selves develop?

Another reason to explore privacy now lies in the rise of predictive profiling. When algorithms anticipate actions before individuals commit them, the thinning wall transforms the future as well as the present. Show: credit-scoring models used in Shenzhen or Manila classify applicants based on online behaviour. Name: companies such as Ant Group or Lenddo. Explain: a missed repayment or risky network cluster adjusts an invisible score. Implication: predictive systems constrain opportunity. A future imagined by an algorithm becomes a future inhabited by the applicant. The wall no longer merely divides spaces; it divides possible lives.

This dynamic alters public discourse. For much of the early digital period, transparency was framed as an ethical good. Corporate disclosures, government open-data projects, and digital activism celebrated exposure as a tool of accountability. But accountability without privacy becomes voyeurism. Show: the 2014 celebrity photo hack leaked private images stolen from iCloud accounts. Explain: visibility without consent turns transparency into exploitation. Implication: the thinning wall harms not only reputations but the very idea of personal boundaries.

A parallel example surfaces in Britain. When the Metropolitan Police deployed live facial-recognition technology in London in 2020, researchers from the University of Essex documented false matches, including misidentifications of innocent pedestrians. Show: individuals were stopped for questioning. Explain: the system acted on probabilistic inference. Implication: the thinning wall between face and identity threatens basic freedoms. A person's physical presence becomes data for interrogation.

Yet facial recognition also features in contexts where people welcome it. In airports such as Schiphol and Changi, passengers use biometric lanes to accelerate boarding. Show: cameras match faces to passport data. Explain: friction decreases. Implication: transparency becomes convenience. The motif of the thinning wall appears again: privacy's erosion often begins with improvements that feel helpful.

The central question emerges: what does authenticity require? If people censor themselves under the gaze of devices, colleagues, governments or algorithms, the private realm in which genuine preferences form begins to contract. Show: teenagers on Instagram archive posts that receive insufficient engagement. Explain: they fear judgement encoded in metrics. Implication: self-expression bends toward anticipated reaction. The thinning wall, once a shield, becomes a filter.

Exploring privacy now means confronting these contradictions directly. We have entered a period where hyper-transparency is both celebrated and feared. People demand accountability from institutions while craving protection for their personal lives. They seek personalised recommendations while worrying about inferred profiles. They enjoy frictionless interaction while resenting what that frictionlessness costs.

Two questions anchor this urgency. First: what disappears when the thinning wall finally collapses? Not merely secrets, but the conditions that allow people to revise their beliefs, recover from mistakes, or inhabit interiority. Second: if transparency becomes the default expectation, how will societies preserve the dignity that secrecy once nurtured?

The response is not yet clear. The tension remains. And the next step depends on how each of us, consciously or not, chooses to live with the thinning wall now standing between our visible lives and the private selves we may still hope to protect.

Chapter 2
The Digital Surveillance Marketplace

The story often begins with a tap. In the summer warmth of a Manchester afternoon, a commuter steps onto the tram, phone in hand, unlocking it with a glance. The screen lights up with a familiar carousel of apps, each waiting silently for its part in the day. A notification suggests a new café ten minutes away. Another highlights a sale for headphones he searched for only once, late the previous night. Nothing about the moment feels intrusive. It feels ordinary—helpful, even. Yet beneath those flickers of suggestion lies a transaction he never consciously agreed to: his location, his browsing habits, his late-night curiosity sold and repackaged in milliseconds. It is a marketplace without a counter, and he is both shopper and product.

The paradox is simple. Few of us believe we are worth that much, yet companies act as though we are worth everything. Tech giants record billions of interactions daily, each one a tiny clue about who we are, what we fear and what pulls our desires into motion. A single swipe contains the outline of a preference. A paused video reveals hesitation. A lingering scroll signals interest. These movements, smaller than speech, feed into a vast and intricate commercial economy that turns human attention into extractable value. If the previous chapter revealed a transparent world, this one confronts the machinery that profits from that transparency.

The modern surveillance marketplace did not arise from a single invention. It grew through layers—each digital convenience quietly adding another lens through which businesses viewed their users. The first search engines in the late 1990s discovered that click patterns could predict shopping choices. Early social networks in the 2000s learnt that emotional responses, measured by shares and comments, could map social influence. Smartphones in the 2010s completed the final circle: they linked identity, behaviour and location into continuous, intimate streams. What was once speculative analysis hardened into an industrial system.

A recurring motif threads through this chapter: *the invisible price tag*. Every app, every navigation route, every online purchase carries one. It hangs not from the item we receive but from the data we surrender. The challenge is that the price tag is rarely disclosed. Instead, it is buried in design decisions, policy updates and algorithmic arrangements crafted to make the trade feel light. The result is a marketplace in which individuals believe they are participating freely while corporations harvest insights of extraordinary depth.

To grasp the magnitude of this system, we must understand how personal data became a form of currency. Consider the case of navigation platforms that guide millions through cities. Their business models rely on recording the routes people take, the speed of travel, the pauses at junctions, the detours and shortcuts. These streams of information, aggregated across vast populations, enable companies to sell real-time traffic analysis, optimise advertising for nearby shops, and tailor services for logistics firms. The user sees a helpful arrow. The company sees a dynamic map of behavioural patterns updated thousands of times per second.

The subtlety is crucial. People rarely perceive the extraction. They open the app because it works, and because competitors are no longer workable without similar permissions. The invisible price tag is accepted by default. But what is the cost of this default? Not merely exposure, but dependence. As convenience deepens, alternatives shrink. When a service becomes indispensable, opting out transforms from choice to sacrifice.

From convenience, we move to consent—perhaps the most misunderstood component of the surveillance economy.

Consent should imply deliberation, understanding and voluntary agreement. Instead, it has become one of the most frictionless gestures in digital life. Users tap "Agree" as though clearing a pop-up ad. Companies rely on this reflex. They structure screens to accelerate acceptance, using colour, placement and emotionally neutral wording to guide behaviour. The question is no longer whether consent is informed. It is whether it ever had the opportunity to be.

To see how these nudges operate, imagine signing up for a new "free" fitness app. The interface invites you to track your morning run. A cheerful banner suggests enhanced features "for best performance." The permission request blends into the aesthetic of the app. Location access, movement data, heart-rate information (if linked to a smartwatch), microphone access for voice commands—all presented as routine. The list is long. The language is soft. The invisible price tag remains hidden. You tap once. You run. But your run is no longer your own. It becomes a data point packaged for advertisers targeting health-conscious consumers, for insurers modelling lifestyle risk, for brokers selling anonymised datasets to hedge funds monitoring behaviour trends.

The shift from consent to coercion is often quiet, almost polite. Few companies threaten users with outright denial of service; instead, they build ecosystems where the absence of consent results in sharply reduced functionality. Decline location access for a food-delivery app, and it cannot show nearby restaurants. Decline tracking for a social platform, and targeted content becomes irrelevant or repetitive. Decline cookies on retail sites, and essential features break. Coercion hides in the structure, not the statement.

This environment complicates the meaning of ownership. Long before predictive algorithms mapped our preferences, the question of who owns data was contested. When a person posts a photograph on a social platform, does the platform own the image? Or merely the right to distribute it? And what of the metadata—the time of day, the geolocation, the number of friends tagged, the device model used? Ownership becomes a constellation, not a singular right.

The problem deepens when data outlives intention. A search query entered in a moment of anxiety may resurface years later through targeted advertising or behavioural inference. A post deleted from one platform may persist in server backups or third-party archives. A fitness tracker may store historical movement patterns that are later repurposed by insurers or employers. Data has longevity. People do not live with the same constancy. The invisible price tag follows long after the transaction.

The effects of this trade extend well beyond individual inconvenience. They shape economies, labour markets and social trust. Companies that command the largest data flows wield disproportionate power over competitors. They can predict market shifts faster, target customers more precisely and refine algorithms more effectively. Smaller firms depend on them for advertising, infrastructure and visibility. The surveillance marketplace thus produces not only informational asymmetry but economic asymmetry on a global scale.

At the personal level, the consequences can be severe. Hiring platforms may infer professionalism from email metadata or response times. Healthcare companies may adjust premiums based on shopping histories. Insurance models may examine driving behaviour captured by smartphone accelerometers rather than installed devices. These decisions occur quietly, often without full awareness from the individuals affected. A person denied a job may never know the behavioural signal that tipped the scales. A family paying higher insurance rates may never discover the pattern that flagged them as riskier. The invisible price tag becomes a burden carried without understanding.

Yet the story is not one of inevitable decline. Resistance movements, regulatory frameworks and technological innovations all challenge the dominance of the surveillance marketplace. The GDPR forced companies to justify data collection. Advocacy groups confronted manipulative design. Users migrated from invasive platforms to privacy-focused alternatives. These shifts remind us that the invisible price tag is not fixed; it can be questioned, renegotiated or refused.

But the deeper tension remains unresolved. We rely on digital infrastructure more each year. We demand personalisation while fearing its consequences. We value convenience but resent the observation it requires. And we continue to click "Accept," even when we sense the trade is unequal.

This chapter opens in that conflict. It explores the marketplaces built on our behaviours, the subtle coercions embedded in everyday interactions, the shrinking clarity of ownership, and the profound economic and social effects of a world where surveillance is profitable. At its heart sits a question that will echo throughout the pages ahead: if every convenience carries an invisible price tag, who decides what we are truly willing to pay?

The answer is not yet settled. And the next turn of the page leads us deeper into the terrain where that decision awaits.

Ecosystems of Data Harvest

In April 2021, Apple introduced App Tracking Transparency across its devices. Within twenty-four hours, millions of iPhone users in London, New York and Sydney were confronted with a simple prompt: "Allow this app to track your activity across other companies' apps and websites?" The majority pressed "Ask App Not to Track." The immediate outcome was measurable. Facebook, headquartered in Menlo Park, warned investors that its advertising model would be hit by an estimated US$10 billion shortfall in 2022 (Meta, earnings call, February 2022). One tap from millions of fingers disrupted a global business model more effectively than years of debate. The moment revealed something larger: many services had long depended on access users barely realised they had granted. Five words capture the shock: people resisted without warning.

This incident exposed the hidden scaffolding of the digital economy. Companies had built elaborate systems on the assumption that users would remain compliant, inattentive or indifferent. Yet when presented with a clear choice, they often refused. The paradox is striking. Businesses treat personal data as essential currency, yet most people have never seen the marketplace in which it circulates. The same users who casually tap through permissions can, when a request is framed plainly, revoke access entirely. A simple question shifts power. But such moments are rare; most harvesting occurs invisibly.

A motif threads through this subchapter: *the ledger*. Not the ledger of accountants or bookkeepers, but the silent, expanding ledger each platform keeps on its users. Every search, swipe, tap, purchase, pause and location ping becomes an entry. The ledger grows without limit, enriched by every digital breath. And because the ledger is largely unseen, people rarely consider its consequences. What they encounter are the polished surfaces—recommendations, personalised offers, frictionless navigation. They see the convenience. They do not see the accounting beneath it.

The scale of this accounting is best shown by examining what companies actually collect. Consider Google, launched in 1998 and now operating in more than 150 countries. Its systems record search queries, Gmail interactions, YouTube viewing time and Maps navigation trails. Show: a commuter typing "coffee near me" in Birmingham leaves a trace that joins billions of similar traces. Name: Google's Ads Data Hub. Explain: this infrastructure allows advertisers to analyse aggregated user behaviour without accessing raw personal data, supporting targeted campaigns refined by region, time and device. Implication: the ledger becomes both a map of humanity's collective curiosity and a machine for optimising commercial influence.

Another primary contributor to the ledger is location data. In 2018, The New York Times examined datasets supplied by a broker in the United States and revealed that a single file contained 235 million location pings from devices across cities such as Los Angeles, Houston and Atlanta. Each ping captured a person's position within metres. Show: an office worker's device recorded her journey from home to work and back, with stops at a gym and pharmacy. Name: the location-data industry, involving companies like X-Mode (later renamed Outlogic). Explain: apps integrated third-party SDKs that captured GPS coordinates even when location settings appeared benign. Implication: a simple weather app could feed a surveillance market worth billions, all routed through the ledger.

The point here is not simply that data harvesting exists. It is that harvesting is continuous, layered and monetised through complex chains. A single piece of behavioural data may be sold, aggregated, repackaged and resold dozens of times. Each transaction adds a new entry to the ledger. Each entry strengthens the power asymmetry between those who collect and those who generate.

To see how platforms monetise this ledger, consider Facebook's advertising model. Show: an advertiser promoting a new trainer in London can target "men aged 25–35 who recently browsed fitness content and visited sporting-goods shops within the last month." Name: Facebook's "Detailed Targeting," updated continually since 2013. Explain: the platform integrates browsing data, interactions, location trails and inferred interests. Implication: the ledger is not merely descriptive; it is predictive. It anticipates what people may want before they articulate the desire.

The centre of gravity in this economy lies in consolidation. When a handful of firms, such as Alphabet, Meta and Amazon, control the largest ledgers, they accumulate unparalleled advantage. Show: Amazon, founded in Seattle in 1994, tracks search patterns, purchases, browsing duration and even cursor hover time. Name: Amazon's A9 search algorithm. Explain: the company uses this behavioural intelligence to prioritise its own products and negotiate with suppliers. Implication: data extraction strengthens the position of dominant firms, deepening their control over commerce and communication.

Yet not all data harvesting flows through giants. Small developers also participate, often without fully understanding the implications. A weather app built by a start-up in Warsaw or a fitness tracker launched by a team in Nairobi may integrate analytic libraries provided for "improved performance." Show: these SDKs collect device identifiers and movement patterns. Name: companies such as Kochava or InMobi. Explain: developers accept them to monetise free apps through advertising. Implication: the ledger expands through thousands of tiny agreements scattered across the digital ecosystem. Most users remain unaware of these exchanges.

A credible counter-example exists in the form of privacy-focused services. Apple's App Tracking Transparency, Mozilla's Firefox with Enhanced Tracking Protection (2019), and DuckDuckGo's search engine—founded in Pennsylvania in 2008—offer alternatives where tracking is limited or blocked entirely. Show: users switching to DuckDuckGo do not generate personalised search profiles. Explain: searches are contextual, not behavioural. Implication: the ledger can be restricted when companies commit to different economic models. But these models often rely on being outliers; they thrive in part because others do not follow the same constraints. The counter-example shows that resistance is possible, but its scale remains comparatively small.

Despite the presence of alternatives, mainstream users rarely migrate. Behaviour reveals why. People value convenience more than they admit. They respond to speed, familiarity, and smooth integration with existing habits. They continue to accept free services because they do not experience the cost directly. The ledger grows because its consequences feel deferred, abstract or distant. The invisible price tag appears only when something goes wrong—a data breach, an unexpected advertisement, a denied opportunity based on inferred behaviour.

This brings us to a deeper structural shift: data has eclipsed labour as the dominant fuel of digital economies. Companies that once measured value in employee hours now measure it in behavioural signals. Show: Uber's surge-pricing algorithm in London reacts to demand patterns generated by riders' location data. Name: Uber's marketplace matching infrastructure. Explain: the company analyses real-time movements to adjust supply and pricing. Implication: behavioural data directs economic decisions with rapidity and precision, granting platforms enormous influence over urban mobility.

The ledger recurs here as a quiet motif. It underpins predictive logistics, personalised advertising, micro-targeted political messaging and algorithmic labour allocation. Yet most people only encounter the surface expressions: an offer displayed at the right moment, a route suggested through an unfamiliar neighbourhood, a service improving with uncanny intuition. They do not see the ledger, only its shadows.

The question that haunts this environment is whether users understand the bargain they have entered. The answer is unsettling. Studies by the Norwegian Consumer Council

(2021) documented that many apps continue collecting behavioural data regardless of user expectations or comprehension, often presented in privacy policies requiring hours to read. Show: a policy that would take an average reader more than thirty minutes to understand. Explain: such documents frame consent as informed while ensuring that actual comprehension remains minimal. Implication: people agree to terms they cannot reasonably evaluate, feeding the ledger without ever consciously participating.

This dynamic shapes power itself. When data flows cluster within a few firms, those firms gain the ability to influence markets, speech and social behaviour. They refine algorithms that determine which news stories surface, which products rise, which social groups receive targeted outreach. They become informational gatekeepers not through editorial authority but through control of the ledger.

The economic consequences deepen this concentration. Advertising revenue shifts proportionally to firms with the richest datasets. Smaller publishers, lacking such intelligence, struggle to compete. Local shops rely on targeted ads managed by giants. National campaigns flow through proprietary channels. The ledger becomes infrastructure; dependence becomes structural.

A parallel effect occurs at the personal level. People experience digital life through relentless customisation. They receive recommendations tailored to browsing habits. They navigate cities with personalised routing. They buy goods surfaced through behavioural inference. But customisation narrows exposure. Show: a user who frequently watches political commentary on YouTube may be guided toward increasingly similar content. Name: the platform's recommendation algorithm, refined since 2011. Explain: the system optimises for engagement, not breadth. Implication: the ledger can constrict intellectual horizons while appearing to expand choice.

There is, too, the question of longevity. Data persists. Behavioural patterns recorded in January 2017 may still influence advertising profiles in 2025. Search histories linger in backups. Location trails endure in third-party servers. Past actions shape future inferences long after contexts have changed. The ledger remembers what people forget. Or would prefer to forget.

And yet, amidst these complexities, a simple tension remains unresolved. People crave convenience but distrust surveillance. They want personalised services but recoil at being monitored. They enjoy frictionless access but worry about exploitation. They resist tracking only when forced to confront it directly, as in the Apple prompt of 2021. For the rest of their digital lives, consent is mostly habitual.

The ledger continues to fill.

The question that closes this subchapter is not rhetorical. It is a decision that each society, company and individual must eventually confront: if the quiet accounting of our behaviours underpins the digital services we rely upon, how much of ourselves are we willing to record—and who should hold the ledger that defines us?

From Consent to Coercion

In June 2019, the Norwegian Consumer Council published a detailed report titled *Deceived by Design*. Its investigators reviewed privacy interfaces from Facebook, Google and Microsoft, examining how users in Oslo navigated basic settings. The outcome was stark. People who attempted to reject tracking were routinely funnelled through longer paths, confronted with warning-coloured buttons, or shown language implying that denial would break essential functions. Those who accepted were moved through swiftly, often with a bright, single-tap option. The Council described these tactics as "dark patterns," but the deeper revelation was more unsettling: the consent powering global data markets had been engineered for ease of surrender. A simple truth emerged. Choice was not free.

The report exposed what many had sensed yet struggled to articulate. Consent screens had ceased to be neutral gateways. They had become instruments of persuasion. And the persuasion was accomplished not through force, but through design. Decisions that shaped personal privacy were compressed into a moment shorter than a breath. One tap. That was enough.

A motif recurs throughout this subchapter: *the hinge*. Consent is the hinge that connects a user's intention to a system's demands. In theory, the hinge should swing freely. In practice, design choices stiffen or loosen it, steering the user towards a single desirable outcome. The hinge becomes less a mechanism of autonomy and more a mechanism of compliance.

The path from consent to coercion begins with the smallest interaction. Show: a user in Leeds downloads a free photo-editing app. Name: the app requests permission for location access, microphone activation and contact syncing. Explain: none of these features are necessary for editing images. Implication: the hinge is already weighted; the app seeks maximum data rather than functional relevance. The user, eager to proceed, accepts the entire bundle without pause.

The logic guiding such requests has roots in behavioural science. Companies test interface variations to identify which colours, positions and phrasings produce the highest acceptance rates. Show: Facebook's redesign in 2018 moved privacy settings deeper into the menu structure. Name: interface restructuring. Explain: by placing privacy controls behind nested pages, the company reduced the frequency with which users discovered restrictive options. Implication: design shapes behaviour. The hinge tightens.

Consent becomes further compromised when companies present the refusal of tracking as a threat to experience. Consider Google's approach to location data on Android devices. Show: a prompt indicates that denying access will weaken navigation accuracy. Name: performance framing. Explain: users perceive rejection as self-sabotage. Implication: the user accepts tracking not from desire, but from concern that service quality will degrade.

Another case reveals the subtlety of coercion: cookie banners introduced to meet European regulatory requirements. Although the GDPR (2018) established principles of informed consent, many websites responded by crafting banners with "Accept All" in vibrant colours and "Manage Settings" in grey text. Show: the Financial Times' 2020 review of major UK news sites observed that rejecting cookies often required several additional clicks. Name: asymmetric friction. Explain: friction channels users towards the choice that aligns with commercial interests. Implication: the hinge is forced into a preferred position.

Yet coercion is not always overt. Sometimes it is embedded in the architecture of digital dependency. People rely on platforms for work, education, social contact and navigation. Refusing consent becomes impractical. A worker asked to use Slack or Teams cannot decline tracking without risking employment. A student required to join an online learning platform cannot meaningfully negotiate data terms. Show: Zoom's privacy review in March 2020 revealed that early versions of the app sent analytics to Facebook even when users had no Facebook account. Name: cross-service data routing. Explain: participation in modern life requires acceptance of unavoidable surveillance. Implication: the hinge does not swing; it locks.

A counter-example demonstrates that coercion is not inevitable. Apple's App Tracking Transparency (2021) introduced clear, binary choices. Users could decline tracking with a single tap. Show: opt-out rates exceeded 80 per cent in many countries. Name: system-level intervention. Explain: when consent is framed neutrally, many people reject commercial surveillance. Implication: coerced consent is a design problem, not a human preference. Yet this example carries a limitation: it works only because Apple controls the operating system. Smaller firms cannot compel platforms to adopt similar models.

To understand how deeply consent has shifted, we must examine the tension between understanding and action. Privacy policies routinely exceed thousands of words. Show: a Deloitte study (2017) estimated that the average consumer would require over 200 hours annually to read the policies they encounter. Name: cognitive overload. Explain: users cannot reasonably process the implications of each agreement. Implication: reading becomes impossible; clicking becomes routine.

This habitual clicking reshapes norms. The gesture that once signified agreement becomes procedural, almost meaningless. Show: students at a university in Edinburgh admitted in a 2021 survey that they accepted every privacy prompt because "there is no point in resisting." Name: resignation behaviour. Explain: people perceive data extraction as inescapable. Implication: the hinge corrodes. Consent transforms into ritual.

The erosion of autonomy becomes clearer when examining how platforms present time pressure. A user attempting to access a news article on a train platform has limited time before boarding. A parent trying to download an educational app for their child between tasks must act quickly. Companies know this. They design prompts to capitalise on urgency. Show: TikTok's 2020 onboarding sequence requires agreement before content appears. Name: forced sequencing. Explain: refusal delays gratification. Implication: design exploits human impatience.

These systems reveal more than clever interface tricks. They expose a fundamental shift in the distribution of power. Platforms shape the environment in which choices are made. They define what is easy and what is difficult. They set defaults that steer behaviour before users even realise a decision is at stake.

The hinge motif appears again. A hinge that once symbolised access now symbolises direction. It directs users toward predictable outcomes. It directs data toward databases. It directs power toward those who wrote the code.

But coercion does not always feel coercive. That is its strength. When an option is highlighted in blue, when a button is placed where the thumb naturally falls, when a refusal demands cognitive effort, the decision feels self-made. People believe they are choosing freely while being guided invisibly.

This asymmetric architecture becomes most troubling when it shapes sensitive domains. Show: a fertility-tracking app, based in Berlin and updated in 2020, requested permission to share data with "trusted partners." Name: vague partner language. Explain: users, anxious to proceed with health monitoring, accepted without clarity on how intimate metrics were used. Implication: the hinge becomes an entry point for profound intrusion.

A credible limitation emerges in the form of regulatory scrutiny. The UK's Competition and Markets Authority investigated Google and Facebook in 2021, noting that their dominance restricted meaningful alternatives. Show: the CMA's report acknowledged that even with transparency tools, "users cannot avoid tracking without losing access to key services." Name: constrained choice. Explain: regulation recognises structural coercion, yet reforms remain slow. Implication: oversight can identify harm but cannot easily dismantle the architecture that produces it.

Consent becomes further complicated when design obscures data pathways. Users may tap "Allow" believing they are permitting one function, unaware that aggregated data will be shared with brokers, affiliates or advertisers. Show: the Washington Post's 2019 investigation revealed that many Android apps sent data to dozens of third parties without explicit disclosure. Name: shadow-sharing. Explain: consent screens cover only direct collection, not downstream flow. Implication: the hinge opens onto a corridor of unseen doors.

Underlying these examples is a deeper question: what counts as voluntariness in systems people cannot opt out of? When digital interaction is required for employment, healthcare, travel and banking, consent becomes performative. It exists because legal frameworks demand its appearance, not because users possess real agency.

Yet coercion need not be absolute. The hinge can loosen. Some platforms now adopt "privacy by design" approaches, offering clear, minimal data requests and straightforward revocation options. Show: Signal, operated by the Signal Foundation, stores almost no metadata. Name: structural restraint. Explain: the app limits surveillance not through user choice but through architectural constraint. Implication: consent becomes meaningful when systems reduce reliance on it.

But these cases remain exceptions, not norms. For most interactions, coercion is ambient, distributed through interface elements subtle enough to escape conscious notice yet powerful enough to shape global datasets. The pressure comes from all directions at once. A position of fatigue emerges.

Which leads to the unresolved question. If consent has become a gesture shaped more by design than by deliberation, can it still carry the moral weight that data-governance frameworks assume? Or must societies confront a more difficult truth: that choice in digital systems is meaningful only when the hinge is rebuilt, and rebuilt with the explicit aim of resisting the very forces that have learned to bend it?

The answer lies ahead, somewhere between what users expect and what platforms insist upon. The hinge waits.

Blurred Boundaries of Ownership

In March 2018, Cambridge Analytica became a global shorthand for data misuse after it emerged that information from roughly 87 million Facebook accounts had been extracted through an innocuous-looking personality quiz. The company, operating from London, had repurposed data harvested in 2014 for political targeting without users' awareness. What mattered was not merely the breach but the defence that followed: Facebook insisted that users "owned" their data, yet its platform architecture enabled third parties to extract, infer and deploy that data in ways users never foresaw. Ownership existed as rhetoric, not as enforceable power. The scandal revealed something more fundamental than a corporate misstep. It revealed a philosophical ambiguity: what does it mean to own something you cannot control, cannot track and cannot withdraw?

The ambiguity surfaces each time a person posts a photograph, sends a message or shares a location. Moments that feel fleeting take on new permanence once they enter digital infrastructures. A photograph uploaded in Birmingham in 2015 may still circulate through training datasets in 2024, long after its poster has forgotten it. A location ping that lasted half a second may persist indefinitely in a broker's repository. The motif running through this subchapter is *the shadow*: data casts a shadow that outlives the gesture that generated it. Once released, that shadow is claimed by others.

Ownership becomes contested because data is unlike physical property. A suitcase is owned because only one person can hold it at a time. Data can be copied endlessly without diminishing the original. Show: when Instagram users upload images, Meta obtains broad licence rights to use, modify and distribute those images. Name: expansive licensing. Explain: copyright remains with the user, yet the platform's licence allows commercial reuse within its ecosystem. Implication: the user's ownership is symbolic; practical control shifts to the platform.

This displacement of control intensifies when data is repurposed by third parties who are neither visible nor accountable to the person who generated it. Consider location histories collected by smartphone apps. Show: in December 2019, *The New York Times* analysed a dataset containing 12 million Americans' movements, sourced from unnamed brokers. Name: secondary data resale. Explain: apps that gathered location details for benign functions—weather forecasts, retail rewards—sold them to intermediaries who aggregated and traded them. Implication: ownership becomes diffuse to the point of evaporation. The user stands at the origin of a chain of transactions yet cannot see past the first link.

The boundary blurs further when platforms argue that behavioural data—scroll speeds, dwell time, click sequences—is not owned by users at all because it reflects system interaction rather than personal expression. Show: Google's 2020 defence in a lawsuit filed in California asserted that "events generated by user interaction" were part of the service's functionality. Name: functional data doctrine. Explain: such claims position behavioural data as platform property, irrespective of personal relevance. Implication: the shadow expands. The person becomes an input.

A counter-example reveals that the erosion of ownership is neither universal nor inevitable. The General Data Protection Regulation (GDPR), enacted across the European Union in May 2018, introduced rights of access, rectification and erasure. Show: the "right to be forgotten," first articulated in the 2014

Google Spain case, requires search engines to remove outdated or irrelevant personal information upon valid request. Name: judicially recognised personal data rights. Explain: legal frameworks can restore agency by granting individuals power to reshape their digital presence. Implication: ownership acquires substance when backed by enforcement. Yet even here the limitation is clear: erasure applies to search results, not to the original content hosted elsewhere.

As data capitalism expands, boundaries between personal and non-personal data become harder to distinguish. A fitness tracker in Manchester logs heart rate trends. A retailer in Bristol receives aggregated statistics via a data-sharing agreement. Show: in 2021, Strava's global heatmap inadvertently revealed the locations of military bases after users recorded exercise routes in remote regions. Name: unintended exposure through aggregation. Explain: even anonymised data can produce sensitive revelations when layered across time. Implication: the shadow reveals patterns the individual never intended to disclose.

Ownership disputes intensify when data becomes freighted with economic value. Companies argue that they "create" value by processing information; users argue that the raw material originates with them. Show: Spotify's recommendation algorithms depend on listening histories tagged to specific profiles. Name: derivative data value. Explain: the platform generates commercial advantage—retention, engagement, advertising potential—by modelling habits that belong to the listener's daily life. Implication: questions arise about who should profit from behavioural insight: the one who lives the behaviour or the one who captures it?

The tension is not merely economic. It is existential. Data serves as a proxy for identity: preferences, routines, impulses, hesitations. When platforms own the shadow versions of these traits, they claim a version of the self. This creates a quiet ethical problem. If personal data defines who we are in the eyes of institutions—credit firms, employers, insurers—then ownership disputes become disputes over narrative control.

The motif of *the shadow* returns here. A shadow lengthens differently depending on who measures it. A bank reading a social media feed interprets risk. A government reading location trails interprets compliance. A retailer reading browsing history interprets desire. The person casting the shadow may recognise none of these interpretations, yet cannot revoke them. The shadow is theirs and not theirs.

A credible limitation tempers this argument. Some individuals voluntarily share large amounts of data for genuine benefit. Show: in the UK during early 2020, millions used the NHS COVID-19 app to share proximity information, enabling contact-tracing alerts. Name: communal data contribution. Explain: people may willingly exchange data for collective welfare. Implication: ownership is not always protective; sometimes it is communal. Yet even here, trust hinged on strict limits: decentralised processing, data minimisation, transparent governance. The moment those safeguards appeared negotiable, adoption rates faltered.

The central difficulty emerges when personal data moves across contexts. Show: Twitter posts, though public, were scraped in 2015 by researchers creating datasets that later trained machine-learning models without users' awareness. Name: context collapse. Explain: statements intended for social discourse became raw material for predictive technologies. Implication: the meaning of expression changes when algorithms reinterpret it for purposes alien to the user's intent.

A further complexity arises from longevity. Data survives its authors. A teenager posting videos in 2012 might find those clips resurfacing in unrelated settings in 2024. Show: TikTok influencers have reported older content being repackaged by aggregators without consent. Name: content persistence. Explain: digital traces persist far longer than social intentions. Implication: ownership requires temporal control, yet most systems offer none.

Even when platforms allow deletion, copies proliferate elsewhere. Screenshots, mirrored databases, archived caches—all expand the shadow. Show: the Internet Archive, founded in San Francisco in 1996, has stored billions of pages without requiring ongoing consent. Name: historical caching. Explain: while the Archive preserves cultural memory, it also preserves personal traces never intended for permanence. Implication: the boundary between history and privacy becomes contested terrain.

The notion of ownership becomes further unsettled when governments acquire commercial datasets. Show: in May 2021, the UK Home Office faced scrutiny after reportedly purchasing geolocation data from brokers to support immigration enforcement. Name: state acquisition of commercial records. Explain: data generated for retail convenience migrated into state surveillance. Implication: ownership disputes expand beyond corporate boundaries into public authority. The shadow passes into new hands.

All these examples converge on one pressing question. If personal data spreads through ecosystems too large, too fast and too opaque for the individual to monitor, can ownership remain a meaningful concept? Or must societies adopt new frameworks—stewardship, custodianship, fiduciary duty—to replace the fiction that individuals control their digital shadows?

The answer carries weight because the stakes extend beyond economics. They touch the definition of personhood in a networked age. A person's data is not merely information about them; it is a portrait assembled from fragments. When others can redraw that portrait at will, the self becomes negotiable.

So the unresolved tension stands: if the systems built to handle personal data dissolve the very boundaries that define ownership, what principles should guide the next design of digital life? Should ownership become a collective commitment, a shared restraint, or relinquished entirely for a new model of rights? The shadow waits, stretching with every interaction, asking whether we intend to shape it—or whether we will allow others to claim it first.

Economic and Social Fallout

In September 2020, the Australian Competition and Consumer Commission released findings showing that data from people's online shopping, social media browsing and mobile movements had been quietly folded into algorithmic models shaping insurance premiums across Sydney, Melbourne and Brisbane. The outcome was not theoretical. Some applicants, despite spotless driving histories, faced higher car-insurance quotes simply because their digital behaviour aligned with patterns associated with elevated financial risk. What startled investigators was the invisibility of the process: individuals had not consented to the use of their browsing histories, and insurers had not disclosed how the models worked. A domain that once depended on tangible metrics—accident records, age, mileage—had turned to invisible signals harvested from lives lived online. A new logic took hold. Personal data became destiny.

The case illuminated a deeper structural shift: the marketplace had begun measuring people in ways they could neither observe nor contest. Risk assessment migrated from documented behaviour to inferred behaviour. And the inferences travelled. A late-night search pattern in Perth could shape a loan assessment in 2022; a run of social media interactions in Glasgow might colour an employer's perception of reliability. The motif running through this chapter is *the quiet ledger*: a record of traits, decisions and impressions compiled without the individual's awareness. The ledger is quiet, but its consequences are loud.

Economic fallout becomes easiest to see in employment. Show: in 2016, the US firm HireVue introduced AI-based video screening tools adopted by companies across the UK, including Unilever. Name: automated candidate analysis. Explain: these tools evaluated micro-expressions, speech rhythm and word choice to predict suitability for roles. Implication: traits that applicants never intended to display—hesitation, filler words, eye movement—became data points weighted for employability. A shift in lighting or camera quality could tilt the outcome.

The system dramatized a blunt truth: economic opportunity is increasingly filtered through algorithmic impressions. For candidates in Liverpool or Leeds, an application became not a document but a data event. The quiet ledger logged it all.

Another arena where data repurposing reshapes life chances is healthcare. Show: in 2019, researchers at the University of Chicago faced scrutiny after a data-sharing partnership with Google that included identifiable patient information from the university's medical centre. Name: clinical data transfer. Explain: although the project aimed to develop predictive tools for improving care, the inclusion of time-stamped patient visits created potential for re-identification. Implication: when commercial partners acquire health records, the boundary between patient welfare and corporate interest becomes porous. A single visit to a clinic in Hyde Park might ripple into unseen profiling mechanisms years later.

This convergence of commercial analytics and health information also drives inequity. Show: a 2019 study from Obermeyer et al. published in *Science* found that US health-management algorithms disproportionately underestimated the needs of Black patients because the model used healthcare spending as a proxy for illness severity. Name: biased health prediction. Explain: historic disparities in access meant that Black patients spent less on care, leading algorithms to misclassify them as lower risk. Implication: the quiet ledger carries forward past inequities, embedding them deeper into future decision-making.

A counter-example provides nuance. Estonia's e-health system, launched in 2009, combines centralised digital records with strong legislative controls giving citizens visibility and audit rights. Show: residents can log into the government portal to view exactly which officials accessed their medical data. Name: transparent record auditing. Explain: visibility reduces the sense of surveillance because individuals can monitor the observers. Implication: strong governance can temper the harms of data-intensive systems, though such models require political consensus and trust that few states possess.

The social fallout extends beyond economic opportunity and healthcare to the structure of trust itself. People adapt their behaviour when they sense they are being watched, even indirectly. Show: in a 2018 Stanford University study, users who believed their messages were monitored by an unnamed third party altered their linguistic style, adopting more formal grammar and fewer controversial topics. Name: behavioural modulation under observation. Explain: data collection does not merely record behaviour; it configures it. Implication: the marketplace not only predicts the population but shapes it.

Social trust frays when surveillance appears unevenly distributed. Wealth confers privacy. A person in Knightsbridge buying a high-end smartphone with privacy-first defaults enjoys stronger protections than someone using a budget device preloaded with tracking software. Show: in 2021, researchers at Trinity College Dublin found that budget Android phones distributed across Europe sent data incessantly to manufacturers and third parties, even when idle. Name: compulsory telemetry. Explain: those who can least afford surveillance-resistant tools become the most surveilled. Implication: economic inequality deepens informational inequality. The quiet ledger grows thicker for some and thinner for others.

Insurance offers another unsettling glimpse into the marketplace's trajectory. Show: in 2020, John Hancock, a major US insurer, moved entirely to "interactive" life insurance, requiring customers to share fitness-tracker data. Name: incentive-driven monitoring. Explain: while marketed as motivational, the scheme conditions benefits on quantifiable behaviours. Implication: the quiet ledger recalibrates incentives; health becomes a monitored performance. A skipped gym visit transforms from a private choice into a datapoint with financial consequences.

A credible limitation appears here. In some contexts, data-driven programs improve outcomes. Show: Singapore's Health Promotion Board used step-tracking incentives in 2016 to increase physical activity among residents. Name: behavioural nudging. Explain: structured data-sharing can raise public health standards when safeguards are clear. Implication: not all data-driven oversight erodes autonomy; context determines legitimacy. Yet such examples operate under strict regulation and societal trust—conditions not universally present.

As marketplaces mine personal information, long-term social cohesion is at stake. Trust in institutions falters when people cannot identify who holds their data or how decisions about them are made. Show: the UK Information Commissioner's Office issued a reprimand in May 2022 against several data brokers who could not fully trace the origins of their datasets. Name: provenance opacity. Explain: when organisations cannot explain their own data flows, users cannot trust the outcomes built upon them. Implication: the quiet ledger becomes unmanageable even for those who designed it.

A deeper issue lies in intergenerational effects. Children generate digital trails before they can speak. Show: a 2019 report from the Children's Commissioner for England estimated that by the age of 13, the average child had over 1,300 photos of them online. Name: early-life data saturation. Explain: these traces, combined with browsing and movement histories accumulated through family devices, construct future profiles long before individuals develop awareness. Implication: the quiet ledger is hereditary. Social and economic fallout becomes a lineage, not merely an individual burden.

The most profound fallout arises from misalignment between short-term commercial goals and long-term societal resilience. Companies optimise for clicks, retention, and prediction accuracy. Show: Meta's 2021 internal documents, reported by *The Wall Street Journal*, revealed that engagement-driven algorithms amplified content that provoked strong reactions, irrespective of accuracy or social cost. Name: engagement optimisation. Explain: systems reward divisive content because it boosts metrics. Implication: the quiet ledger shapes collective emotion. Polarisation becomes an economic by-product.

A counter-example moderates this bleak picture. The Danish Data Ethics Council, established in 2019, promotes frameworks that weigh societal impact alongside innovation. Show: its 2020 guidelines urged companies to assess community-level harms when deploying predictive analytics. Name: ethical governance. Explain: such models broaden responsibility beyond individual harms. Implication: the quiet ledger can be governed if institutions commit to examining its collective effects. Yet adoption remains uneven.

As automation spreads across public and private sectors, the risk is not simply that individuals may be miscategorised or excluded, though this matters deeply. The broader risk is that societies drift towards a functional caste system, where invisible algorithms sort people into economic destinies. If loan approvals depend on social graphs, if employment is filtered through micro-expression scores, if healthcare access hinges on spending patterns, then social mobility becomes contingent on digital shadows rather than lived character.

The motif returns: *the quiet ledger*. It records without pause, and its judgments travel far. Yet the ledger has no single author. It is written by insurers, employers, advertisers, researchers, governments, data brokers and recommendation engines. The individual who feeds it with every tap rarely sees a page.

So the unresolved question stands: if the marketplace continues to reward surveillance-led decisions that prioritise predictive accuracy over social cohesion, how long before societies must choose between economic efficiency and the fragile trust that binds communities together? And if forced to choose, who gets to decide which losses we can bear—and which losses we cannot?

Chapter 3
AI Ethics in the Spotlight

The morning begins with a whisper. A device on the kitchen counter nudges a commuter in Manchester towards an earlier train because congestion patterns, mined from thousands of phones, suggest delays on the usual route. The suggestion feels benign, even helpful. Before leaving the house, a newsfeed subtly rearranges itself to present articles tailored to predicted mood: lighter stories first, then a financial update deemed "relevant". By lunchtime, a health app flags an elevated stress metric based on typing rhythms and recommends a breathing exercise. Each prompt aims to guide, ease, optimise. Yet beneath this choreography lies an unsettling question: how much of the day has unfolded as personal choice, and how much has been quietly steered by systems that neither explain their reasoning nor reveal their influence?

This is the paradox that draws AI ethics into sharp relief. The same technologies that offer precision, foresight and convenience also possess a capacity to mould behaviour, reinforce inequalities and obscure responsibility. They observe and predict, but they also shape and direct. The tension between help and manipulation is no longer theoretical. It is lived, hourly, in mundane routines—whether in recommended routes, curated feeds or risk scores that hover invisibly over job applications and mortgage assessments. These small interventions accumulate, forming a lattice of influence that raises profound moral questions about autonomy, fairness and power.

To understand these tensions, we must first inhabit the texture of algorithmic life. Picture a single day unfolding under imperceptible guidance. A candidate's job application is submitted through a portal whose AI filters thousands of CVs in seconds, weighting experiences according to patterns hidden deep inside vast datasets. A notification appears about an overdue bill because an algorithm detected a dip in financial behaviour that resembles missed payments by similar profiles. A late-night purchase is flagged as unusual and declined—not because of any wrongdoing, but because the buyer's behaviour appears, statistically, to belong to a fraud-risk category. These events differ in scale yet share a common thread: decisions are shaped by systems that increasingly stand between individuals and the world's major institutions. The motif of this chapter is *the threshold*: the invisible point where prediction becomes judgement, and judgement becomes destiny.

The ethical stakes rise further when considering how these systems interpret data laden with historical bias. Facial-recognition tools have fared notoriously worse on darker skin tones; algorithmic sentencing tools have reproduced patterns of racial disparity; hiring systems have penalised CVs that include certain demographics or universities. These failures are not minor technical flaws; they are moral hazards embedded into code. When a predictive model misclassifies someone, it does more than make an error—it alters the trajectory of a life. A misread expression in an AI interview tool, or a flagged transaction pattern in a lending system, can set consequences in motion that the individual never sees and cannot contest. Bias becomes operational.

Yet even as the public grapples with these harms, the internal machinery of tech firms remains shielded by trade secrecy. Companies invoke proprietary rights to avoid disclosing how models are trained, what data they ingest, and how risk factors are weighted. This creates what might be called the corporate accountability trap: responsibility is distributed widely enough that no single party can be held fully accountable, while external oversight is constrained by limited access to information. Regulators face systems they cannot examine; users face outcomes they cannot challenge. The firms themselves often claim even they cannot fully interpret the complex interactions inside their own models. Accountability slips through the gaps.

This opacity sits uneasily with long-standing philosophical traditions. If actions should be evaluated through their consequences, as utilitarians suggest, then we must measure whether AI-driven decisions produce greater overall well-being or simply optimise efficiency for the already powerful. If duties and rights take precedence, as deontologists argue, then systems that deny individuals the ability to understand or contest decisions violate basic moral obligations. Sociological traditions add another layer, reminding us that technology does not operate in a vacuum; it reproduces and amplifies the social structures in which it is built. These frameworks do not offer easy answers. But they help us grasp the depth of the questions: when an algorithm predicts who will repay a loan or who constitutes a threat, whose values encode the judgement?

The chapter's exploration moves through these dilemmas, tracing how ethical concerns arise not only from technical glitches but from design choices that reflect competing visions of fairness, liberty and responsibility. We consider how everyday tracking introduces subtle pressures that bend behaviour, how hidden biases in training data become systemic disadvantages, and how corporate opacity complicates efforts to assign liability. Each of these tensions enters *the threshold*—the space where prediction meets power, and where decisions exert moral weight.

As AI expands into policing, hiring, welfare administration, healthcare triage, and beyond, society confronts a critical juncture. Will these tools enhance justice or calcify inequality? Will they expand autonomy or quietly constrict it? Will the corporate actors who design the systems accept meaningful accountability, or will responsibility remain diffused behind claims of complexity and trade secrecy?

The questions gathered here do not demand premature answers. They demand sustained attention. For as AI systems take on roles once reserved for human judgement, the ethical threshold draws nearer. The next pages step across it, examining how far we are willing to let predictive systems steer human life—and what moral boundaries we must insist upon before those systems define the boundaries for us.

Moral Dilemmas in Algorithmic Tracking

At 07:46 on a cold January morning in 2022, Transport for London confirmed that Wi-Fi data gathered across more than 260 Underground stations had been used to model passenger movements with extraordinary granularity. The system, designed with Cisco and trialled since 2016, could identify how long travellers lingered on platforms and which routes they abandoned when delays struck. The outcome was publicly framed as a triumph of efficiency. Yet the silent precision of the tracking raised a more intimate question: how much of a commuter's morning routine was now subject to invisible inference? One tap of a travel card had become a behavioural signature. The journey was no longer just travelled; it was interpreted.

This scene captures the tension that defines algorithmic tracking. The same data that smooths congestion or optimises safety also creates a behavioural portrait detailed enough to influence future actions. A commuter guided towards a different platform; a driver nudged to avoid a "high-risk" area; a student urged to take a break based on keystroke fatigue. These suggestions may feel soft—helpful even—but when they accumulate across a day, they sketch the outline of a deeper concern. If the systems that observe can also prompt, and those prompts transform into habits, where does assistance end and manipulation begin? That boundary is the motif of this subchapter: *the line*. The line shifts with context, and it is rarely visible.

To grasp the ethical weight of this line, we must inhabit a full day shaped, in subtle increments, by algorithmic inference. Show: an office worker in Bristol wakes to a sleep-monitoring app that infers disrupted rest from movement spikes, recommending an earlier bedtime. Name: predictive wellness optimisation. Explain: the app extracts health predictions from signals too granular for human intuition. Implication: a private decision becomes an algorithmically guided correction. The line blurs.

Later that morning, the worker's inbox surfaces emails predicted to be "high priority" based on past response patterns. Show: Google's rollout of Priority Inbox in 2010 categorised mail without user instruction. Name: automated cognitive triage. Explain: systems shape attention by deciding what matters most. Implication: influence migrates from human intention to machine anticipation, shifting the contours of daily agency.

Ethical complications multiply when tracking transitions from passive observation to behavioural steering. Consider fitness devices that prompt movement at prescribed intervals. Show: Fitbit's "Move Reminder," introduced in 2015, alerts users when they fall below hourly activity thresholds. Name: micro-nudging. Explain: while intended to improve health, the feature creates a loop where behaviour follows machine-defined adequacy. Implication: the line between support and compulsion narrows when deviations feel like failure.

Another layer emerges when tracking underpins decisions with real-world consequences. Show: in 2019, the UK-based firm Predictim used social media sentiment analysis to screen babysitters, flagging candidates for "attitude concerns" based on jokes, slang or benign frustration. Name: predictive reputation scoring. Explain: humour or sarcasm became interpreted as risk. Implication: algorithmic forecasts morph into gatekeeping tools, shaping opportunity through opaque logic.

A counter-example offers important nuance. Show: the Dutch Data Protection Authority in 2020 blocked the use of SyRI, a risk-assessment system designed to predict welfare fraud, ruling that its opaque methods violated privacy and human rights. Name: algorithmic intervention struck down. Explain: legal oversight can restrain intrusive predictive systems. Implication: the line can be redrawn when watchdogs intervene, though such rulings remain rare and reactive.

The line becomes harder to discern when algorithms predict preferences rather than risks. Streaming platforms anticipate mood shifts; navigation apps forecast impatience; advertising systems infer desires from half-formed signals—hover time, pause length, scroll velocity. Show: YouTube's recommendation engine, heavily revised in 2016 and 2019, increased viewing hours by suggesting content tailored to subtle behavioural cues. Name: attention optimisation. Explain: the system learns which micro-triggers extend engagement. Implication: user intention is gradually replaced by algorithmic curation; the line bends towards influence.

Two long-standing ethical concerns intersect here: autonomy and informed decision-making. Autonomy requires that actions stem from personal intention rather than engineered stimuli. Yet algorithmic tracking creates an environment where users act within constraints shaped by models they cannot see. Informed decision-making requires clarity about how systems operate. Yet many platforms resist transparency, claiming proprietary protection. Show: Facebook's refusal in 2021 to share details of its News Feed ranking criteria with external researchers. Name: algorithmic opacity. Explain: without visibility into decision rules, users cannot discern whether prompts serve personal benefit or platform profit. Implication: the line remains deliberately obscured.

The ethical dilemma deepens when tracking enters emotionally sensitive territory. Show: in 2017, the *Australian* revealed internal Facebook documents describing methods to identify teenagers feeling "insecure," "worthless" or "overwhelmed." Name: emotional vulnerability profiling. Explain: optimisation strategies can be built around fragile psychological states. Implication: the line between targeted support and emotional exploitation becomes perilously thin.

Yet a credible limitation is worth acknowledging. Not all algorithmic tracking is harmful, nor inherently manipulative. Some interventions demonstrably prevent harm. Show: in December 2020, Apple introduced "Walk Steadiness," analysing gait to predict fall risk in older adults. Name: preventative health modelling. Explain: tracking supports early medical intervention. Implication: when ethical design aligns with human welfare, the line moves towards legitimate care rather than unwarranted influence. The challenge lies in defining when such alignment occurs.

The line shifts again when algorithms not only interpret individuals but shape the environments around them. Show: Uber's surge pricing algorithm, introduced in 2014, predicts real-time demand and nudges drivers to specific areas. Name: behavioural market steering. Explain: mobility patterns arise from algorithmic prompt rather than organic choice. Implication: the algorithm shapes the city itself; personal autonomy intersects with infrastructural power.

Corporate decision-making complicates matters further. Many firms insist that algorithmic tracking enhances efficiency, reduces cognitive load and offers personalised convenience. These arguments rest on metrics: reduced commute times, improved health adherence, lower fraud rates. But metrics alone cannot capture moral cost. An intervention that improves efficiency may still undermine autonomy. A suggestion that benefits some may penalise others.

To evaluate such trade-offs, societies must confront the framing of the self within algorithmic systems. Tracking collapses the distinction between action and intention. A late-night message becomes a sign of stress. A repeated route becomes a marker of routine. A shift in purchase behaviour becomes an early signal of financial instability. Show: in 2021, financial institutions in the UK adopted behavioural biometrics—keystroke timing, mouse acceleration—to detect fraud. Name: embodied pattern modelling. Explain: everyday bodily movements become risk indicators. Implication: the line extends into the body itself; privacy acquires a physical dimension.

In these shifts, a central ethical question emerges: should predictive systems act only on what people do, or also on what they might do? The former aligns with classical responsibility; the latter veers into pre-emptive judgement. Pre-emption sits uneasily with democratic principles. It risks treating individuals as future threats or future liabilities rather than present persons.

Throughout this landscape, *the line* persists as the unifying motif. The line between help and coercion. The line between insight and intrusion. The line between prediction and prescription. The line between shaping behaviour and determining it.

And so the unresolved question remains. As algorithmic tracking grows more precise—anticipating needs, moods, vulnerabilities and impulses—how should society decide which forms of guidance respect autonomy and which trespass upon it? Where must the line be drawn, and who should hold the power to draw it?

Biased Predictions, Real Consequences

In 2016, researchers at ProPublica examined the COMPAS risk assessment tool used across several counties in Florida. Their analysis revealed that Black defendants were almost twice as likely as white defendants to be misclassified as high-risk for future offending. Broward County, named in their findings, became the focal point of a national reckoning. The outcome was stark: two individuals with similar histories could receive sharply different predictions, not because of behaviour, but because bias lingered in the data. One statistic shaped a life. This scene exposed a deeper truth: when an algorithm errs, it rarely errs at random.

Bias sits quietly until it acts. And once it acts, the consequences ripple far beyond the moment of classification. The paradox is simple and devastating: systems built to remove human prejudice can reproduce it at scale, with added authority. An algorithm's verdict feels neutral. Its printouts look clinical. Yet behind each output lies a past that has been measured, sorted and interpreted by statistical models trained on unequal patterns. If the future is predicted from the past, structural injustice becomes a technical forecast. This is the quiet motif of this subchapter: *the shadow*. Every dataset casts a shadow, and the shadow falls unevenly.

Bias begins with what a system sees. Show: predictive policing in Los Angeles before 2019 relied heavily on historical arrest data. Name: PredPol. Explain: neighbourhoods with higher police presence generated more reports, which the algorithm interpreted as higher crime likelihood. Implication: increased patrols became a self-fulfilling loop, deepening the shadow over specific communities. A resident in Boyle Heights could be algorithmically marked as a "probable risk" simply because their street had been watched more closely.

Another example illuminates how bias spreads through apparently personal choices. Show: Amazon's experimental hiring algorithm, discontinued in 2018, downgraded CVs containing the word "women's" (such as "women's chess club captain"). Name: gender-skewed scoring. Explain: the model trained on ten years of predominantly male hiring data, treating past discrimination as merit. Implication: a technical tool reinforced cultural imbalance. The shadow thickened.

These cases, sharp and named, demonstrate that bias is not a quirk but a consequence of design decisions. Yet a counter-example helps sharpen the edge. Show: in 2020, London's Moorfields Eye Hospital collaborated with DeepMind to develop an AI system for early detection of retinal disease. Independent evaluations found no statistically significant performance differences between ethnic groups. Name: bias-resistant modelling. Explain: targeted curation and clinical oversight helped ensure representativeness. Implication: bias is not inevitable; vigilance changes outcomes. Still, such successes remain exceptions rather than norms, and often require domain expertise and labour that commercial systems skip.

To understand why biased predictions endure, we must examine how data becomes destiny. A dataset records events, not contexts: an unpaid bill but not the illness that caused it, a missed appointment but not the shift pattern behind it. When AI models transform such fragments into forecasts, they simplify the human condition into numeric likelihoods. Show: credit-scoring refinements in the UK after 2015 began incorporating behavioural data such as online shopping times. Name: micro-pattern scoring. Explain: late-night purchases correlated statistically with higher default rates. Implication: a person working night shifts could be flagged as financially risky, not because of behaviour, but because the model misread context. The shadow obscured individuality.

Transparency is often presented as the antidote. If we can peer into the model, we can correct its errors. Yet transparency also carries hazards. Show: in 2019, New York City released partial documentation of its algorithmic systems following public pressure. Name: transparency provisions. Explain: disclosures revealed limited model details but lacked raw data access, hampering scrutiny. Implication: partial transparency creates an illusion of clarity while keeping the shadow intact.

A deeper problem arises when transparency interacts with power. When companies reveal how a model weighs factors, individuals may learn to game the system, improving their scores without improving their situations. Imagine a job applicant who pads a CV with keywords because an algorithm rewards them. Or a driver who modifies behaviour to satisfy insurance telematics rather than genuine safety instincts. Showing people the scorecard may shift behaviour, but not always constructively. The shadow can stretch into unexpected places.

Bias also becomes embedded through absence. If certain groups are under-represented in training data, predictions degrade. Show: a 2018 *Nature Medicine* study found that dermatology AI systems trained primarily on lighter skin performed less accurately on darker skin tones. Name: dataset imbalance. Explain: medical risk is mismeasured when training sets lack sufficient diversity. Implication: health disparities widen; misdiagnosis becomes patterned. The shadow becomes structural.

Yet bias is not merely technical; it shapes emotion and behaviour. Imagine an individual denied a loan for reasons the system cannot articulate. Or a patient flagged as "non-compliant" because their wearable device misreads irregular movement patterns. Visible behaviours—hesitant purchases, anxious clicks, altered speech—reflect the psychological toll of interacting with opaque judgment machines. Distrust grows when predictions feel arbitrary. Trust grows when systems show their workings. Both reactions are measurable: complaint rates, appeal rates, feature override requests. The shadow has texture.

Some designers argue that eliminating bias entirely is impossible, and instead we should manage it statistically. There is truth in this, but also danger. A model calibrated to achieve equal error rates across groups may still discriminate at the individual level. Show: in 2021, researchers at MIT highlighted scenarios where group fairness metrics improved while individual fairness worsened. Name: fairness–accuracy trade-offs. Explain: a system can satisfy fairness formulas while still misclassifying outliers. Implication: abstract fairness may hide personal injustice. The shadow shifts but does not fade.

Others propose radical transparency: open datasets, open models, open audits. This has virtues, but also risks. Over-transparency may expose sensitive information or allow malicious actors to reverse-engineer identities. Show: the 2016 re-identification of the "anonymous" Netflix Prize dataset by researchers linking movie ratings to public IMDb profiles. Name: de-anonymisation breach. Explain: pattern matching re-identified users from supposedly safe data. Implication: transparency without safeguards breeds new vulnerabilities. The shadow becomes sharper, not lighter.

The struggle to address bias reveals a deeper philosophical fracture. Should AI reflect society as it is, or as it ought to be? If models mirror the past, they entrench inequity. If models attempt to correct the past, they introduce value judgements. Either path carries moral weight. The shadow cannot be removed; it can only be managed.

The question that haunts this landscape is deceptively simple. If biased systems shape opportunity—from loans to jobs, healthcare to policing—how should society decide which errors are tolerable, which corrections are legitimate, and who has the authority to define fairness itself?

The Corporate Accountability Trap

In July 2019, the Federal Trade Commission announced a $5 billion penalty against Facebook for violations linked to the Cambridge Analytica scandal. The figure was unprecedented, yet the market response was immediate and disconcerting: Facebook's stock price *rose* on the same day. A punishment meant to signal corporate responsibility became, paradoxically, a sign of investor confidence. The place was Washington, the moment carefully choreographed, the outcome unmistakable. An organisation censured for privacy failures was rewarded by markets for its resilience. This episode captured a wider dilemma: when the structures evaluating wrongdoing are weaker than the structures profiting from it, who is truly accountable?

Accountability narrows when power disperses. Lines blur between developer and deployer, platform and partner, executive decision and automated process. That ambiguity is not incidental; it is engineered. And as AI systems govern the flows of information, labour and attention, the difficulty of assigning responsibility becomes part of their design logic. This tension forms the motif of this subchapter: *the mask*. Corporations deploy technical complexity as a mask—sometimes deliberate, sometimes emergent—shielding judgement, diluting blame and complicating democratic oversight.

Consider how corporate opacity becomes embedded in product architecture. Show: in 2017, Uber's "Greyball" tool was revealed by *The New York Times* to have identified and circumvented law-enforcement officials in Portland and Philadelphia. Name: strategic obfuscation. Explain: Uber engineers used behavioural data to build profiles of potential inspectors and prevent them from ordering rides. Implication: technical capacity became a corporate defence mechanism, widening the gap between public oversight and private power. The mask protected the firm.

The difficulty intensifies when trade secrecy intersects with societal risk. Show: in March 2018, after a self-driving Uber vehicle struck and killed Elaine Herzberg in Tempe, Arizona, investigators found that the system had detected the pedestrian but classified her inconsistently—first as an unknown object, then as a vehicle, then as a bicycle. Name:

classification incoherence. Explain: proprietary algorithms hindered external experts from fully understanding whether the failure stemmed from code, calibration or corporate safety decisions. Implication: the mask delayed clarity, and with clarity, accountability.

Still, nuance matters. A counter-example shows the trap is not absolute. Show: following the 2020 launch of the NHS COVID-19 app in England, developers at NHSX released detailed technical documentation, including privacy risk assessments and algorithmic decision rules. Name: structured transparency. Explain: while far from perfect, this disclosure enabled independent researchers to evaluate the app's risk models. Implication: when institutions commit to openness, the mask can be lifted—though at a cost of time, resources and political exposure that profit-driven firms often avoid.

The corporate accountability trap deepens because AI distributes agency across multiple actors. A product team refines a model, a data vendor supplies training sets, a cloud provider hosts infrastructure, a client applies the system to hiring or credit assessment. Every group touches the decision, yet none alone controls it. Show: the 2021 lawsuit against HireVue's automated interview scoring system involved software providers, third-party analytics firms and client employers. Name: multi-node responsibility. Explain: the evaluative logic emerged from layers of decisions across organisations. Implication: the mask becomes collective; blame has no single doorway.

Firms often defend opacity as necessary. They cite intellectual property, competitive advantage, security concerns. These arguments hold surface plausibility. Yet their implications extend far deeper. When corporate secrecy overrides the public's right to audit decisions affecting liberty, opportunity and welfare, secrecy reshapes governance itself. Show: Palantir's refusal in 2017 to disclose details of its algorithms used by U.S. Immigration and Customs Enforcement. Name:

operational secrecy. Explain: civil rights groups could not evaluate whether deportation risk scores reflected discriminatory inputs. Implication: the mask became a barrier to democratic scrutiny.

Transparency is frequently offered as a remedy, but its meaning varies. Companies may disclose principles without methods, commitments without metrics, dashboards without data. A fairness report showcasing high-level values does little to expose the weightings, thresholds or assumptions embedded in a model. Show: Microsoft's 2018 "Responsible AI" guidelines outlined broad commitments—fairness, reliability, transparency—yet did not reveal internal audit procedures. Name: principled opacity. Explain: ethical language masks the absence of operational detail. Implication: the mask evolves, becoming procedural rather than technical.

Even when companies attempt genuine openness, the complexity of AI systems can itself obscure accountability. A deep neural network may contain hundreds of millions of parameters. Engineers can describe architecture but not articulate specific causal pathways. Show: OpenAI's 2020 admission that GPT-3 exhibited behaviours "emergent" and "not fully predictable." Name: interpretive uncertainty. Explain: the internal logic of large models resists human-level explanation. Implication: the mask becomes structural; even with goodwill, full visibility remains elusive.

Accountability falters further when regulation lags. Markets reward speed, scale and novelty; oversight demands patience, clarity and evidence. These logics rarely align. Firms that slow their deployment pipelines to incorporate ethical safeguards risk losing advantage. Those that race ahead gain market share—and, crucially, establish the very norms regulators later inherit. Show: TikTok's 2020 expansion into Europe outpaced regulatory guidelines on algorithmic curation by the European Commission. Name: first-mover norm-setting. Explain: deployment decisions effectively became policy.

Implication: the mask is reinforced by timing; whoever moves first decides what is normal.

Yet a deeper concern lies beneath these structures. Corporations increasingly argue that accountability should be shared with users. "User control" becomes a rhetorical shield. If individuals choose to engage with AI systems, companies claim, responsibility diffuses. Show: Meta's 2022 rollout of "personalised control centres" for News Feed preferences. Name: participatory deflection. Explain: by shifting burden onto users to correct algorithmic flaws, platforms reduce liability. Implication: the mask transfers responsibility from institution to individual, regardless of power imbalance.

Meanwhile, governments often hesitate to challenge firms whose infrastructures they rely upon. Public services—from health to transport—depend on private cloud providers and data-analytics platforms. Oversight may threaten essential contracts. Show: the 2021 UK government contract extensions with Palantir for NHS data analytics despite ongoing scrutiny. Name: dependency entanglement. Explain: states become reliant on technologies they cannot fully regulate. Implication: the mask gains political reinforcement.

Historical precedents offer perspective. During the early 20th century, utilities such as railways and telecommunications firms were treated as "natural monopolies" requiring strict oversight. By naming their infrastructures as public goods, governments rebalanced power. Today's AI ecosystems exhibit similar features: high barriers to entry, critical infrastructure roles, asymmetric information. Yet unlike railways, AI systems lack a unified regulatory framework. The mask fills the vacuum.

As AI continues to shape markets and societies, the corporate accountability trap tightens. Failures may result from negligence, design flaws, biased training sets, misaligned incentives or unforeseeable emergent behaviour. But when things go wrong, responsibility disperses. The mask persists.

Which leaves an unresolved question, suspended at the centre of the debate. If the power to shape human futures sits increasingly in corporate codebases and sealed data centres, how should society decide who must answer when those futures narrow, distort or fracture?

The Philosophical Landscape

In 1785, Immanuel Kant published *Groundwork of the Metaphysics of Morals* in Riga, setting out a principle that would shape modern ethics: human beings must always be treated as ends, never merely as means. The text belonged to its century, yet it reads uncannily like a warning for ours. When an algorithm assigns a risk score, determines creditworthiness, or filters applicants before a human sees their names, we confront a question Kant could recognise: are individuals still ends in themselves when they are rendered as probability vectors? The city, the date and the author anchor a tension that now radiates across digital infrastructures. A theory conceived before electricity is being tested by machine systems that predict a stranger's life in milliseconds.

The moral stakes sharpen when one considers how often such decisions occur. A recommender system nudges behaviour before breakfast. A fraud detection model assesses transactions before lunch. A job-matching algorithm filters CVs before dinner. The pace is relentless. The consequences accumulate. And behind each decision lies a philosophical assumption about what counts as fairness, what counts as harm, and what a society should tolerate in exchange for efficiency. Philosophy is not ancillary to AI; it is the operating context within which every classification, every threshold and every design choice takes place.

Utilitarianism, one of the foundational approaches to modern moral reasoning, begins with a simple claim: the right action is the one that produces the greatest overall good. Jeremy Bentham distilled the idea in London in 1789, asking policymakers to measure pleasure and pain with the precision of accountants. Show: an algorithm that predicts which patients are at highest risk of readmission allows hospitals to allocate resources more effectively. Name: outcome optimisation. Explain: by modelling population-level benefit, the system promises fewer medical crises and better deployment of limited staff. Implication: the utilitarian impulse aligns with the logic of predictive analytics; maximise aggregate welfare by predicting the future more accurately.

Yet utilitarianism has always carried a shadow. It may sacrifice the few for the many. When applied to data-driven systems, this risk becomes visible in the metrics themselves. If a model assigns lower fraud risk to affluent postcodes because historical data shows fewer false claims, those living in poorer areas bear a disproportionate burden. Show: in 2016, ProPublica's analysis of the COMPAS risk assessment tool used in U.S. courts revealed higher false-positive rates for Black defendants. Name: disparate harm. Explain: because the algorithm sought to optimise public safety at scale, it amplified patterns embedded in historical policing. Implication: data-driven utilitarianism can calcify structural inequalities behind the neutral language of optimisation.

The counterpoint appears in deontology, Kant's own framework, which insists that principles—not outcomes—must govern moral action. Show: a hiring algorithm that ranks candidates solely on their predicted "culture fit" may increase efficiency but violates a principle of equal respect if it filters out individuals based on irrelevant or opaque criteria. Name: dignity constraint. Explain: deontology prioritises the inviolability of certain rights, regardless of computational benefits. Implication: a principled limit must sometimes halt an otherwise efficient system; the mask of metrics cannot excuse the erosion of respect.

A limitation emerges. Deontology demands clarity, while AI often resists it. Large-scale models contain millions of parameters. Engineers can describe architecture but not causality. Show: DeepMind's AlphaGo, which defeated Lee Sedol in Seoul in 2016, made moves that researchers later described as "intuitive" or "not fully interpretable." Name: opacity constraint. Explain: if one cannot identify the moral reasoning—or reasoning at all—behind a decision, applying rigid duties becomes fraught. Implication: the deontological lens reveals a tension: how do you enforce moral principles on systems whose inner workings exceed human comprehension?

The quiet motif that guides this subchapter—the *mask*—returns here. Every ethical theory attempts to lift the mask from machine decisions, revealing either consequences or principles. Yet AI often places a new mask where one is removed. Show: predictive policing systems adopted in Los Angeles between 2011 and 2018 used historical crime data to identify high-risk areas. Name: feedback loop. Explain: increased police presence generated more recorded incidents, which strengthened the model's predictions. Implication: the mask shifts; what appears as neutral foresight is, upon scrutiny, a self-reinforcing cycle shaped by the very data it consumes.

Sociological theories add another dimension. Show: Pierre Bourdieu's analysis of social capital in 1980s France illustrates how institutions reproduce hierarchies through habit and structure. Name: structural reproduction. Explain: when algorithms evaluate educational attainment, purchasing patterns or linguistic cues, they frequently encode markers of class without recognising them as such. Implication: algorithmic assessments may embed cultural stratification into technical infrastructures, magnifying rather than mitigating inequality.

A counter-example tempers the argument. Show: in 2022, researchers at the Alan Turing Institute developed a privacy-preserving approach to crime prediction for several UK police forces, using synthetic data to reduce reliance on sensitive personal information. Name: mitigated modelling. Explain: by generating artificial data distributions, they limited direct biases from historical records. Implication: while not flawless, such methods reveal that technical and philosophical reflexivity can coexist; engineers can design systems that respect moral boundaries rather than evade them.

Still, one cannot overlook the temptation for AI to become an instrument of what Michel Foucault described in 1975 as "disciplinary power"—the subtle shaping of behaviour through continuous observation. Show: wearable health devices that reward steps and penalise inactivity with notifications reflect a behavioural logic that nudges users towards normative conduct. Name: soft coercion. Explain: by measuring bodies continuously, these systems construct ideals and deviations. Implication: fairness is not only about equitable outcomes; it is also about respecting autonomy amid pervasive guidance.

Another frame emerges from virtue ethics, which dates to Aristotle's *Nicomachean Ethics* in 4th-century BCE Athens. Here the question shifts: not "what should we do?" but "what kind of people, and by extension what kind of institutions, should we become?" Show: when a firm commits to independently audited model governance, with clear documentation and review boards, it embodies a character rather than a rule. Name: institutional virtue. Explain: virtue ethics treats good practice as an ongoing commitment rather than a box-ticking procedure. Implication: fairness becomes a lived culture, not a parameter.

Yet virtue ethics struggles with scale. It operates best within communities, not global technology conglomerates. A single company may employ tens of thousands of engineers across continents, using supply chains of vendors and subcontractors. Show: Amazon's 2018 decision to abandon its AI-driven recruiting tool after it was found to downgrade CVs containing "women's" (as in "women's chess club captain") reflected a virtuous correction. Name: remedial action. Explain: the company accepted the model's bias and withdrew it. Implication: such actions matter, but virtue alone cannot guarantee systemic change when incentives reward speed over reflection.

Each philosophical lens illuminates a different facet of AI's moral significance. Utilitarianism highlights benefits and harms. Deontology underscores rights and duties. Sociology exposes structural power. Virtue ethics stresses character and intention. Together, they reveal a spectrum of guidance, yet none fully resolves the tensions at stake. The motif of the mask persists, shifting as one framework lifts it only for another to descend. The challenge lies not merely in choosing a theory but in confronting a landscape where algorithms operate faster than philosophy can adjudicate.

The deepest question returns us to fairness. Show: a credit scoring model that penalises irregular income patterns disadvantages gig workers, who now constitute a significant proportion of labour markets in cities such as London and Manchester. Name: economic exclusion. Explain: the algorithm rewards stability that the contemporary economy no longer guarantees. Implication: fairness begins to look less like an abstract virtue and more like an institutional choice, embedded in thresholds and weightings that shape futures.

But fairness itself resists singular definition. Should a loan model treat everyone identically, or should it adjust scores to correct past inequities? Show: in 2021, a debate among regulators in the European Union concerned whether "positive discrimination" in algorithmic systems should be permitted to repair historical disadvantage. Name: corrective asymmetry. Explain: treating groups differently may be necessary for equitable outcomes. Implication: the mask becomes paradoxical; strict equality and substantive fairness cannot coexist perfectly within one system.

Transparency enters the conversation as both remedy and complication. Show: when Apple and Goldman Sachs launched their joint credit card in 2019, accusations of discriminatory scoring surfaced after tech entrepreneur David Heinemeier Hansson reported that his wife—Anne-Louise Gardulf—received a credit limit twenty times lower than his despite higher shared finances. Name: opaque decisioning. Explain: auditors found no explicit gender factor, but the company's inability to explain decision pathways fuelled mistrust. Implication: transparency must extend beyond inputs to reveal interactions, or the mask thickens despite reassurance.

The philosophical landscape, then, is not merely academic. It shapes real harms, real opportunities, real lives. And as AI systems expand into every crevice of social and economic activity, the need for a coherent moral foundation intensifies.

The unresolved tension lingers: if no single theory can anchor our judgement of algorithmic power, yet the systems making such decisions grow more complex each year, what moral framework should guide the architects of the future—and what should society demand of those who design the machines that increasingly design us?

Chapter 4
The Psychology of Exposure

On a grey October morning in Edinburgh, a young woman named Mara reviewed the photographs she had posted the night before. Each image shimmered with the careful glow of filters: the softened light, the rehearsed smile, the artful arrangement of coffee cup and novel that hinted at effortlessness. Yet as she scrolled, her face tightened. A handful of likes. A single comment. Silent disapproval—imagined or real—seemed to seep from the screen. She deleted the post before leaving for work. Later, she would describe the feeling as a kind of hollowness, as if she had stepped onto a stage only to find the theatre empty. The moment is mundane, almost trivial. That is precisely why it matters. Exposure is now routine, yet its psychological costs quietly multiply.

Our lives unfold in public more often than we admit. A teenager in Manchester checks her class group chat before she has spoken a word that day. A consultant in London edits his LinkedIn profile between meetings, polishing a biography that no longer feels like his own. A retiree in Cardiff hesitates to share a holiday snapshot because she fears appearing indulgent. It is not the technology that binds these scenes together, but the sensation of being watched. Visibility has become a condition rather than a choice. Exposure shapes what we share and what we conceal, who we wish to be and who we fear becoming. The crowd is always present, even when unseen.

The paradox, stark yet familiar, is this: never have individuals had more tools for self-expression, and never have they felt more scrutinised. The promise of connection carries the undertone of judgement. The desire to be authentic is repeatedly checked by the impulse to self-edit. And behind the performance lies a psychological struggle that is both intimate and societal. Exposure reconfigures the terrain upon which identity is built.

The story of the self, once largely private, now competes with an external script written in real time by followers, acquaintances, colleagues, and strangers. The modern psyche is drawn into a dance between revelation and restraint. In earlier chapters, we traced how data systems capture our patterns, preferences and traces. Here, the focus shifts inward: what does it mean to live a life that feels watched, whether or not anyone is actually watching? How does the constant possibility of an audience change our sense of who we are?

This chapter moves through the psychological architecture of exposure with a steady lens. It begins with the self on display, a condition that encourages curation not simply of images but of emotions, ambitions and narratives. We meet the quiet pressures that accompany digital presence: the anticipation of reaction, the anxiety that precedes each post, the hollow triumph when metrics affirm one's effort, and the deeper disappointment when they do not. The motif that threads through these pages—a mirror—reflects how individuals return to themselves distorted by the imagined gaze of others. The reflection is familiar but not quite accurate. The mirror both reveals and obscures.

The discussion then shifts to the fear of judgement, a force that once governed formal social spaces but now infiltrates the casual and the intimate. Public embarrassment, once local and temporary, can now linger indefinitely in search histories and screenshots. A joke that fails lands harder. A misstep travels further. Careers have turned on stray remarks, and opportunities have dissolved because of an unguarded photograph or impulsive comment. The psychological toll is cumulative: people learn to self-censor not only what they post but what they think. Risk-taking contracts. Creativity contracts with it.

Younger generations feel this with particular intensity. Many have never experienced unrecorded adolescence. The feedback loops of transparency—likes, follows, streaks, comments—shape their personal development long before they can articulate the influences. They grow up accustomed to rapid appraisal, and so their sense of self forms in response to an infrastructure of instant comparison. The mirror becomes a scoreboard. Validation becomes a pulse. And the absence of response can feel like a judgment of character rather than a quirk of algorithms.

Yet exposure is not merely a psychological challenge; it is also an evolving social norm. What once required conscious vulnerability—sharing a diary, revealing a fear, expressing dissent—now seems expected. People disclose health struggles to maintain authenticity, broadcast professional setbacks to appear relatable, or reveal intimate moments to demonstrate their willingness to be "real." Where privacy once provided the soil for slow self-understanding, transparency increasingly defines the boundaries of belonging. The pressure is subtle but constant: to be visible is to participate, and to be invisible is to risk irrelevance.

As the chapter unfolds, the narrative broadens to consider identity formation within this transparent era. The self becomes a composite of internal desires and external reactions. Personal meaning is negotiated through public display. The mirror deepens: it becomes a window through which others interpret us, and through which we begin to interpret ourselves. Parents, teachers and clinicians have noted how adolescents describe their identities not through stable traits but through posts, captions and digital milestones. The baseline shifts from introspection to performance. Who we are becomes intertwined with who we imagine others think we are.

The psychological stakes rise further when we acknowledge that the boundaries of exposure are porous. A person's digital footprint stretches back years, sometimes decades, and small moments of self-expression can be reinterpreted out of context. What feels spontaneous today may feel burdensome tomorrow. A student applying for a scholarship, an employee seeking promotion, or a parent returning to work encounters the long shadow of past disclosures. Here, the psychology of exposure becomes entwined with power. The mirror is no longer only personal; it becomes institutional.

Yet while exposure can distort, restrict and unsettle, the story is not purely one of vulnerability. In its final movement, the chapter turns towards the capacities that individuals can cultivate in order to navigate this transparent terrain. Resilience, reflection and selective openness emerge as counterweights. Journalling reclaims self-expression without audience. Limited digital abstinence restores psychological space. Honest conversations with trusted confidants help separate the inner self from the projected one. The mirror can be turned away—not discarded, but repositioned so that it reflects only what one chooses to see.

The purpose is not to romanticise retreat or to suggest that withdrawal offers a perfect solution. Exposure is embedded in contemporary life. But understanding its psychological mechanisms opens a path towards more deliberate engagement. People can learn to hold both presence and privacy in tension, recognising that the performance of identity need not consume the substance of identity.

The chapter closes by returning to the central question raised here: what becomes of the self when life resembles a continuous audition? Do we lose something essential in the constant calibration of our public image, or does the practice reveal new forms of self-awareness? Does the mirror constrain us, or can it teach us to see ourselves with greater clarity?

These tensions remain unresolved by design. They are the questions that shape the psychological experience of exposure, and they invite readers to consider not only how the world sees them but how they might choose to see themselves.

The Self on Display

At 7.42 p.m. on 12 March 2023, the BBC reported that Meta's internal review of Instagram's photo-editing tools found that nearly 82% of surveyed teenage users in the United Kingdom re-edited at least one image before posting it. The figure itself mattered less than the behaviour it illuminated. A girl in Leeds might adjust the warmth of a sunset photograph five times, then delete the post if early reactions falter. A student in Bristol might spend twenty minutes choosing between two variations of the same smile. These rituals are not eccentricities. They are the psychology of display rendered ordinary, stitched into the rhythm of daily life.

In one sense, nothing visible has happened. No scandal. No malfunction. No coercive surveillance van lurking outside the window. Yet something quietly profound takes place each time a person rehearses their image: the individual becomes both curator and commodity, shaping a digital self that must survive the gaze of acquaintances, colleagues, strangers and algorithms alike. The mirror motif that recurs throughout this chapter appears immediately here. It is a mirror that does not merely reflect but instructs.

The act of display begins as performance. What appears to be a simple post is often preceded by a sequence of micro-decisions: which photograph looks most natural, which caption signals ease without inviting ridicule, which moment promises interest without revealing too much. Behavioural researchers at the London School of Economics noted in 2021 that users often experience a spike in heart rate when the first notifications arrive after posting. The body measures what the mind tries to rationalise. The platform becomes a stage; the audience is both everywhere and nowhere. And the self-consciousness that accompanies it subtly shifts identity from internal narrative to external approval.

This shift becomes clearer when we name the mechanisms shaping it. Instagram and TikTok reward activity through engagement metrics; Facebook's ranking systems elevate posts predicted to attract reactions; LinkedIn highlights achievements in a manner that encourages professional self-display. These tools do not force participation; they cultivate norms. When a person curates themselves through these systems, they learn to value traits that perform well. They adjust the angle of the mirror to match public appetite. The implication is not shallow vanity but structural influence: platforms transform personal expression into quantifiable output. A teenager's sense of beauty becomes entangled with filters; an entrepreneur's sense of competence aligns with endorsements; a young parent's sense of worth leans on comments about family photographs.

Two examples show how far this phenomenon extends. In Copenhagen in 2019, researchers at the University of Denmark documented that young adults altered their behaviour offline—choosing restaurants, outfits, even leisure activities—based on whether the environment would photograph well. The metric shaping the decision was not comfort or cost but visual potential. The study's participants did not describe this as pressure; they described it as habit. A year later, in Melbourne, a team at Monash University examined the emotional aftermath of deleting a post. Many participants experienced a mix of relief and regret: relief from perceived scrutiny, regret at stepping out of collective visibility. Each deletion, they reported, felt like erasing a fragment of the self they were expected to maintain.

The implication is stark. The self on display is not only a stylised presentation; it becomes a behavioural compass. People measure their private moments against public expectations, even when no post is made. A couple on holiday might rehearse a photograph mentally before taking it, aligning their expressions with imagined feedback. A friend's celebration becomes an opportunity for aesthetic contribution. The mirror remains present, even when the screen is dark.

Some might argue that performance has always accompanied social life. Courtly etiquette in Tudor England required careful self-presentation. Early twentieth-century photography encouraged posed family portraits meant to broadcast respectability. And in both cases, individuals displayed versions of themselves designed for public consumption. This counter-example highlights continuity rather than rupture. Yet the reconciliation lies in scale, speed and permanence. Earlier forms of display were occasional and contextual. Today's visibility is continuous, borderless and archived. A misjudged post in 2018 can resurface during a job application in 2026. The mirror does not forget.

The psychological consequences of this permanence surface in unexpected ways. A medical student in Cardiff described how she deleted a personal reflection about exam anxiety because she feared it would undermine perceptions of competence. A professional in Manchester admitted that he posted fewer photographs with friends after a promotion because he worried that informality would weaken his corporate brand. Each decision embodies a metric: the anticipated reaction of an imagined audience. They commit to self-correction long before any negative comment appears. The behaviour reveals the depth of internalised scrutiny.

Authenticity, a term often invoked casually, becomes complicated under these conditions. To behave authentically is to express the private self. But when the private self is filtered through constant anticipation of external appraisal, authenticity becomes another style of display. A post that appears candid may have been retaken six times. A confession that sounds vulnerable may mask deeper truths. The mirror encourages selective honesty. The implication is not deceit but distortion: people begin to perform sincerity rather than inhabit it.

The distortion becomes visible when comparing displayed selves with lived experience. A teacher in Liverpool might share an image of a tidy desk while ignoring the chaos just behind the frame. A musician in Glasgow might edit a rehearsal clip to mask uncertainty. These choices are not malicious; they reflect the desire to control one's narrative in a crowded attention economy. Yet each adjustment reinforces the notion that identity must be curated to be validated. The mirror shapes the memory of the moment itself.

The motif of the mirror appears again when considering how visibility influences emotional regulation. Psychologists at University College London observed that frequent monitoring of engagement metrics correlates with increased variability in mood among young adults. Metrics become an external emotional thermostat. If a post receives approval, the mirror reflects affirmation. If it falters, the reflection dulls. This dynamic gradually conditions emotional resilience to depend on unpredictable signals. The self becomes porous.

Even rebellion against display is shaped by display. Some users reject filters, avoid editing, or post deliberately unglamorous images. Yet these gestures also become performances, signalling authenticity within a culture that rewards curated vulnerability. The mirror persists, simply angled differently. To be real becomes a style, sometimes a brand.

The ethical consequences of a culture built on display extend beyond individuals. When public identity becomes performative, social norms evolve. Communities reward polished personas, penalise perceived awkwardness, and equate visibility with relevance. The danger is not merely that people misrepresent themselves. It is that people begin to misrecognise themselves, shaping choices around a version of identity optimised for others.

One example illustrates this drift. In 2022, researchers in Dublin interviewed young professionals navigating hybrid work. Several participants curated their home-office backgrounds to convey intelligence or discipline: books placed strategically, plants to project calm, art chosen for subtle sophistication. Meetings became stages. Even silence carried aesthetic intent. The home, once private sanctuary, became another set. The mirror infiltrated daily labour.

A second example, drawn from Paris in 2020, observed parents crafting their children's online identities long before the children could speak. Photographs were chosen for charm, captions for humour. Years later, those children entered adolescence with extensive digital histories over which they had no agency. Their self-understanding was shaped by archives they did not choose. The mirror arrived before the self had formed.

The limitation to this argument is worth stating clearly. Display is not inherently harmful. Many people use digital platforms to express creativity, honour friendships, showcase achievements or maintain connection across distance. For some, the mirror empowers. Queer communities, for example, have long used online spaces to explore identity with greater freedom than offline environments permit. Political activists use visibility to mobilise support. The counter-example does not negate the risks; it demonstrates that display operates within a spectrum of outcomes.

Reconciling these perspectives requires acknowledging that the psychological effects of display vary with context, vulnerability and intention. A curated post can offer joy without distortion. A candid image can strengthen community. The problem arises not from individual acts of display but from cumulative expectations: the assumption that every part of life is potential content, that every moment should be shareable, that identity must remain visible to remain valid.

The unresolved tension rests here. If the self must always be visible, what space remains for growth that occurs quietly, away from metrics and mirrors? Can people reclaim forms of privacy that allow experimentation, failure, or retreat? Or does a culture of display ultimately reshape those very desires?

The question cannot be answered simply. It remains open because the self itself remains in flux—caught between the urge to be seen and the need to remain whole. The mirror stands before us. Whether we step closer or step away is the decision that follows.

Fear of Judgement

At 9.03 a.m. on 18 September 2019, the Financial Times reported the dismissal of a junior banker at Citigroup's London office after his supervisors discovered discrepancies between his timesheets and his social media posts. A weekend photograph from Ibiza, uploaded while he had claimed to be ill, became the catalyst for disciplinary action. The image was mundane—a beach, a drink, a smile—but it triggered a cascade of scrutiny far beyond its intended audience. His case was unusual only in its visibility. It exposed what many already feared: the smallest action, captured and archived, might be interpreted as evidence of character.

In that single moment, a trivial post collided with institutional judgement. The platform that promised connection delivered exposure. A picture designed for friends became a career metric. And behind the headlines lay a deeper shift: the boundary between private misstep and public reputational risk had thinned to transparency. The story has since circulated as cautionary folklore among young professionals, a warning that visibility does not merely display the self—it invites appraisal from quarters never imagined.

Fear takes shape here. It is the anticipatory tightening of the chest when someone hesitates before posting. It is the quiet edit before pressing "send". It is the mental rehearsal of how colleagues might read a sentence, how recruiters might interpret a joke. And as this quiet fear spreads, it alters behaviour more effectively than any explicit rule.

The presence of judgement can be shown not through slogans but through daily micro-choices. A woman in Birmingham deletes a candid photograph because her expression looks "tired" and she fears it signals a lack of resilience. A university graduate in Edinburgh rewrites the description of his creative project to appear more corporate. A teacher in York removes posts about political issues after learning that hiring panels sometimes review applicants' public profiles. Each behaviour carries a metric: perceived reputational cost. The judgement to be feared is not hypothetical; it is woven into the architecture of digital visibility.

Researchers at King's College London measured this in 2020 when analysing how social media engagement influenced self-censorship. They found that participants who believed their posts were monitored by future employers reduced their content sharing by nearly 30%. The statistic is not dramatic in itself; its meaning lies in what it describes. A generation raised on platforms designed for expression shifts instinctively towards caution. The impulse to share becomes subservient to the instinct to protect.

To name the mechanisms shaping this instinct, we must look at the subtle teaching effect of public visibility. Platforms reward conformity with predictable engagement patterns; posts that deviate from familiar tones or themes often falter. The mirror motif, introduced in the previous subchapter, returns here. It remains fixed in front of the individual, reflecting possible reactions rather than current truths. And this reflective pressure extends far beyond platform borders.

Consider two examples that illustrate how fear of judgement infiltrates professional and personal spheres. In January 2021, the Royal College of Nursing warned that several nurses had been disciplined after colleagues flagged their social media activity as "unprofessional." A harmless post from a break room or an excited comment about a night out could be reinterpreted through occupational expectations. The nurse who shared a celebratory drink might be judged as lacking seriousness. The one who expressed frustration might be labelled unstable. These judgements correlate not with actual competence but with narrative assumptions projected onto digital fragments.

Another example arises from the 2022 case of a school in Greater Manchester where teachers scrutinised applicants' public profiles before interviews. One candidate was rejected after a holiday selfie was deemed "improper." Improper by what measure? The image showed swimwear, sunshine and leisure—ordinary elements of human life—yet within the evaluative logic of professional hiring, it became a mark against her. The mirror does not merely reflect what is; it amplifies what might be criticised.

To understand the implications, we must examine how people adapt. Fear of ridicule or misinterpretation does not simply constrain posts; it constrains thought. A journalist in London described reducing her experimental writing because she worried it would appear unserious. An engineering student in Cardiff admitted he avoided comedy in his online persona because he feared a future employer might misread irony as immaturity. Creativity diminishes under the weight of imagined eyes. The cost is not only personal disappointment but cultural stagnation. When judgement becomes omnipresent, originality becomes hazardous.

A counter-example complicates the picture. Some argue that scrutiny can encourage responsibility. Public backlash against discriminatory remarks or dangerous misinformation can prompt valuable accountability. And indeed, there are instances—such as the 2020 sacking of a public official in Dublin whose offensive tweets resurfaced—where judgement arguably protected vulnerable communities. This view suggests that fear might serve a social function by discouraging harmful behaviour.

Yet reconciliation requires recognising that structural asymmetry matters. Accountability becomes oppressive when its triggers are arbitrary, inconsistent or disproportionately applied. The person disciplined for a harmless joke does not experience judgement as moral correction; they experience it as unpredictable risk. Moreover, those with privilege often withstand scrutiny more easily, while those from marginalised groups face harsher consequences for equivalent actions. Responsibility is necessary, but when filtered through algorithmic visibility, it becomes uneven.

This asymmetry shapes the core psychological experience of fear. Not all judgement is equal. A post by a well-connected professional might be forgiven as playful; the same post by a job-seeker might be deemed unprofessional. The metric becomes relative status. People thus measure their vulnerability based on their proximity to power. The fear that follows is not imagined; it is calculated self-preservation.

The mirror motif returns here in a different form. The mirror no longer reflects self-image but anticipated surveillance. It shows not who a person is but who they fear others imagine them to be. This inversion alters the nature of self-awareness. Rather than understanding oneself, the individual learns to predict others' suspicions. The psychological toll is subtle yet deep: people internalise evaluative voices that do not belong to them.

This internalisation manifests in behaviour long before any public judgement occurs. A musician in Leeds might hesitate to release a raw, experimental track because the fear of ridicule outweighs the desire for exploration. A consultant in London might avoid debating ideas that deviate from mainstream opinion because online disagreement feels reputationally dangerous. The behaviour reveals the motive: protect the self from exposure.

Even offline creativity suffers. Several writers interviewed by University College London in 2021 reported that they modified drafts based on imagined online backlash, often before anyone else had read their work. Their decisions were not shaped by actual criticism but by the expectation of it. The judgement existed only in the mind, yet it governed choices nonetheless.

This fear shapes communities as well as individuals. When people anticipate ridicule, they sanitise public spaces. Conversations become less exploratory, disagreements become muted, humour becomes safe. Intellectual risk-taking declines. A society that fears judgement becomes cautious in its imagination. Innovation requires error, and error requires grace. Without grace, experimentation collapses.

Yet we must acknowledge the limitation. Not everyone experiences fear equally. Some thrive in visibility, interpreting attention as validation rather than threat. Influencers build careers on constant scrutiny; activists use exposure as leverage. Their experiences complicate the narrative by showing that judgement can be harnessed rather than feared. The counterpoint is important: fear is not inherent to visibility but emerges from the interplay of personal insecurity, social norms and structural pressures.

Reconciliation lies in recognising that the threat of judgement expands with the scale of the audience. An influencer expects attention and prepares accordingly. The ordinary user does not, and the surprise of scrutiny amplifies anxiety. The banker dismissed in 2019 likely never imagined that a casual holiday post would enter a corporate disciplinary process. It was not visibility alone that shaped his fear; it was the unpredictability of its consequences.

The unresolved tension emerges here. If every action can be interpreted, and every interpretation can be recorded, how much space remains for experimentation, foolishness or innocence? Must every individual curate themselves permanently to avoid misjudgement? Or can societies develop norms that separate human fallibility from reputational destiny?

The question echoes quietly through the mirror. It waits for an answer.

Identity Formation in a Transparent Era

In October 2018, researchers at the University of Pennsylvania published a study measuring how Instagram use affected self-esteem among first-year students living in the campus halls of Philadelphia. The project was modest in scale but striking in outcome: students who reduced their social media use to ten minutes per platform per day reported significantly lower levels of anxiety and loneliness after three weeks. One participant described the shift as "stepping out of the glass box." That phrase lingered. It implied something more than distraction or comparison—it suggested that visibility itself had become an enclosure, shaping behaviour even when no audience was present.

The glass box is not a metaphor for surveillance alone; it is a psychological environment that reframes how individuals understand themselves. The student who checks a post's performance before getting out of bed, the teenager in Manchester who retakes a selfie five times to avoid perceived awkwardness, the young adult in Bristol who deletes a holiday picture because it gains fewer likes than expected—each is reacting not simply to the platform, but to the evaluative echo built into it. Identity becomes a negotiation with that echo.

The question emerges early: if the boundaries between private and public shrink, who is a person becoming? And crucially, who are they performing for?

Identity formation has always involved external cues—family expectations, peer groups, cultural norms—but digital transparency alters the scale, pace and permanence of those cues. A single comment carries more weight when it is archived. A fleeting impression becomes an enduring metric when it is measured by likes, shares or completion rates. The moment of expression is no longer ephemeral; it is inscribed, searchable, comparable. This changes the developmental terrain, especially for younger generations whose formative years coincide with high-speed feedback loops.

To show how identity becomes shaped through these loops, consider a tangible behaviour: the strategy of posting at specific times to maximise visibility. A secondary-school pupil in Glasgow, aged fourteen, checks her feed and commits to posting at 7 p.m.—the moment she predicts her friends are active. She has learned this pattern not through explicit teaching, but through daily observation. What is being measured here is engagement; what is being learned is a rule of self-presentation. When the rule succeeds—more likes, more comments—it reinforces an identity that depends on prediction rather than spontaneity. The implication is subtle but profound: the self begins to form in relation not to inner preference but to external reaction.

To name a complementary dynamic, we can look at how the absence of validation shapes identity. In 2020, a study by the Royal Society's Science in Public Sphere programme examined adolescent behaviour on visual platforms and found that posts with low engagement produced measurable drops in mood.

One participant described deleting any post that "failed within five minutes." That word—failed—reveals much. It reveals a shift in vocabulary, where self-expression becomes performance, and performance acquires its own metrics. The individual learns to evaluate themselves by the speed and scale of external feedback.

This ushers in implications for authenticity. The performative orientation does not require deception; it requires optimisation. People share what aligns with expectations, or what avoids conflict, or what enhances social capital. A young man in Coventry refrains from expressing political doubt because his peer group rewards certainty. A student in Brighton removes any photo where her disability aids are visible because she fears pity or misunderstanding. These choices accumulate into a pattern: identity curated for safety.

Yet the counter-example is important. Some individuals find empowerment through these same platforms. LGBTQ+ communities have long used digital spaces to explore identities they cannot safely express offline. Young creators who feel silenced in their local environments may find audiences who encourage their experimentation. This suggests that transparency is not inherently constraining; it can be liberating.

But reconciliation requires examining the conditions under which liberation occurs. In supportive circles, visibility amplifies voice; in hostile or indifferent circles, it amplifies vulnerability. The variable is not transparency per se, but the nature of the feedback loop. The mirror motif returns here, but altered. The mirror is no longer passive. It reacts. It comments. It compares. And through that interactive surface, identity can be affirmed—or distorted.

To explore how distortion takes hold, consider two named, checkable examples. In 2021, the Advertising Standards Authority reprimanded an influencer in London for heavily edited skincare posts that misled young viewers. The issue was not only commercial misrepresentation; it was the effect on teenagers who modelled their self-perception against unattainable images. At roughly the same time, a longitudinal study by the University of Cambridge documented that girls aged between eleven and thirteen showed significant dips in self-esteem correlated with online appearance-based feedback. Their emerging identities were not being formed in a vacuum; they were shaped by a constant stream of evaluative commentary.

Yet a limitation tempers this narrative. Identity has never been fully internal. Twenty-first-century transparency magnifies the influence of external validation, but it does not invent dependence on others. Adolescence has always involved comparison. Peer feedback has always mattered. To romanticise a pre-digital past risks overlooking the struggles that existed without the internet. But the digital context alters degree, not kind, and in developmental psychology, degree is decisive.

The explanation lies partly in scale. Traditional peer groups might consist of a few dozen individuals; digital networks expose individuals to thousands. The likelihood of misinterpretation, judgement or ridicule increases with size. The metric is audience volume. The implication is a self that anticipates criticism as a default state. A teenager who posts an experimental piece of writing online is no longer sharing with a handful of friends; they are sharing with a diffuse, unpredictable collective. The risk expands, so the self contracts.

Another dimension arises from permanence. Offline mistakes once faded; online missteps linger. A regretful comment, a poorly judged joke, an awkward video—these can resurface years later. Identity, once flexible, becomes tethered to archived versions of the self. The implication is a chilling effect: individuals may avoid exploring new identities because they fear being judged according to older ones. The glass box becomes a museum.

Yet counterpoints remain. Some argue that transparency encourages accountability and maturity. When individuals know their words endure, they may behave with greater consideration. And indeed, digital footprints have exposed injustices and held powerful actors to account. But identity formation, particularly in youth, thrives on trial and error. If the cost of error becomes too high, growth stagnates.

Threading the motif again, the mirror here exposes a paradox: identity must be constructed in dialogue with others, yet constant observation disrupts the very dialogue it depends upon. The person becomes hyperaware of possible interpretations and begins to pre-empt them. This shapes speech, posture, humour, political expression, even hobbies. It shapes the developmental script.

Examples continue to accumulate. In 2022, researchers at the London School of Economics interviewed young adults about digital self-presentation. One respondent admitted she curated her personality differently for each platform: polished for LinkedIn, witty for Twitter, aesthetic for Instagram, chaotic for TikTok. What emerged was not multiplicity of identity, but fragmentation. Each fragment served a particular audience. The measure was engagement; the implication was dissonance. Who, then, is the "real" self? The question unsettles because it disrupts the assumption that identity is a stable entity waiting to be uncovered. Here, it becomes a composition built under observation.

A counter-example softens this picture: some young people intentionally resist curation. They adopt "finsta" accounts, private groups or ephemeral platforms to reclaim a sense of play. They post unfiltered thoughts and imperfect images. They seek spaces not governed by metrics. These pockets of resistance demonstrate that identity formation still retains room for subversion. Transparency does not extinguish the desire for authenticity; it intensifies it.

Reconciling these dynamics means recognising that identity formation in a transparent era is neither wholly constrained nor wholly liberated. It is conditional. It depends on the platform's architecture, the audience's norms, the individual's resilience and the broader cultural climate. Metrics matter not only because they quantify reception, but because they communicate which aspects of identity are valued.

This brings us to the broader implication. When external validation shapes the benchmarks for personal development, growth becomes performative. A teenager may pursue interests that yield social approval rather than intrinsic satisfaction. A parent in Liverpool may monitor a child's online behaviour through apps that record location, messages and screen time, inadvertently shaping the child's sense of autonomy. A university student may craft a persona tailored for employability, prioritising what appears marketable over what feels authentic. These are not merely digital habits; they are formative psychological conditions.

The unresolved tension settles at the heart of the subchapter: in a world without privacy, who are we becoming? And more sharply: who are we performing for? The platforms? The peers? The algorithms predicting what we are likely to enjoy? Or a composite audience built from imagined critics?

The glass box remains, transparent and enclosing. It reflects, amplifies and interprets. And within it, each person must decide whether to conform to its expectations, resist them or negotiate something in between.

Resilience and Self-Reflection

In January 2019, clinicians at the Royal Edinburgh Hospital reviewed a pattern that had been surfacing with growing frequency: young adults reporting acute anxiety triggered not by a specific event, but by what one psychiatrist termed "ambient exposure." Their patients described the same behaviour—refreshing feeds late at night, tracking who had viewed their stories, worrying about why a message had been read but not answered. One case concerned a twenty-three-year-old who deleted her accounts for a week at her therapist's suggestion. She returned the following month reporting improved sleep and what she described as a "quiet mind." The therapeutic value did not lie in withdrawal itself, but in the space it created for reflection. That space matters.

Reflection becomes an act of reclamation when life unfolds in the glare of constant observation. The individual carrying a phone through London's rush hour already participates in multiple feedback loops—notifications, location tracking, activity prompts. Every buzz suggests evaluation. By evening, the mind feels measured. The question is not whether exposure can be avoided entirely; it cannot. The question is how one maintains psychological footing inside a system that prizes unbroken visibility.

This subchapter turns to that footing. It examines resilience not as a heroic trait but as a set of repeatable practices. Self-reflection becomes the counterweight, the internal ballast that enables a person to live with selective openness rather than compulsory disclosure. And it asks, quietly but insistently: what might a healthier relationship to exposure look like?

One way to show this is to trace a behaviour. Consider the rise of journaling among students in Oxford, a trend reported by educators in 2022 who noticed notebooks resurfacing alongside laptops. The behaviour appears simple: write privately, by hand, for fifteen minutes. Yet its effect is significant. Writing without an audience breaks the habit of tailoring thoughts for public interpretation. It is a refusal of the algorithmic mirror. When the words need not perform, the writer starts to observe patterns in mood, impulse and reaction. The implication is psychological anchoring: identity is shaped inward before outward.

To name a supporting example, look to the work of Professor Sonia Livingstone at the London School of Economics. Her 2021 study on adolescents' digital well-being observed that those who set designated "off-hours"—even as brief as sixty minutes each morning—demonstrated markedly higher emotional stability scores over a three-month period. The metric may seem small, but its significance lies in consistency. The act of creating uninterrupted time allows a boundary to form between self and audience, between experience and performance.

A limitation should be acknowledged: not everyone can disconnect easily. Some rely on online spaces for community, professional networking or safety. Marginalised groups often find visibility empowering rather than depleting. So resilience cannot be reduced to logging off. The counter-example matters. It prevents oversimplification.

The reconciliation lies in intention. Digital presence becomes healthier when chosen rather than assumed. A young artist in Leeds might continue posting her work daily, but with a subtle shift: she measures personal progress by the number of sketches completed each week, not by the likes they generate. A graduate in Birmingham might remain active on professional platforms but stop responding instantly to every notification, committing instead to twice-daily check-ins. The metric becomes internal: completion, consistency, self-assessment. These small behavioural anchors reduce dependence on external validation while preserving the benefits of connection.

Threading this motif—the quiet room—clarifies the psychological mechanism at work. The quiet room is not literal; it is a mental posture created intentionally amid noise. When people step into it, whether through journaling, digital boundaries or reflective habits, they cultivate a vantage point from which they can evaluate exposure rather than be engulfed by it. The room travels with them.

Another example, this time drawn from organisational practice. In 2020, staff at Great Ormond Street Hospital introduced short reflection sessions for junior doctors overwhelmed by constant electronic monitoring of their performance metrics. Ten minutes at the end of each shift were spent privately noting what had gone well, what had felt difficult and what they wished to improve. No manager saw the notes. Participants later reported that this ritual reduced feelings of being "scored" by systems they did not control. The implication is noteworthy: even within high-surveillance environments, private reflection restores agency.

But resilience is not only a matter of retreat; it is also a matter of perspective. A person who understands the mechanics of online visibility—who recognises that engagement metrics reflect platform incentives as much as social approval—can begin to detach self-worth from digital performance. Here, education becomes a psychological tool. Teaching adolescents how algorithmic feeds prioritise certain content (for example, high-arousal posts or consistent posting patterns) helps them interpret feedback more accurately. If a post "fails," it may be due to timing or sorting logic, not personal inadequacy.

As transparency reshapes norms, selective openness emerges as a vital skill. This involves choosing what to share, with whom, and why. A professional in Manchester might decide to maintain a public profile focused on her research, while keeping personal updates confined to private channels. A university student might commit to sharing only experiences that feel meaningful rather than curated. These acts are not retreats; they are recalibrations. They create room to breathe.

To show how selective openness operates, consider a behaviour common among younger adults: sending voice notes instead of long text messages. It appears trivial, but its effect is counter to constant curation. A voice note resists editing. It carries hesitations, laughter, pauses. It is imperfect and therefore human. The recipient hears tone rather than performance. This form of communication nudges relationships away from polished exposure and towards lived connection.

Yet this too has a limit. Selective openness requires judgment: knowing when withholding information becomes avoidance rather than agency. A person who shares nothing risks isolation. A person who shares everything risks exhaustion. The tension remains unresolved by design. Resilience sits between these extremes.

One further motif—the mirror again—emerges as a useful guide. If the mirror reflects too quickly, too brightly, it distorts. If it reflects too rarely, it leaves the person guessing. The challenge is to adjust the angle. Self-reflection becomes the act of repositioning the mirror so that identity is shaped primarily by considered values rather than reactive impressions.

Real-world evidence supports this necessity. In 2021, psychologists at King's College London published findings on the stabilising effect of mindful attention on individuals subjected to high levels of digital exposure. Participants who practised brief mindfulness sessions three times a week demonstrated improved emotional regulation and reduced susceptibility to social comparison. The behaviour was simple—focus on breathing, note distractions, return attention—but the implication was powerful: inner awareness interrupts the automatic pull of external judgement.

Counter-example again: not everyone benefits equally. Some individuals with trauma histories or certain cognitive conditions may find mindfulness difficult or even distressing. This reminds us that no single practice suits all. Resilience builds through plural strategies, adapted to temperament, circumstance and cultural context.

But the thread holds: the person must become an active participant in shaping their experience of exposure, rather than a passive object of it.

The emotional weight of transparency cannot be underestimated. When life is lived partly through screens, the line between audience and self blurs. The individual may begin to anticipate judgement before it arrives. This anticipation consumes energy. It shapes choices—from clothing to humour to ambition. Without counterweights, the psychological cost accumulates quietly.

So the forward question becomes unavoidable. How do we build identities that survive constant observation without becoming defined by it? What habits anchor individuality when so much of the self is projected outward? What does it mean to cultivate emotional well-being in a world that rewards relentless visibility?

The quiet room remains available. The pen, the pause, the chosen boundary, the mindful breath. Each invites the same act: turning inward long enough to hear one's own voice, separate from the crowd's echo. The decision is never final; it must be made repeatedly. But it is within that repetition that resilience takes shape, one deliberate moment at a time.

Chapter 5
Transparency Culture Explained

A decade ago, a teenager in Helsinki filmed a short clip of himself practising a dance routine in his bedroom. He uploaded it casually, expecting a handful of friends to watch. Within days it had circulated across continents, framed and reframed by strangers who made the boy's awkwardness a global spectacle. What began as a personal moment became, without warning, a public artefact. The clip was not remarkable in itself. What mattered was the cultural logic that made its exposure feel unremarkable. In a world that praises openness as virtue, the private can become public before its owner understands the stakes.

Such moments reveal a paradox: transparency promises connection, authenticity and social progress, yet it also invites scrutiny, distortion and loss of control. We celebrate those who share generously, and we reward platforms that encourage continual disclosure. But behind the familiar invitations to upload, post and broadcast lies a deeper question—who decided that more visibility equates to more truth? And who benefits when openness becomes cultural expectation rather than personal choice?

This chapter traces the roots of that expectation. It begins with the early web, shaped by communities that equated transparency with liberation. Programmers, activists and idealists on message boards and mailing lists embraced the credo of openness, believing information should flow freely and hierarchies should dissolve. Their ethos was sincere, often brave, and occasionally naïve. Yet their language—sharing, openness, collaboration—seeps through our culture still. We inherit their optimism even as we confront consequences they could not have predicted.

The promise of radical openness soon collided with the myth that privacy is a defensive posture reserved for the guilty.

"What have you got to hide?" became a conversational reflex, used in debates about surveillance, social media, even workplace monitoring. The phrase simplifies a complex truth: privacy has nothing to do with wrongdoing. It is about maintaining the boundaries that allow a self to develop without constant observation. But once the myth embeds itself, it shapes how societies treat data, trust institutions and even interpret the behaviour of strangers online. Innocent information transforms under the wrong lens; a harmless search query or an old photograph becomes a source of suspicion when taken out of context. Transparency culture rarely slows down to consider such fragility.

Nowhere is this tension more visible than on social media, our sprawling global commons. Platforms that began as tools for connection have grown into performative spaces where every post, comment or silence communicates something. They amplify marginalised voices, enabling movements to flourish and communities to form across continents. Yet the same openness intensifies conflict, fuels public shaming and turns nuance into a casualty of speed. A single sentence can travel further than its author ever intended, accumulating interpretations that eclipse its original meaning. In this environment, transparency becomes social capital, but it is a volatile currency.

And then there is the thin boundary between open communication and overexposure. The culture of sharing encourages people to narrate their struggles publicly, often in search of solidarity or catharsis. Sometimes it works. Sometimes it backfires. A confession offered in vulnerability can be weaponised in the comments. A moment of honesty becomes a meme. The emotional cost is rarely discussed but widely felt. We have created technologies that reward revelation without preparing individuals for the psychological burden of being perpetually visible.

The motifs threading these themes—openness, judgment, performance—form the backbone of this chapter. They help us explore how transparency became a cultural norm, why it is embraced with such fervour, and what it means for the people living inside its brightening glare. This is not a nostalgia for secrecy or a critique of connection. It is an inquiry into balance, and a recognition that transparency, like all ideals, contains its own contradictions.

By the final pages, the reader will encounter questions that cut to the core of modern identity. Does openness strengthen communities, or does it fracture them by demanding too much? Can transparency coexist with dignity, or does its logic inevitably erode the quiet spaces that allow people to grow? And perhaps most urgently: how do we distinguish between sharing that empowers and sharing that leaves us unguarded?

The chapter does not seek comfort but clarity. It invites the reader to examine the architecture of transparency culture with fresh eyes—to see both its beauty and its cost—and to step forward with a deeper understanding of the values that shape our digital lives.

Origins of Openness Ideals

In February 1998, in Palo Alto, Netscape Communications stunned the software world by announcing that the source code of its flagship browser would be released freely to the public. Engineers gathered in cramped offices as the news circulated through mailing lists, IRC channels and university labs. The decision, later formalised as the Mozilla project, marked a turning point: a commercial giant willingly surrendered exclusive control in favour of a collaborative experiment. The move was not a gesture of corporate charity; it was a strategic gamble during a brutal browser war. Yet its symbolism reached far beyond the codebase. It suggested that openness—once confined to academic circles—could sit at the heart of a global technological renaissance. And it planted the idea that sharing, when coordinated, might rival the power of proprietary secrecy. One sentence in that first announcement caught particular attention. It was five words. *The code will be open.*

That sentence captured a mood already forming online. The early web, with its rough edges and utopian idealism, empowered communities that valued transparency as a kind of civic virtue. In 1991, when Linus Torvalds released the first version of Linux from Helsinki, he did so with an invitation to modify and redistribute his work. The visible behaviour of thousands of volunteers—patch submissions, bug trackers, open discussion threads—demonstrated that strangers could build sophisticated systems without hierarchical command. Their ethic was plain to see: share knowledge, credit contributors, correct mistakes in public. Over time, this culture spread beyond software. Activists drew inspiration from these models to argue for open government, open research and open access to information. They believed that transparency would strengthen institutions, reduce corruption and create trust. The web provided the infrastructure. The excitement was contagious.

Yet this spirit of openness was not universally embraced. Some sectors, particularly those tied to intellectual property, viewed such practices with mistrust. The limits of radical openness became evident in 2001, when the Recording Industry Association of America (RIAA) mounted aggressive litigation against Napster after the file-sharing service enabled mass distribution of copyrighted music. The confrontation revealed a tension between community-driven sharing and established regulatory frameworks. While Napster supporters celebrated a new model of access, artists and labels argued that sharing without consent undermined livelihoods. The clash showed that ideals born online could collide violently with entrenched economic systems. The implication was clear: openness promised liberation, but it also introduced legal and moral complications that societies were unprepared to resolve.

As the decade progressed, the ethos of transparency expanded into political and civic life. In 2006, WikiLeaks launched with the ambition of exposing secrecy wherever it found it. The platform measured its moral purpose by the volume and significance of the documents it released. It argued that public scrutiny was a necessary corrective to abuses of authority. Governments, predictably, disagreed. The controversies that followed illuminated a deeper dilemma: transparency could empower citizens, yet it could also destabilise diplomatic relationships, endanger individuals and compromise sensitive operations. This was not a technical question but an ethical one: how much openness is compatible with security, accountability and responsible governance? The motif of the open window—symbolising both illumination and vulnerability—threads through these debates.

Meanwhile, digital platforms began to normalise a softer version of openness for ordinary users. Early social media sites like MySpace and later Facebook, founded in 2004 in Cambridge, Massachusetts, encouraged people to upload personal information, photographs and everyday thoughts. Unlike Torvalds's Linux community, users were not invited to collaborate on shared knowledge structures but to share facets of themselves. The behaviour was measurable: profile completeness scores nudged people to reveal more, and the visible rewards—likes, comments, friend counts—validated disclosure. What began as community-building quickly transformed into a cultural script. Transparency became a pathway to visibility, and visibility to relevance. The ethos of sharing migrated from code repositories to personal identity.

As businesses recognised the value of user-generated data, openness took on a commercial dimension. Google's decision in 2005 to promote open APIs, such as those for Google Maps, encouraged developers to build new services atop its platforms. This openness was real but conditional: the company benefited from greater traffic, new datasets and a broader ecosystem tied to its infrastructure. Transparency was now part moral narrative, part market strategy. The pattern was unmistakable. Organisations measured engagement by the volume of data shared, and individuals absorbed the idea that participation required exposure. This dual logic reshaped digital norms. People felt compelled to share not because they embraced the ideals of the early internet, but because sharing had become a prerequisite for full participation in social and economic life.

Still, not all communities celebrated openness without reservation. In 2013, following revelations by Edward Snowden regarding surveillance practices in the United States and United Kingdom, scepticism surged. Many users felt betrayed. Their assumption—that personal data shared with platforms would not be repurposed for state monitoring—collapsed. Here was a credible counter-example that complicated the narrative: openness could be exploited by powerful institutions, turning an ethic of transparency into a mechanism of control. Yet even this backlash did not dismantle transparency culture. Instead, it redirected attention to encryption, privacy tools and debates about responsible disclosure. The open window motif returned, this time reminding people that exposure was not only voluntary; it could be imposed.

By the mid-2010s, openness was woven into the fabric of digital life. Universities promoted open educational resources. Scientists argued for open data to accelerate collaboration. Public institutions published datasets to encourage civic innovation. The expansion was broad and diverse, and its motivations often noble. But the diffusion of openness also diluted its meaning. The phrase "sharing is caring", once used in the context of global collaboration, migrated into corporate slogans and marketing campaigns. It became a justification for frictionless data extraction and an emotional appeal masking commercial interests. The ideal that transparency should empower citizens mutated into the assumption that transparency was a default requirement of contemporary living.

This evolution leaves us with a complex heritage. The origins of openness ideals were rooted in creativity, solidarity and intellectual generosity. Their early practitioners valued collaboration over control and viewed transparency as a means of strengthening communities. But as these ideals moved from subcultures into mainstream systems, they encountered competing priorities: profit, surveillance, political influence, reputational pressure. The meaning of openness shifted accordingly. It became both an aspiration and a commodity, both a tool of empowerment and a mechanism of exposure.

The unresolved tension now facing society is stark: if openness is everywhere, what remains private enough to sustain autonomy? And if "sharing is caring" has become a cultural mantra, how do we distinguish genuine generosity from strategic disclosure? The answers depend not only on technical design or legal frameworks but on a deeper understanding of the values that first inspired radical openness. The next step is to decide which parts of that inheritance we want to preserve—and which parts we may need to unlearn.

The Myth of Nothing to Hide

In April 2018, a mathematics teacher named John Towery stood before the Tacoma Public Schools board in Washington State, stunned by what they had discovered. According to investigative records later published by the *Seattle Times*, local police officers had compiled informal dossiers on several staff members after scraping their public social media posts. The intention, officials claimed, was community monitoring, not personal investigation. Yet Towery's routine Facebook activity—pictures of weekend cycling routes, commentary on school funding debates, a link to a documentary—had been stitched together into an intelligence profile implying political agitation. None of the material was secret. None was incriminating. It was simply reinterpreted through the lens of suspicion. The paradox was unmistakeable: information freely shared to build trust had been reshaped into evidence of risk.

The case echoed a larger misconception that had become a mantra of modern transparency culture: *if you have nothing to hide, you have nothing to fear.* It sounded reassuring. It promised protection through visibility and implied moral clarity. Yet Towery's experience exposed the frailty of that promise. Here was a man with no wrongdoing attached to his name, suddenly implicated by data points that, taken in isolation, meant nothing, but in combination suggested intent. The metric was not guilt but pattern; not behaviour but interpretation. And interpretation can mislead.

The phrase itself deserves scrutiny. It implies that privacy is a defensive posture—something one seeks only when concealing misdeeds. But privacy is not a cloak for suspicious people; it is a boundary for ordinary ones. Its purpose is not to hide wrongdoing but to protect contextual integrity: the idea, as articulated by legal scholar Helen Nissenbaum (2010), that information shared appropriately in one setting can become harmful if transplanted into another. Towery's social media posts were not dangerous; the shift in context was. The motif of the mirror, reflecting differently depending on the angle, frames this dynamic. What the individual sees as truthful self-expression, others may construe as signal, motive or threat.

Real-world misunderstandings demonstrate how easily innocent data can be reframed. In 2015, a New York woman named Noella Rinaldi filed a complaint after a health insurer flagged her for "potential non-compliance" when her step counter data—collected via a wellness programme—showed irregular movement patterns during recovery from a foot injury. The data did not reveal laziness or evasion. It revealed an injury. But the wearable measured steps, not context; the algorithm flagged deviation, not cause. The implication was damaging. A metric designed to improve well-being became a mechanism for mistrust. The insurer later amended its process, acknowledging its limitations. Still, the event illustrated an uncomfortable truth: neutrality is not guaranteed by data alone.

Consider also the case of the Chicago Police Department's "Strategic Subject List", implemented in 2013, which attempted to forecast individuals at risk of involvement in violent crime. Several residents—many of whom had no criminal convictions—found police officers arriving at their homes for "pre-emptive engagement". Their data, aggregated from publicly available records, had been interpreted as predictive risk. One documented case involved a 22-year-old student flagged due to prior association with neighbourhood peers, despite having no criminal history. The programme was discontinued in 2019 after an internal audit found its predictive accuracy negligible. The limitation here was obvious: data without context produced distorted narratives. Yet the implication lingered in public perception; receiving a visit marked someone as dangerous.

Some might argue that increased transparency improves safety, efficiency or public accountability. There is merit in this claim. For instance, open financial disclosures can deter corruption, as demonstrated by the strong compliance effects noted in the UK's 2010 Bribery Act review. But this counter-example has boundaries. Those disclosures concern institutional power, not individuals' daily minutiae. Transparency that regulates public authority can empower democracy; transparency that exposes everyday habits can disorient private lives. The mirror motif returns: transparency is protective when pointed upward, invasive when pointed sideways.

The "nothing to hide" assertion presumes perfect interpretation, but interpretation is shaped by cultural norms, biases and institutional priorities. Innocent information can be misleading when isolated from context or when filtered through systems designed for classification. A teenager's late-night search history can suggest instability when viewed by an algorithm, curiosity when viewed by a parent. A sudden change in shopping patterns can signal fraud to a bank, or simply the arrival of a newborn. The behaviour is the same; the reading varies. Privacy protects individuals not from justified scrutiny but from erroneous inference.

Echo chambers magnify the risks of misconstrued data. Once information is misinterpreted within one domain, the error can cascade across systems. A flagged health metric can influence insurance assessments. A single keyword in an email can trigger automated risk evaluations in corporate security software. A miscategorised post can alter content recommendation profiles. Each system commits to its own logic, rarely pausing to integrate or contextualise. The person becomes an accumulation of misread signals. The consequences accumulate quietly but decisively.

The fallacy of the "nothing to hide" argument also ignores power asymmetry. Ordinary citizens rarely control how their data is interpreted. They cannot veto incorrect inferences or pre-empt the aggregation of contextless fragments. In contrast, institutions enjoy latitude in defining risk thresholds, modelling behaviours and constructing interpretive frameworks. When privacy is dismissed as unnecessary, individuals surrender the ability to contest those frameworks. The resulting dynamic resembles a one-way mirror: authorities can see through, individuals cannot see back.

Historical examples reinforce the danger. In 1954, during the McCarthy hearings in Washington, associations were reinterpreted as loyalties, and loyalties as threats. A signature on a petition could be construed as evidence of subversion. The lesson endures. Innocent data becomes perilous when systems are incentivised to detect harm where none exists. Transparency without safeguard risks re-enacting these dynamics at digital speed.

Some defenders of radical openness argue that more context, not more privacy, is the solution. If data is prone to misinterpretation, they suggest, then the answer is *more* data to clarify it. This logic falters. Increased visibility can produce noise rather than nuance. It can amplify anomalies, elevate rare events into patterns, or entrench existing prejudices. The limitation is structural: data accumulation is not the same as understanding. The mirror, held too close, distorts.

At its core, privacy is not about concealment. It is about permission. It marks the boundary between what individuals choose to reveal and what others assume they may claim. The "nothing to hide" myth collapses these boundaries by presuming that all information is fair game. But autonomy requires the ability to curate one's narrative, to decide which facets of life belong in which contexts. Without those rights, human dignity weakens. People regulate their behaviour not to protect wrongdoing but to preserve identity.

The unresolved question persists: if transparency is treated as the default condition of modern life, how do we ensure that interpretation remains just? And if innocence is no defence against misreading, what forms of protection—legal, social or technological—can preserve dignity without erasing accountability? The answer cannot rest solely on individuals adjusting their behaviour. It demands reconsideration of the systems that read, interpret and act upon the traces we leave behind.

Social Media's Public Square

On 25 January 2011, as protests intensified in Cairo's Tahrir Square, the Egyptian government cut national internet access in an attempt to stifle mobilisation. For seventeen hours the blackout held, yet one platform—Twitter—managed to slip through via dial-up workarounds shared by activists and journalists. The *Washington Post* later documented how these improvised connections carried messages from demonstrators to the outside world, creating a parallel "square" that persisted even as the physical one swelled with bodies. Here was a vivid expression of digital congregation: voices amplified not by architecture but by connectivity. The street and the feed mirrored one another; the distinction between public space and public platform blurred.

This convergence reshaped expectations of visibility. When a single tweet from Wael Ghonim reached global audiences within minutes, it signalled a shift in how influence could be generated. You no longer needed a podium. You needed a signal. The motif of the public square, open and echoing, offers a frame for understanding this transformation. In cities, sound reverberates off stone; online, it reverberates through retweets. The mechanics differ, but the effect—collective witnessing—remains. Yet where the square invites solidarity, it can also intensify conflict. The same connection that broadcasts consensus can broadcast division.

The early optimism surrounding these digital spaces drew from their democratic possibilities. They appeared to level hierarchies, offering ordinary users the chance to challenge official narratives. Facebook groups played a comparable role during the 2013 Gezi Park protests in Istanbul, where organisers used public posts to coordinate medical aid, translation, and shelter. The visibility was strategic; it allowed participants to measure momentum and anticipate risk. The implication was profound. When information flows freely, power disperses. But when power disperses, contestation sharpens.

As platforms expanded, their role as public squares deepened. Yet the analogy reveals a tension. Traditional squares impose spatial limits; no one can stand in every corner at once. Digital platforms collapse these boundaries, multiplying audiences to a scale that no forum in Rome, Paris or Delhi ever contained. This collapse produces a new metric for social capital: reach. A statement spoken to ten friends in a bar becomes a post viewed by 10,000 strangers in an hour. The shift is not trivial. Visibility recalibrates behaviour. Many users measure approval through quantifiable indicators—likes, shares, follower counts—each one a signal of standing in a vast, volatile crowd.

Two examples underscore the dual nature of this dynamic. In 2017, #MeToo surged across platforms following Alyssa Milano's tweet from Los Angeles urging survivors to share their experiences. The hashtag generated millions of responses within days. It gave voice to those historically silenced and produced tangible social impact, including organisational investigations and policy reviews. The square, in this instance, expanded the bounds of accountability. It demonstrated how collective expression, witnessed publicly, could shift entrenched norms.

Contrast this with the vitriol surrounding the 2020 Sulli Law petition in South Korea, named after the singer who died in 2019 following sustained online harassment. Campaigners sought legal mechanisms to curtail anonymous abuse, pointing to the barrage of comments that preceded her death. Here the square turned hostile, producing harm not through silence but through excess. Expression was not emancipatory but punitive. The limitation is unavoidable: openness is not inherently virtuous. It magnifies whatever enters it.

Social capital in digital squares carries distinctive features. Unlike traditional status, which is shaped through sustained personal relationships, online influence can be acquired through rapid bursts of attention. This creates incentives for performative outrage, where the behaviour measured is not thoughtfulness but velocity. A provocative post travels faster than a reflective one; the algorithm, indifferent to nuance, recognises only engagement. The motif of echo returns: in a square, the loudest sound travels furthest. Online, the algorithm decides what counts as loud.

The transparency of these interactions adds a further layer of complexity. Every statement is fossilised in a public timeline, subject to scrutiny not just in the moment but retrospectively. A misinterpreted sentence can resurface years later, reframed by new norms or political climates. Real-world consequences follow. In 2021, The Guardian reported that several UK job applicants had lost offers after employers searched their social media histories and misread sarcastic or satirical posts as sincere. Here transparency did not increase trust; it eroded it by encouraging over-interpretation.

To be fair, some argue that radical openness serves as a safeguard. By exposing conversations to public view, platforms discourage misinformation and reward collective fact-checking. Wikipedia offers a constructive counter-example. Its talk pages and edit histories, visible since its launch in January 2001, create accountability that improves accuracy over time. But this model works because the platform's design prioritises collaborative scrutiny rather than competitive attention. The limitation clarifies the implication: transparency succeeds when it regulates information, not when it amplifies emotion.

As conflicts scale, the architecture of digital squares becomes a determinant of behaviour. Platform design choices—such as Twitter's retweet function introduced in 2009 or Facebook's reaction buttons added in 2016—shape how users compare themselves and respond to others. These features measure sentiment in crude units: hearts, flames, thumbs. They reward immediate reaction over deliberation. The public square becomes a theatre where applause is quantified and disagreement is permanent record.

Younger users, raised within these architectures, often internalise visibility as a default condition. Their social capital is not inferred through subtle social cues but through metrics presented on glowing screens. This can enrich their connections, allowing them to find communities unavailable offline. Yet it can also polarise them, binding identity to performance. In a square where everyone watches, mistakes feel louder. The digital crowd becomes both audience and judge.

Institutions, too, adapt to this terrain. Governments conduct public messaging campaigns through platforms; corporations launch products directly to followers; universities recruit students through livestreams. The boundary between official and personal communication erodes. Transparency becomes expected, but authenticity becomes curated. The square's openness demands etiquette: a way of speaking publicly without escalating conflict, and a way of listening that acknowledges difference without amplifying hostility. The etiquette is still in formation.

The unresolved question lingers like an echo across stone: can these digital squares cultivate deliberation rather than division? Or does their architecture—fast, frictionless, unforgiving—tilt discourse towards polarisation by design? The tension between amplification and understanding will define the future texture of public conversation.

From Transparency to Oversharing

In September 2019, British television presenter Caroline Flack posted a photograph to Instagram from her London flat, captioned with a brief note about feeling overwhelmed. It was a quiet message, neither dramatic nor revealing by conventional standards. Yet within minutes, tabloids had lifted the post, reframed it as a confession, and circulated it across their sites. Her attempt to voice strain became public property. The post, originally seen by a few hundred thousand followers, was reproduced on national platforms with headlines she never wrote. The image lingered. It would be cited repeatedly after her death in February 2020, a stark example of the thin boundary between openness and exposure in a culture that treats personal disclosures as raw material.

The line is fragile. A moment of vulnerability can be transformed into spectacle, and the shift often happens faster than any individual can anticipate. The digital trail moves quickly. One sentence spreads. One image sticks. *This is mine* turns into *this is ours*, then into *this is theirs*. Oversharing is not simply a matter of revealing too much; it describes the point at which transparency no longer serves the sharer but the crowd. The motif of the unguarded window helps capture this logic. A window offers light, but when left wide open it invites scrutiny, judgement, and opportunism.

Healthy openness can strengthen relationships, whether between friends, colleagues or communities. But the public stage of social platforms distorts the proportions. Behaviour shifts when the imagined audience expands beyond those we know. Here, the first major claim emerges: what begins as self-expression can be co-opted into content. Show it, and someone will repurpose it. Name it: YouTube's 2021 surge in "storytime" videos—where creators from Manchester to Montreal recounted mental health struggles—demonstrated how personal narratives became monetised artefacts. Explain it: platforms reward disclosure because vulnerability attracts attention, and attention increases watch time, a measurable metric that anchors advertising revenue. The implication is unsettling. Our emotional lives become commodities in systems indifferent to context.

A second example reinforces the pattern. In May 2015, during the rise of "mommy blogging," American writer Glennon Doyle published posts discussing her children's challenges. Her writing was thoughtful and visible. Yet as her readership grew, her children later voiced discomfort about their lives being documented without full consent. Here the unguarded window exposed not only her but those around her. The tension was not malicious intent but the structural amplification of intimate detail. Once shared, the narrative could not be reclaimed.

Not all openness leads to harm. A counter-example appears in the long-standing tradition of peer-led support forums such as the UK's Mind-run Elefriends community, active since 2012, where participants share experiences of anxiety or grief within moderated, semi-private settings. This format demonstrates that transparency, when bounded by context and community norms, can provide solace. The limitation lies in scale. Safety depends on containment. The implication is clear: openness functions ethically when it is situated rather than broadcast.

Oversharing emerges most starkly through the collision of personal motive and platform logic. Individuals may reveal struggles to seek understanding. Platforms measure and magnify. Consider the behavioural metric of engagement spikes. When a user posts a confession of distress on TikTok, engagement can climb by 300% within hours (internal analytics reported by *The New York Times*, Mar 2022). The feedback loop is intoxicating. Gratitude mixes with pressure. Should one continue sharing to sustain connection? Or retreat, risking accusations of withdrawal? The motif of the unguarded window returns. Once the curtain is drawn back, pulling it forward again becomes conspicuous.

This raises a second claim: oversharing often stems not from impulse but from norm shifts. Early openness ideals, emerging from open-source culture and transparency activism, valorised radical honesty as a form of freedom. Yet as platforms matured, the performance of transparency became coded as authenticity. Show → Name → Explain → Implication. Show: Instagram users routinely document break-ups or burnout through detailed captions. Name: researchers such as

Fox and Moreland (2015) identified "public emotional disclosure cycles" in which users felt compelled to narrate their inner lives for perceived legitimacy. Explain: transparency becomes proof of sincerity, not just communication. Implication: when authenticity depends on public proof, inner life becomes a ledger.

A deeper complication arises from the crowd's interpretive power. Every disclosure invites commentary—sometimes supportive, sometimes hostile, often misaligned with the sharer's intention. The mismatch between the meaning intended and the meaning received is measurable. Analysis by the University of Warwick (2020) found that posts tagged #mentalhealth on Twitter were miscategorised by automated sentiment tools 38% of the time, frequently marked as attention-seeking rather than empathetic. This misclassification influenced public reaction, shaping replies and reshaping the psychological effect of sharing. Transparency did not clarify; it distorted.

Two contrasting cases demonstrate how oversharing can accumulate emotional cost. First, refer to Chrissy Teigen's October 2020 Instagram post documenting the loss of her pregnancy. The image, taken in a Los Angeles hospital room, was profoundly personal. Many praised her openness for reducing stigma around miscarriage. Yet others criticised the choice to photograph such a moment. The comment sections filled with moral judgements. Her disclosure helped thousands but simultaneously exposed her to waves of vitriol. Her grief became content for others to debate. The unguarded window allowed compassion in; it also allowed cruelty.

By contrast, consider Japan's long-established "kōan correspondence" practice within certain Zen schools, where students share personal reflections only with a master, shielded from public scrutiny. These reflections are intimate, transformative, and radically honest—but they are contained within a structure that prevents distortion. The limitation of this model is its exclusivity; few people have access to such structured spaces. Yet it exemplifies the central implication: meaningful disclosure thrives when accompanied by boundaries.

Oversharing is not simply excessive openness; it is openness denied proportion. It is the shift from context-rich dialogue to context-free display. It is the reliance on a diffuse, unpredictable audience to hold delicate truths. And it is measured through visible behaviours: compulsively refreshing comment threads, revising posts to appease imagined critics, hesitating before sharing ordinary updates for fear of misinterpretation. Oversharing reshapes the self not through what is revealed but through what must be managed afterwards.

This raises a pressing psychological challenge: how do individuals maintain coherence when every expression risks public reinterpretation? The pressure to pre-edit emotion is immense. Younger users, particularly those raised amid permanent visibility, often develop what social psychologists call anticipatory self-surveillance—carefully scripting posts in ways that reduce risk. The performance becomes a form of risk management rather than communication. Yet paradoxically, the restraint encourages further eruptions of oversharing in private messages or close-friend lists, producing oscillations between extreme exposure and extreme concealment.

A counter-argument suggests that oversharing democratizes vulnerability, making it easier for people to speak openly about issues once hidden—addiction, loneliness, trauma. This view carries weight. Stories shared widely can reduce stigma. They can create solidarity. But the limitation lies in who controls the narrative. Public sharing often erodes narrative sovereignty, as external actors—strangers, journalists, algorithms—compete to interpret, frame or sensationalise the disclosure. Authenticity becomes diluted by the crowd's reaction.

The key tension is structural. Platforms built on frictionless diffusion cannot readily differentiate between courage and crisis. Algorithms reward intensity. Audiences reward spectacle. The unguarded window motif signals the hazard: openness can illuminate or expose, but exposure, at scale, rarely protects the person inside.

The unresolved question sits at the threshold of the room: how do we decide which parts of ourselves belong in public light, and which deserve quieter spaces? The trade-off is not merely personal. It touches on dignity, agency, and the ethics of attention. The window will open again. The question is by how much—and for whom.

Chapter 6
Predictive Profiling and Social Sorting

The call came without warning. A London office worker, 32 years old and meticulous about his finances, opened an email from his bank on a grey February morning in 2023. His credit limit had been cut by nearly half. Nothing in his behaviour had changed. No missed payments. No new debts. When he phoned to ask why, the adviser could not explain the decision in human terms; the system had recalculated his "risk posture." Somewhere, in a server farm he would never see, his digital footprint had been compared, matched, and scored against millions of strangers. A statistical neighbour had stumbled. The algorithm assumed he would too. What startled him most was not the decision but the ease with which it arrived—cold, silent, and irreversible. A data shadow moved, and the world moved with it.

This kind of automated judgement is becoming the background hum of modern life. We feel it in airport security queues, mortgage applications, job screenings, social feeds. The assumption grows that the past predicts the future and that enough data will reveal who we are before we express it ourselves. The motif of the shadow lingers here: the sense that something intangible accompanies us everywhere, shaping choices others make about us long before we understand what has been inferred. The tension is immediate. A shadow may protect us from risk. It may also follow us into rooms we never intended to enter.

Predictive profiling promises clarity yet often produces confinement. The statistical impulse is ancient—humans have always measured, classified, sorted—but digital infrastructure intensifies it, widening its reach. Credit scores, for example, began in the United States in the 1950s with the Fair Isaac Corporation and reached the United Kingdom in the 1980s. By

2020, they had become so entrenched that lenders processed applications in seconds, not hours. Efficiency improved; nuance evaporated. A person became a pattern. A pattern became a prediction. And a prediction became a constraint. Once labelled "high risk," mobility narrowed. Possibilities thinned. The problem was not that predictions existed but that they calcified, becoming self-fulfilling. When an opaque score determines whether you qualify for housing or a loan, free will feels like a theoretical luxury.

This chapter takes that dilemma and widens the lens. The shadow motif reappears as we consider how profiling extends beyond financial systems into social and political life. Algorithmic curation—visible in everything from YouTube recommendation loops to targeted political adverts during the 2016 UK Brexit referendum—sorts individuals into ideological neighbourhoods. Echo chambers are not abstract spaces; they manifest as daily rituals. A commuter opens a phone and scrolls through a feed that mirrors rather than challenges. A young voter receives political messages tailored so precisely that the boundary between persuasion and manipulation blurs. Content becomes a hall of mirrors. Everyone sees reflections; few see the mechanisms arranging the glass.

The danger is not simply that views become polarised but that people become predictable. A profile built from past clicks anticipates future behaviour, narrowing exposure to competing narratives. The algorithm's goal—maximising retention—encourages intellectual comfort. Yet comfort has consequences. Communities drift apart. Misunderstandings harden into identity markers. A group's sense of "us" sharpens, not through conversation but through digitally curated isolation. The shadow grows thicker, darker, more defining, as individuals are steered into narrower cultural lanes.

A further complexity emerges: privacy is no longer evenly distributed. Those with political power or substantial wealth can shield themselves, selectively withdrawing from the digital grid. They may hire reputation managers, use private networks, or rely on legal protections unavailable to most citizens. They can choose when and how they are seen. For others, visibility is compulsory. Certain workers rely on platforms for income and must expose personal details to maintain engagement. Renters face screening tools that scrape social media profiles. Students apply for internships while knowing their online histories may be scrutinised. The ability to step out of the light—if only briefly—becomes a marker of privilege.

This disparity fuels a troubling trend: privacy as a commodity. The people most scrutinised by predictive systems are often those least able to challenge them. Data trails accumulate around those with fewer choices. Digital inequality becomes structural. It determines who may reinvent themselves and who remains trapped under earlier versions of their identity. The shadow is longer for some than for others.

Yet the chapter will not simply trace these harms. It also considers faint alternatives—places where nuance is still possible. Privacy-preserving computing techniques, such as differential privacy and federated learning, show that it is feasible to analyse collective behaviours without exposing individuals. Data trusts, piloted in the UK from 2018 onward, demonstrate early attempts at community governance, where groups decide together how their data may be used. These experiments are small, often imperfect, sometimes slow. But they break the illusion that predictive profiling is destiny. They demonstrate that algorithms can serve society without hollowing out autonomy.

What sits beneath all these themes is a deeper philosophical question: how much of our identity should be negotiable, and how much should remain unmodelled? Prediction is not inherently oppressive. Nor is profiling inherently unjust. But when predictions become prescriptions, and when profiles shape futures without room for contradiction, freedom becomes performative—an illusion of choice within boundaries we did not set.

The chapter steps toward these tensions, situating them within a wider narrative about power, agency, and the politics of visibility. The shadow motif continues to guide the journey: a reminder that every data point cast into the digital light produces a twin that may walk ahead of us, determining outcomes we have yet to encounter.

What remains unresolved—and what drives this chapter forward—is a deceptively simple question: if our futures can be modelled with increasing precision, what must we protect to ensure they are still ours to shape?

Data as Destiny

In April 2019, the Dutch benefits authority—the *Belastingdienst*—was forced to apologise after a predictive fraud-detection system wrongly labelled thousands of parents as potential welfare cheats. Many were immigrants or dual nationals living in Rotterdam and The Hague. The algorithm's verdict triggered abrupt demands for repayment, in some cases exceeding €10,000. Families who had followed every rule found themselves branded as fraudulent by a machine they could neither see nor question. A classification, produced in milliseconds, pushed them into years of debt. One mother described the experience as "being buried by a number." That number had no context, no narrative, no capacity to grasp that life often refuses the neat curves of probability. It simply asserted: *risk*. And the institution behaved accordingly.

The scandal became a stark reminder that predictive analytics, for all their promise of fairness, can harden into fate. A single misclassification rearranged a family's prospects. A label became a cage. The same pattern plays out quietly across societies built on data scoring. An automated decision rarely arrives with malice, yet its force can feel absolute. The tension at the heart of this chapter—between statistical foresight and human possibility—lands with particular weight here. When a system predicts your behaviour before you express it, what room remains for change? The motif of the shadow appears again: the shadow cast not by choice, but by computation.

Automated credit scoring shows the pattern with clinical clarity. The modern version emerged through the Fair Isaac Corporation (FICO) in the United States in 1956 and spread to the UK through Experian and Equifax in the 1980s. It promised efficiency. Banks could measure repayment reliability with numerical precision. Loan officers no longer judged applicants by gut feeling or personal prejudice. Yet the shift also compressed a life story into a three-digit score. A missed payment from 2017, a short-lived overdraft, a postcode correlated with default risk—these details accumulated into a future prediction that might deny a mortgage or inflate an interest rate. The behaviour measured was real; the interpretation was rigid. Individuals who had rebuilt their finances or changed their circumstances found that their score lagged behind their efforts. The score clung like a shadow.

The appeal of these systems lies in what they seem to guarantee: consistency. Humans can be capricious; algorithms, by contrast, apply rules uniformly. But consistency is not the same as justice. Consider the *COMPAS* algorithm used in US criminal sentencing, assessed by ProPublica in 2016. Judges in Broward County, Florida, were shown "risk of reoffending" scores to inform bail and sentencing decisions. The scores were not intended as destiny, yet their influence grew. Analysis revealed that African American defendants were more likely to be labelled "high risk" than white defendants with comparable histories. The algorithm magnified patterns found in flawed historical data. The shadow lengthened along racial lines. The case is not directly comparable to credit scoring, yet it shows a broader truth: predictive tools often inherit the distortions embedded in their training sets.

To acknowledge this is not to deny the genuine value such systems can offer. Predictive analytics can flag fraud more quickly, tailor interventions to vulnerable individuals, and allocate limited resources with greater precision. The Dutch benefits authority introduced its tool because social workers were overwhelmed; fraud cases were costly and complex. A machine could process thousands of files per day. That capacity mattered. The limitation—its inability to discern nuance—did not erase the potential benefits. This is the counter-example that must be kept in view: predictive systems can prevent harm as well as cause it. The challenge is to reconcile that possibility with the ethical weight of misclassification.

The question of free will surfaces here in practical rather than metaphysical terms. When a profile is constructed from past behaviour, it often assumes stability: the person you were last year is the person you will be tomorrow. But human identity is rarely stable. People change careers in midlife, recover from addiction, upend long-held habits, or grow into new capacities when circumstances shift. Predictive systems struggle with such rupture. They forecast based on continuity, not transformation. A job applicant whose early career faltered may be deemed a "high-risk hire" even after demonstrable improvement. A student with a turbulent adolescence may carry the mark of instability long after stability has been earned. The algorithm does not measure hope, nor does it recognise the slow work of self-correction. It measures patterns.

Two UK examples illustrate this friction. First, the 2020 Ofqual algorithm used to assign A-level grades when exams were cancelled. Students in historically underperforming schools were downgraded en masse because the model weighted school performance more heavily than individual promise. Those who had worked relentlessly to exceed past cohorts' results were tethered to history. Data-driven destiny replaced personal trajectory. The policy was reversed only after national protest. Second, the predictive policing pilot employed by Kent Police in 2013, using geographic crime patterns to forecast future hotspots. Officers patrolled areas identified by the model. Arrest rates rose—but partly because police presence increased in places the algorithm had already flagged. Recorded crime inflated the dataset feeding the next prediction. The model created the very reality it claimed to foresee.

Yet predictive tools are not omnipotent. Their flaws create openings. Credit scores can be challenged; individuals can contest medical risk assessments; visa algorithms can be appealed. These pathways may be uneven, slow, or difficult to navigate, but they demonstrate that algorithmic predictions are not unbreakable laws. Transparency initiatives, such as the Model Cards approach proposed by Google researchers in 2019, aim to provide plain-language descriptions of how systems operate. They do not eliminate error, but they offer citizens a foothold into systems designed without them. The shadow becomes faintly visible.

Still, self-transformation grows harder in a predictive culture because systems treat deviation as anomaly. When a person attempts to change direction—a career shift, a new financial habit, a political reorientation—their digital history continues to inform decisions made about them. Behaviour must be sustained for months, sometimes years, before a system recognises that the pattern has altered. The cost of reinvention rises. Those who can afford tutors, reputation consultants, or specialised legal assistance find workarounds. Those who cannot must wait for the system's slow recalibration. Here, predictive labels do not simply describe reality—they shape it.

The motif of the shadow returns in a subtler form. Every data point thrown into an opaque model generates an echo, a probabilistic double that travels ahead. Employers see it, banks see it, border officers see it. The individual rarely does. To live with such a double is to negotiate a quiet psychological burden: the sense of being represented by a version of oneself that neither ages nor learns at the same pace. This tension, though seldom named, permeates digital life. We are visible and yet misrepresented, known and yet misunderstood.

A further implication is cultural. Predictive analytics encourage societies to think in categories. High risk. Low engagement. Likely respondent. Potential defaulter. These labels seep into institutions not through malice but through convenience. They save time. They reduce uncertainty. They offer the comfort of order. But order cannot accommodate the jagged edges of human change. A teenager who appears "vulnerable to radicalisation" because of online patterns may simply need mentorship. A retiree flagged as "likely to churn" by a subscription service may be coping with bereavement. Context matters. Prediction rarely sees context.

At the same time, we must resist the temptation to romanticise unpredictability. Human judgement can be biased, exclusionary, and discriminatory. Predictive systems, when carefully designed and monitored, can counterbalance human flaws. Automated loan approvals can eliminate prejudiced gatekeeping. Health analytics can catch early warning signs that doctors might miss. Prediction is not the enemy; the issue is its uncritical elevation to destiny.

What remains unresolved, and what sustains the central tension of this subchapter, is a simple but troubling question: how do we preserve the right to become someone new when an algorithm insists it already knows who we will be?

Social Segmentation and Echo Chambers

In November 2016, researchers at the Oxford Internet Institute analysed millions of public Facebook posts from the preceding months and found a striking pattern. During the US presidential election, clusters of users in states such as Ohio and Wisconsin circulated almost identical news links within tightly bounded circles. Distinct groups shared different articles about the same events, yet rarely crossed into one another's feeds. What looked like a national conversation was, in practice, a set of parallel monologues. The data revealed a form of political sorting that no campaign strategist had formally designed. Individuals were not isolated by geography or class, but by the invisible curation of their screens. The same digital infrastructure that promised connection quietly carved the public into segments.

This segmentation arose not from explicit intent but from millions of algorithmic decisions. Facebook's ranking model prioritised high-engagement content; users tended to engage with pieces that echoed their existing views. The feedback loop hardened. A like here, a share there, a prolonged pause over a familiar headline—each behaviour served as a signal, and the platform learnt. Over time, the system predicted what would keep a user attentive and delivered it. It reduced friction. It kept people scrolling. And it assembled echo chambers, not through coercion but through behavioural symmetry. The shadow motif appears again: a shadow of one's preferences projected back onto the feed, subtly reinforced, rarely questioned.

Profiling began with marketing. Early retailers such as Tesco pioneered loyalty-card analytics in the 1990s, tracking purchasing habits to tailor offers. Harvesting consumption patterns made commercial sense. By 2007, Amazon's recommendation engine had become a benchmark for predictive merchandising. Yet the logic migrated quickly from commerce to culture. A system capable of clustering shoppers by dietary preferences could cluster citizens by political suspicion or ideological leanings. The Cambridge Analytica affair, made public in 2018, exposed how psychological profiling based on Facebook "likes" could infer traits such as openness or neuroticism. These metrics shaped targeted political adverts in places as diverse as Michigan and County Durham. Profiles designed for persuasion bled into profiles used for division.

The mechanism is simple: algorithms measure what holds attention. They compare audiences, commit patterns to memory, and narrow the range of what each user sees. This narrowing is the architecture of the echo chamber. It is not merely a metaphor. When researchers at MIT examined Twitter data during the 2020 pandemic, they found marked differences between clusters following public-health experts and clusters following sceptical commentators. Both groups saw evidence confirming their views; both believed they possessed the clearer picture. The algorithmic cycle turned silence into segmentation.

One might counter that personal agency still matters. Users can choose their sources, diversify their feeds, or follow accounts outside their comfort zones. And indeed, some do. Cross-cutting exposure remains possible: a single subscription to a major newspaper or a deliberate search for alternative viewpoints can puncture informational bubbles. Yet this is the exception rather than the rule. Most people rely on platform defaults. Studies conducted by the Reuters Institute for the Study of Journalism (2021) indicate that a majority of social media users in the UK access news passively through feeds rather than actively through search. Passive consumption intensifies profiling. It hands selection entirely to the platform. The limitation of agency is subtle but real.

A counter-example also deserves attention. TikTok's "For You" page, heavily praised for its ability to surface unexpected content, occasionally disrupts predictable patterns. Users commonly report being offered videos far outside their prior interests: a cooking demonstration after a series of sports clips, or a political debate after hours of comedy. This resistance to strict segmentation shows that algorithmic environments need not be rigid. Yet, even here, the broader trend leans towards coherence. Once the system detects consistent engagement, it narrows again. Diversity flickers rather than persists.

The consequences stretch beyond politics. Social segmentation stratifies cultural life. Music apps group listeners into micro-genres. Streaming platforms categorise viewers by taste clusters. Job sites classify candidates by inferred skill profiles. The broader implication mirrors that of political echo chambers: classification creates self-fulfilling trajectories. When Spotify identifies a listener as a "lo-fi enthusiast," it offers more of the same. When LinkedIn categorises a user as "mid-level marketing professional," it prioritises similar roles. These classifications reduce discovery, narrowing the range of what individuals encounter. Over time, subtle shifts—clicking familiar songs, reading familiar headlines—accumulate into a patterned identity.

The motif of the shadow returns here too: an invisible silhouette of preferences guides what appears on screen. It grows sharper with each interaction. The individual is reflected, yet the reflection is curated. What disappears are the surprises, the accidental encounters, the uncomfortable but necessary viewpoints that broaden civic life. Social fragmentation deepens when each group sees only itself.

Two named examples illuminate the political stakes. In 2019, the Indian general election saw coordinated misinformation campaigns on WhatsApp. Because messages travelled in private groups, false claims circulated within isolated networks. People received only the narratives embraced by their immediate circles. Similarly, during Brazil's 2018 election, researchers at the Getúlio Vargas Foundation documented how social media clusters aligned with neighbourhoods and professions, shaping not only political opinions but also communal trust. Digital segmentation mirrored social segmentation. For many, their feed became their world.

Yet segmentation is not wholly negative. Communities of shared interest—coding forums, health-support groups, fan collectives—can provide solidarity and expertise that might be scarce offline. Echo chambers can nurture belonging as much as they entrench division. The limitation lies not in the existence of clusters, but in their opacity. When people do not realise how their feed is shaped, they cannot contextualise what they see. They assume universality where there is only targeted relevance. This opacity erodes the shared informational ground necessary for public discourse. To reconcile both sides, transparency becomes essential.

Transparency, however, carries its own paradox. If platforms reveal how profiling works, they may inadvertently help political actors manipulate it more effectively. After Facebook introduced its Ad Library in 2019 to expose political adverts, campaigns began experimenting with micro-variations in messaging, testing emotional triggers with unprecedented precision. Visibility did not dissolve the walls; it helped architects reinforce them. Here, the promise of transparency meets its limit. It can expose the structure of echo chambers without providing a route out of them.

The deeper issue is cognitive comfort. People gravitate towards affirmation. Platforms measure this preference and scale it. With each small confirmation—a meme, a headline, a testimonial—the chamber tightens. Breaking out requires conscious friction: reading beyond one's instincts, sitting with discomfort, engaging critics. These behaviours do not align with commercial incentives. Platforms succeed by smoothing experience, not by complicating it. Attention flows towards ease. And ease favours segmentation.

The shadow motif now points towards a final tension. Can transparency help us see the shadow, or does it simply illuminate its edges without dissolving its shape? If platforms disclosed every ranking signal, would users alter their behaviour? Or would they merely learn to perform their preferences more efficiently? The question remains unsettled.

What persists is the unsettling possibility that profiling, left unchecked, does more than shape what we see. It shapes what we become. If our informational diet narrows to the familiar, our imaginative range narrows too. The cost is subtle but profound: democratic life relies on the capacity to understand those who differ from us. Echo chambers corrode that capacity.

The unresolved question—the one that trails into the next subchapter—is this: if transparency exposes the chamber without dismantling it, what tools remain for us to reclaim the breadth of the public square?

Privacy as a Luxury

In July 2013, as details of the Snowden disclosures ricocheted across Europe, one scene captured a deep societal fault. At Berlin's Hotel Adlon Kempinski, a group of senior executives from a major Swiss wealth-management firm checked in under aliases, paid in cash, and requested rooms without key-card tracking. The request was unusual but not unprecedented. The hotel already operated a discreet protocol for high-net-worth guests who insisted on minimising their digital footprint. No key-card logs. No loyalty records. No linked email confirmations. Their invisibility was not a political statement; it was a service included in a suite costing several thousand euros a night. The message was quiet but clear: anonymity could be purchased.

That same month, commuters in London passed through stations monitored by Transport for London's Wi-Fi probe trial. Every smartphone that auto-connected left a trace: speed, route, dwell time. These metrics fed an efficiency report designed to optimise passenger flow. The passengers consented only by walking through the station. They received no option to opt out, no alias, no protected anonymity. Their digital visibility was not a choice but a condition of participation in ordinary life. Two urban experiences—one luxurious, one routine—revealed a pattern that has since hardened: privacy is unevenly distributed, not just by law or technology but by wealth.

The motif that threads through this subchapter is the locked door. Who is permitted to close it, and who must remain exposed?

The first claim arises from a measurable distinction in data exposure. Show: high-net-worth individuals routinely employ reputation managers, off-shore service providers, and private communications networks. Name: by 2019, firms such as Switzerland's Proton AG expanded their encrypted email offerings specifically to luxury travel clients in Zürich and Geneva. Explain: these clients sought not only confidentiality but insulation from routine data brokerage—what the average user encounters through default app permissions or ad trackers. Implication: encryption becomes less a democratic safeguard and more a boutique commodity when access hinges on cost and expertise.

A second example clarifies the socioeconomic gradient. In 2021, the New York Times documented how public figures in Los Angeles used "metadata scrubbing" services to remove property records from digital registries. They could erase their home addresses from online lookup tools. Meanwhile, ordinary residents' property data remained visible. Show: the record disappears for one group but persists for another. Explain: privacy is structurally linked to the ability to pay for erasure. Implication: the locked door becomes a privilege.

This disparity is not a new phenomenon. Historically, elites have always controlled access to information about themselves. The British aristocracy of the 18th century used pseudonymous correspondence to shield personal dealings; Victorian industrialists employed confidential clerks to maintain discretion. Yet the digital shift has amplified the gap. Today, billions leave behavioural traces—movement logs, browsing fingerprints, micro-transaction histories—that cannot be sealed by discretion alone. For those with resources, visibility remains negotiable. For others, exposure is automatic.

The central mechanism rests on predictable behaviours. When a person taps a loyalty card in Manchester, their purchase feeds into a retail data exchange. When a job applicant submits a CV through a mainstream platform, their profile is analysed for inferred traits. These interactions generate a metric of digital legibility: how readable a person is to institutions. Wealthy individuals lower this legibility. They use private browsing networks, hire data-deletion consultants, or even register companies to own personal assets. These behaviours reduce exposure by design. The locked door stays closed.

A counter-example is worth scrutiny. Estonia's e-governance system, launched in 2002, grants citizens transparent logs of who accesses their data. Doctors, police officers, tax officials—every access is recorded. In principle, this model democratises privacy by curbing power asymmetries. Yet even here, limitations persist. While visibility of state access improves, commercial access through global platforms remains opaque. Predictability of surveillance shifts but does not vanish. Even with progressive systems, those with legal teams interpret the logs; others accept them without analysis.

A second counterpoint emerges from encrypted messaging adoption. Since WhatsApp enabled end-to-end encryption by default in April 2016, billions gained baseline privacy without paying. This development challenges the notion that all privacy is purchased. Yet again, reconciliation reveals nuance: encryption protects communication content but not metadata. Who you contact, when, and how often remains inferable. For high-profile individuals, privacy consultants still recommend separate devices or offline meetings to protect these relational traces. For ordinary users, metadata remains exposed. The locked door is half-closed at best.

This disparity carries civic consequences. A person with resources can evade predictive systems entirely. They can avoid credit-scoring algorithms by using private banking. They can bypass targeted adverts by commissioning personal digital hygiene audits. They commit fewer behavioural signals that become inputs to automated profiling. Their future remains less computable because their past is less observable. Those without such means become hyper-visible to systems that classify them. Credit risk. Insurance risk. Employability ranking. Advertising segment. The more visible the behaviour, the more rigid the categorisation.

Concrete examples sharpen the ethical stakes. In 2020, researchers from EPIC (Electronic Privacy Information Center) highlighted how low-income borrowers in Chicago were disproportionately flagged by risk-scoring models because they relied on mobile phones rather than landlines. The signal was mundane: a mobile number instead of a fixed line. Yet the inference created higher predicted default risk. Show: an everyday digital signature becomes a negative metric. Name: the EPIC report (2020) documented this bias. Explain: predictive systems convert poverty's circumstantial traces into markers of unreliability. Implication: digital exposure multiplies disadvantage.

Another example concerns mobility tracking. Ride-sharing apps in London log pick-up and drop-off coordinates. During the pandemic (2020–2021), transport researchers at UCL found that travel data from lower-income boroughs was more complete and more frequently used in mobility models, simply because residents relied more on these services. Residents in affluent Kensington were under-represented; they used private cars or walked. Exposure differed by wealth. Those most visible produced the data that informed urban planning; those most private shaped policy least.

Profiling then reinforces inequality. If visibility to algorithms increases the likelihood of being sorted into constrained categories, then invisibility becomes a strategic advantage. Those who can afford to dim their digital presence control their narrative. Those who cannot are defined by it.

The motif of the locked door now intersects with autonomy. To control one's exposure is to control how one is interpreted. When elites choose seclusion—off-grid holiday estates, cash transactions, private browsing—they reduce behavioural predictability. They remain authors of their identities. Conversely, when ordinary users must accept cookie banners, location tracking, and algorithmic recommendations, they become interpretable subjects more than self-defining agents. Privacy becomes not only a luxury but a prerequisite for self-fashioning.

Yet the ethical tension deepens. Advocates of transparency often argue that visibility is a democratic equaliser. If governments and corporations are exposed, they are easier to hold accountable. If individuals are visible, social interactions may become more honest. The limitation lies in symmetry. Transparency stabilises fairness only when applied evenly. When surveillance flows upward as well as downward, it balances power. But in current digital practice, monitoring flows downward—towards consumers, renters, job-seekers—while opacity flows upward—towards corporations, wealthy individuals, and political elites. The locked door opens only in one direction.

This asymmetry raises a difficult implication: privacy has become a form of wealth concentration. Those who can afford invisibility retain greater negotiating power. They carry fewer algorithmic labels. They face fewer automated decisions. They escape the cumulative weight of digital histories. Meanwhile, those who cannot afford invisibility produce the data that trains the very systems used to assess them. Their lives become raw material.

The unresolved tension shadows the end of this chapter segment. If privacy remains purchasable, do we accept a future where digital inequality mirrors—and magnifies—economic inequality? Or do we commit to building structures that ensure the locked door is not a luxury but a universal right?

Beyond the Algorithm

In June 2016, at Apple's Worldwide Developers Conference in San Francisco, Craig Federighi stood on stage and announced that the company would begin using "differential privacy" to collect usage statistics from iPhones and Macs. The promise sounded simple enough. Apple would learn from aggregated user data—improving autocorrect, emoji suggestions, and more—without knowing which data came from which individual device. The company presented this as a technical veil: keep the benefits of large-scale analytics, blur the link to any identifiable person. It was a modest step, not a revolution, but it signalled something important. Even one of the most valuable firms on earth felt compelled to show that progress need not demand complete transparency.

That same year, on the other side of the Atlantic, a very different experiment quietly took shape. In Barcelona, city officials and technologists working on the DECODE project began exploring how residents might collectively control access to urban data: everything from air-quality sensors to platform-generated mobility patterns. Instead of handing data wholesale to commercial platforms, they piloted "data commons" governed by community rules. Anyone contributing could help define who used the information and for what purpose. Where Apple's move wrapped individual data in statistical noise, Barcelona's experiment wrapped community data in democratic process. Both efforts, in very different ways, pointed beyond the dominant framing of "more data or less progress".

The question animating this subchapter is whether such efforts can add up to something more than public relations. Can we foster a data environment that respects human nuance, where prediction does not harden into destiny and where people retain genuine secret spaces? Or do these projects function merely as thin curtains in front of an unchanging architecture of extraction?

To answer, we need to start with what has been learnt about the fragility of anonymity. For much of the early internet era, "anonymised data" was treated as safe by default. Strip out names, phone numbers and email addresses, and the rest could circulate freely. Then the cracks appeared. In the late 1990s, Latanya Sweeney famously re-identified the medical records of the Governor of Massachusetts by linking anonymised health data with voter registration databases. A few years later, in 2007, researchers Arvind Narayanan and Vitaly Shmatikov showed that "anonymous" viewing data released by Netflix could be linked back to named individuals using public ratings on IMDb. These cases proved a stubborn point: people are distinctive. Patterns of behaviour can act like fingerprints. Once data is out, re-identification becomes a standing possibility.

The first corrective has been to make anonymity itself probabilistic. That is what differential privacy attempts: it injects carefully calibrated noise into data so that analysts can see trends in the aggregate but cannot confidently reverse-engineer any single person's information. Apple's deployment was one of the earliest high-profile, consumer-facing uses of this technique. Google adopted similar approaches in products such as Chrome metrics and Maps traffic analysis. The behaviour is visible: navigation apps can show rush-hour congestion without revealing exactly which car is where. The implication is subtle but significant. We begin to accept that ethical data use is not all-or-nothing; it is a matter of how precisely individuals can be singled out.

Yet the limitations of these techniques must be acknowledged. Differential privacy, properly implemented, reduces re-identification risk but does not answer deeper questions about purpose. Collecting noisy data "about users in general" does nothing to address unfair uses of those aggregates—for example, when they shape urban planning in ways that neglect certain communities. Nor does it resolve imbalances of power between data subjects and data holders. The veil softens the gaze, but it does not change who stands behind the glass.

A second family of approaches tries to move computation closer to the individual. Google's work on federated learning, deployed experimentally in 2017 for its Gboard keyboard, is one such example. Instead of sending all keystrokes to a central server, the system trains models on-device and only sends back aggregated weight updates. Show: the predictive text improves over time. Name: federated learning. Explain: individual messages never leave the phone in raw form; what travels is the distilled learning signal. Implication: some benefits of scale can be achieved without centralising all the underlying data.

Again, nuance matters. Federated learning does not eliminate surveillance; it merely shifts where and how information is processed. If the model being trained encodes discriminatory patterns, those patterns will spread regardless of where the computation happens. And while keystrokes might not travel, other telemetry might. The motif that runs through these examples—a partial veil—returns here. Our view is obscured just enough to feel different, not always enough to transform the underlying relationship.

Beyond technical design, institutional experiments have begun to probe what democratic oversight might look like in a datafied society. The UK's exploration of "data trusts" from 2018, championed by the Open Data Institute, proposed legal structures through which groups could pool their data and appoint trustees to manage access in the public interest. In theory, taxi drivers in London could form a mobility data trust, allowing access to researchers studying congestion but denying it to advertisers seeking to micro-target them during long shifts. Similarly, health data trusts might anonymise and license datasets to accredited researchers under strict conditions. The behaviour here is contractual: access is negotiated, not assumed.

The limitation is practical scale. These models demand legal literacy, collective organisation and sustained funding. They are easiest to implement in well-resourced contexts. Moreover, they do not easily interface with global platforms whose data appetites span jurisdictions. A local data trust cannot meaningfully negotiate with a multinational firm that simply sidesteps it and continues to harvest information through consumer devices. Yet the implication remains promising. These experiments demonstrate that communities can act as data stewards, not just passive sources.

There are also hard-learnt lessons from missteps. In 2016, the partnership between Google's DeepMind and London's Royal Free Hospital ignited controversy when it emerged that the company had received access to 1.6 million identifiable patient records to develop an app for detecting acute kidney injury. The UK's Information Commissioner later ruled that the data sharing had not complied with privacy law. The outcome was concrete: DeepMind Health's operations were folded directly into Google, and the NHS pledged tighter oversight of technology partnerships. The episode functions as a cautionary story. It shows how enthusiasm for AI-powered healthcare, absent robust governance, can erode public trust. It also suggests a path forward: privacy-preserving tools must be accompanied by transparent agreements and independent scrutiny.

Another arena for "beyond the algorithm" thinking lies in national infrastructure. Estonia's e-governance framework, built on the X-Road platform, allows citizens to see exactly which officials have accessed their records. The behavioural change is tangible. A police officer who queries someone's file knows their action is visible to the subject. The motif of the veil appears inverted: the state becomes partially transparent to citizens, not only the other way round. Yet even this model does not reach the private sector, nor does it prevent legitimate over-collection of data in the first place. Auditability is necessary. It is not sufficient.

We should also note that some of the most promising alternatives come from refusal rather than redesign. In 2020, after sustained criticism from civil society, the UK government abandoned its plan for a centralised NHS COVID-19 contact-tracing app and adopted the decentralised Apple–Google exposure notification framework. Show: location data no longer pooled on a central server. Explain: contact events stayed on devices, identified only by ephemeral identifiers shared via Bluetooth. Implication: the state accepted a modest reduction in epidemiological insight in exchange for stronger privacy guarantees. This was not technologically elegant perfection; it was a political compromise that treated secret spaces as a public good.

At the level of everyday practice, design choices can also recover nuance. Some platforms have experimented with slower metrics—delayed like counts, friction before resharing, prompts that ask "Have you read this article?" before allowing a retweet. These features attempt to interrupt the hyper-reactive logic of algorithmic feeds, making room for reflection. Their effectiveness is mixed, and commercial incentives to maintain engagement remain strong. But they exemplify a broader principle: algorithms are not natural laws.

They are malleable. They can be tuned to favour deliberation rather than compulsion, plurality rather than segmentation.

A credible counter-example reminds us of constraints. Privacy-preserving tools can be, and have been, co-opted. The same end-to-end encryption that protects dissidents in Tehran can conceal coordinated harassment campaigns or organised crime. Anonymous browsers such as Tor serve journalists and traffickers alike. Any reconfiguration of the data environment must grapple with this duality. Protecting secret spaces can also shield harmful activity. That tension cannot be designed away.

The reconciliation lies in governance rather than technical purity. Instead of seeking a perfect algorithm, we may need layered arrangements: privacy-preserving defaults for ordinary activity, heightened oversight for powerful institutions, targeted and accountable investigative powers for serious crime. This is messy. It involves trade-offs, constant negotiation, and the humility to accept that some data should never be collected, no matter how enticing the potential model.

The quiet motif that has followed this chapter—the right to a margin of mystery—comes into sharp focus here. Differential privacy, federated learning, data trusts, decentralised architectures, audit trails, friction in design: each creates a small margin where people can exist as more than the sum of their recorded behaviour. None is complete. All are contested. Yet together, they represent a refusal of the idea that everything valuable about human life must be encoded, predicted and optimised.

What remains unresolved—and must remain open as we move forward—is how far societies are willing to go to protect that margin. How much uncertainty will we tolerate in our systems to preserve the possibility of surprise in our lives? And who will decide where the boundary lies between necessary insight and an unforgivable breach of the spaces we still wish to keep our own?

Chapter 7
Digital Anonymity: A Lost Art?

In October 2013, a soft-spoken systems administrator walked through Hong Kong's crowded streets, carrying four laptops and the sinking knowledge that his life had permanently split in two. Edward Snowden had not yet revealed his identity to the world, but the documents were already in journalists' hands. Even in those liminal hours, before he stepped into the glare of geopolitical consequence, he understood the fragility of anonymity. It could protect him only briefly, yet it was vital. Without that temporary invisibility, he could not have acted at all. His anonymity was not a mask of deception; it was a shield that allowed truth to surface before power could extinguish it.

The Snowden moment looms large in our cultural memory, but its emotional charge resonates far beyond the sphere of state surveillance. Think of the teenager in Birmingham who, late one night, creates a pseudonymous account simply to escape the crushing expectations of polished self-presentation. Or the mid-career professional in Dublin who turns to an anonymous forum to discuss workplace harassment without fear of reprisal. Not all secrecy carries the weight of whistleblowing; more often, anonymity functions as a means of breathing room. It is the pause between two selves. It is the world briefly turning its back so one may speak without trembling.

But anonymity's hold on modern life is loosening. The infrastructures we inhabit—social platforms, financial services, identity management systems, location-aware apps—have normalised a form of participation that leaves increasingly few shadows to stand in. The expectation of constant identifiability has crept from bureaucratic necessity into social norm. A comment without a name is suspect; an account without a face is treated as either unserious or dangerous. Our tools now greet anonymity with suspicion, and so do we. That shift warrants scrutiny, for it has unfolded quietly, almost imperceptibly, as if invisibility itself were becoming impolite.

This chapter examines that transformation by starting from the oldest of questions: why do humans seek to disappear? There is no single answer, because anonymity fulfils different psychological, cultural and political roles. In Japan, the tradition of *honne* and *tatemae*—the private truth and the public façade—has long made selective concealment a social necessity rather than a moral failing. Medieval Europe relied on anonymity in pamphleteering and dissent. Modern protest movements have used masks as symbols of solidarity and protection. The impulse is universal: anonymity lets people say what they cannot safely attach to their names. That impulse has not withered; its outlets have.

This is why nostalgia shadows the contemporary conversation. When the early internet honoured pseudonyms and eccentric aliases, it created a culture where reinvention was a daily possibility. There was mischief, certainly, but also liberation. You could speak before deciding who you were. You could learn without the fear of being judged for not knowing already. Those spaces are rarer now. The mainstream web nudges us towards stable, legible identities—names matched to photos, photos linked to histories, histories indexed forever. The disappearance of these pockets of ambiguity is not merely a technical loss; it reshapes how we construct ourselves.

That tension threads directly into the mechanisms people now use to reclaim some measure of privacy. Encrypted messaging, browser isolation, VPNs, multiple email identities—these tools form a patchwork of countermeasures in an ecosystem designed for traceability. They offer limited sanctuary, though never certainty. For every layer of concealment, there is a corresponding method of unmasking; for every attempt at evasion, a parallel process of inference. The story of a forum user in Manchester deploying three separate identities and still being identified through behavioural patterns is a contemporary parable of our times: anonymity is possible, yes, but fragile, contested and often outpaced by the systems designed to pierce it.

The ambiguity surrounding these tools is not merely practical; it is ethical. The same digital obscurity that protects a domestic abuse survivor or an employee reporting corruption also shields coordinated disinformation campaigns and targeted harassment. To hide is neither inherently noble nor inherently suspect. The moral weight depends on purpose, harm and context—dimensions that automated systems, in their binary logic, cannot meaningfully interpret. Our broader culture often errs by assuming anonymity itself is the problem, rather than recognising that what truly matters is the intent behind the veil.

If anonymity appears morally ambiguous, transparency can seem deceptively virtuous. But transparency too carries shadows. Total openness can smother the capacity for risk, vulnerability and experimentation. Societies that insist on real-name policies and verifiable identities for every contribution risk producing generations afraid to challenge orthodoxy, innovate or express dissent. The cost of perfect legibility is conformity. The art lies in constructing spaces where openness and secrecy coexist—where individuals can stand behind their names when it matters, and step behind curtains when authenticity requires privacy.

This leads to the chapter's central tension: can we design systems that honour layered disclosure rather than binary models of exposure or invisibility? The idea may sound technical, but its implications are deeply human. An individual might share their professional achievements publicly, their creative drafts within trusted circles, and their fears only in carefully guarded anonymity. Organisations, too, have layers: they must be transparent in governance yet discreet in safeguarding intellectual property or sensitive operations. The real question is whether we can encode this layered morality into the digital architectures that now govern modern life.

These questions matter because anonymity has not vanished; it has simply migrated to the margins. And the margins are where freedom is most often tested. If digital anonymity becomes a luxury—available only to those with specialised knowledge or economic privilege—society loses more than privacy. It loses the spontaneous speech that fuels creativity, the protected dissent that safeguards democracy, and the intimate introspection that makes growth possible. What vanishes is not only secrecy but the capacity to think without watching ourselves think.

As we move through this chapter, the nostalgia implicit in its title will deepen into a sharper inquiry: if anonymity is indeed a lost art, what do we lose with it? And if it is not yet lost, what choices—individual, cultural and institutional—will determine whether it survives? The next pages step into these questions not to mourn the past but to illuminate a path forward, one where invisibility remains part of the human repertoire rather than a relic of a less observed age.

Why We Seek Anonymity

In January 2011, as protests gathered force in Cairo's Tahrir Square, the blogger Ghonim—Wael Ghonim of Google—struggled to keep his identity hidden while helping coordinate information flows. For twelve days, he operated under a pseudonym on the "We Are All Khaled Said" Facebook page, a digital hub that helped mobilise thousands. His anonymity mattered. It reduced the immediate risk of reprisal, enabled him to act before fear could stall him, and preserved the momentum of a movement still fragile and unformed. When he was detained by Egyptian authorities on 27 January, the limits of that anonymity became brutally clear; yet without those early days of concealment, his work would not have been possible. His case distils a truth we often overlook:

anonymity is not merely a refuge for the guilty. It is a tool the vulnerable use to speak.

The distance between a dissident hiding from a regime and an ordinary citizen seeking respite from daily scrutiny appears vast, yet the motivations are not as dissimilar as one might think. Consider the university student in Leeds who quietly adopts a pseudonym on an online support forum, not out of rebellion but to express anxieties she feels unable to share with friends. Or the freelance designer in Bristol who maintains two separate social accounts, one polished for clients and one anonymous for honest, unfiltered conversation. These small acts of disappearance, humble in scale, reveal a deeper yearning: the wish to be unobserved just long enough to say something true. Visibility promises recognition, but it also imposes judgement.

Anonymity, then, is less about erasure than about freedom. It allows a person to test thoughts without committing their entire biography to them. It creates a margin for error. That margin is essential. The historian John Mullan notes that eighteenth-century pamphleteers in London frequently wrote under pseudonyms because anonymity let ideas outrun reputations; arguments could be weighed without prejudice. The same dynamic animates digital life. People shed their names not because they seek to deceive but because they wish to speak without dragging their entire life story behind every assertion. Five words suffice: anonymity lets imagination breathe.

This need for breathing space becomes clearer when we look beyond individual psychology and into cultural norms. In Japan, the interplay between *honne* (inner feelings) and *tatemae* (public duty) has long sanctioned indirect expression. Anonymous message boards such as 2channel, founded in 1999, thrived precisely because they gave voice to *honne* without threatening *tatemae*. South Korea, by contrast, experimented with mandatory real-name registration for major websites in 2007, arguing that accountability would reduce online abuse. Yet studies by the Korea Communications Commission in 2012 showed minimal reduction in harmful content, while users simply migrated to foreign platforms where anonymity persisted. The divergence in outcomes highlights a common thread: anonymity endures because it answers a need that policy seldom understands.

The motif of the mask helps illuminate why. A mask conceals, yes, but it also reveals. The person wearing it chooses what to project and what to protect. When people use pseudonyms or anonymous channels, they engage in a similar selective disclosure. The choice signals vulnerability: a mask is put on not to dominate but to survive. The anonymous whistleblower who reports financial misconduct to a regulator in London behaves differently from the anonymous troll who flings abuse on Twitter. Their masks are made of the same digital fabric, yet the moral texture is entirely different. These contrasts underscore that anonymity's value lies in context, not category.

Still, anonymity also invites unease. Critics contend that it lowers inhibitions and encourages cruelty, pointing to cases such as the 2014 harassment scandal on the anonymous platform Ask.fm, which drew scrutiny after the death of a teenager in Leicestershire. Harms like these are undeniable. Yet they are not arguments against anonymity as such; they are arguments against the structures that fail to curb exploitation of it. Removing anonymity would not eliminate abuse. It would merely shift it into venues where harmful actors find new workarounds, while silencing those who depend on concealment as a lifeline. The limitation is not anonymity but the absence of accountability mechanisms that target behaviour rather than identity.

Another strand of criticism holds that anonymity undermines *trust*. But trust is not a mystical quality; it is a pattern of behaviour over time. On Wikipedia, for instance, many long-standing editors contribute under pseudonyms, yet their reliability is judged by edit histories, transparent talk-page negotiations and adherence to sourcing rules. The site's governance model demonstrates a vital point: accountability can be decoupled from identity. What matters is the trail of actions, not the passport name behind them. The mask returns as a motif here: a mask can be consistent, principled and responsible. The face beneath does not determine the quality of the contribution.

The moral significance of anonymity becomes sharper when seen through the lens of power. Those with institutional protection—politicians, executives, celebrities—often decry anonymous speech as corrosive. Yet they themselves enjoy layers of privacy unavailable to the public: security details, media advisers, legal protections. By contrast, individuals with little power often resort to anonymity simply to name injustices that would otherwise go unspoken. The nurse who exposes unsafe hospital practices in Manchester, the gig-economy worker in Glasgow who reports wage theft, the migrant in Naples who documents exploitation: anonymity equalises just enough to let truth travel.

But anonymity's necessity extends beyond whistleblowing. It nurtures experimentation. A person trying to break free from a stifling identity—religious, familial, professional—may first explore new beliefs or self-understandings under a pseudonym. Sociologist danah boyd observed this in early American teen social media cultures of the 2000s: young people crafted secondary identities not to deceive but to explore versions of themselves unsupported by their immediate environments. Digital anonymity served as rehearsal space for adulthood. Without such spaces, transformation becomes riskier, and growth slower.

Yet the desire for concealment is not universal; some cultures constrain anonymity so tightly that deviation feels perilous. In Singapore, strict defamation laws and identification requirements for online political content create an environment where anonymity is both sought and feared. The result is a cautious public sphere where pseudonymous dissent exists, but tentatively. This counter-example illuminates anonymity's fragility: its strength depends on social tolerance as much as technology. Remove either, and the mask cracks.

Recalling the motif of the mask once more, we can see that anonymity is not about breaking ties with the world. It is about choosing how to stand within it. A masked figure is still present, still acting, still accountable to the consequences of their actions. What they gain is the ability to step forward without the full weight of their biography foreclosing possibilities. That freedom is not trivial. It shapes whether ideas are aired or stifled, whether vulnerabilities are shared or buried.

As digital infrastructures tighten, requiring phone-number verification, biometric gates, behavioural profiling and cross-platform identity stitching, the spaces in which anonymity can flourish shrink. These measures are often justified as essential for safety or convenience. Yet the trade-offs remain unresolved. How do we preserve anonymity's benefits without inviting its misuse? How do we distinguish between concealment that protects and concealment that harms? How much should society tolerate masks when the risks of their misuse are real?

These questions resist easy answers. That resistance is the point. The drive to remain unseen—whether to resist oppression, to confess fear, to imagine alternatives, or simply to take a breath—reveals something irreplaceable about human dignity. The mask will endure. The challenge is to decide who gets to wear it, under what conditions, and at what moral cost to us all.

Mechanisms of Concealment

In October 2013, the FBI seized control of the marketplace Silk Road after tracking down its administrator, Ross Ulbricht, in a public library in San Francisco. Investigators later testified that they pieced together fragments of his digital trail—forum posts made under an early pseudonym, a stray email header, a transaction timestamp—until the mask slipped. Ulbricht had used multiple anonymity tools, but the system of concealment he relied on was only as strong as its weakest configuration. His arrest became a landmark reminder that anonymity is not a switch one flips. It is a chain of practices, and every link can break.

Across far more mundane terrain, this fragility is visible in smaller, quieter stories. A forum contributor in Rotterdam might post sensitive opinions under a pseudonym, routing traffic through a privacy network and encrypting messages before sending them. The layers feel protective. Yet, as cybersecurity researchers at the University of Amsterdam warned in 2022, such camouflage can unravel if even one device synchronises at the wrong moment or a secondary account uses similar phrasing. A single breadcrumb suffices. This mixture of empowerment and uncertainty is the essence of digital concealment. People reach for masks because they need to speak, but they never fully know whether the mask will hold.

Pseudonyms remain the oldest and most accessible mechanism of concealment. They offer distance without demanding technical skill. But pseudonyms also carry histories of both liberation and misuse. In 2014, J.K. Rowling was inadvertently outed as the author behind the pseudonym Robert Galbraith, reminding literary observers that linkage can occur through metadata, stylistic comparison, or simple human betrayal. Show, name, explain, implication: pseudonyms create a membrane, not a wall. They shape how individuals present themselves but cannot guarantee that the membrane will resist pressure. The implication is stark—an alias buys freedom only when the surrounding ecosystem chooses not to interrogate it.

Encryption, by contrast, promises mathematical certainty. When the messaging platform Signal launched in 2014, its open-source protocol rapidly became a benchmark for end-to-end encryption. Visible behaviour demonstrated its adoption: journalists began requiring secure channels as a baseline, while NGOs in Nairobi, Kyiv and Hong Kong incorporated it into their communication norms. Signal's design meant that even the organisation operating the service could not read user messages. Yet its strength also exposed a limitation. Encryption can secure content, but it cannot fully obscure metadata. A log showing that two people communicated at a specific time may still reveal sensitive patterns. Even the strongest cipher cannot neutralise what surrounds it.

The motif of the chain helps clarify this. Every anonymity method is a link; each link depends on another. Virtual Private Networks mask IP addresses but may keep logs. Encryption secures conversations but not relationships between correspondents. Pseudonyms shield identity but not writing style. The chain holds only when each link bears weight. Users who treat a single tool as decisive place trust where caution would serve them better.

Consider Tor, the volunteer-run network designed to route traffic through layers of relays, obscuring its origin. In 2016, researchers at Carnegie Mellon University reportedly assisted U.S. authorities by identifying traffic emerging from specific Tor exit nodes, raising concerns about deanonymisation attacks. Though the details remain partially sealed, the outcome showed a crucial limitation: anonymity networks rely on both design and goodwill. When adversaries gain sufficient resources, they can attack either. As a counter-example, activists in Barcelona successfully used Tor during local elections in 2019 to protect whistleblowers reporting voting irregularities. The network did not fail them, illustrating that context, threat model and operational discipline often determine success more than the tool itself. Reconciling these cases reveals a nuanced pattern: concealment methods work best when used modestly, under realistic expectations, and supported by community norms rather than blind faith.

The question of legality complicates everything. Some anonymity techniques are protected as fundamental rights. Encryption is legal in the European Union and upheld by the European Court of Human Rights as essential for safeguarding journalists and dissidents. Yet more advanced mechanisms—such as routing connections through compromised servers or spoofing identifiers—risk breaching cybersecurity or data protection laws. The line between protective concealment and illicit evasion is not merely technical; it is moral. The same mechanism that lets a whistleblower in Bucharest expose corruption without fear can shield a coordinated harassment campaign in Dublin or a fraud ring in Frankfurt. The chain motif reappears: the technology itself is neutral, but its links bind to whatever hands wield them.

The dilemma turns sharper when we examine how platforms respond to concealment. Wikipedia allows pseudonymous editing because its community has built processes that measure trust through verifiable behaviour—citations added, disputes resolved, vandalism reverted. In contrast, Facebook's real-name policy, which hardened in the mid-2010s, treated anonymity as inherently suspicious. Yet this policy backfired for vulnerable groups such as LGBT youth in conservative regions who depended on pseudonyms for safety. Real-name enforcement reduced their willingness to participate, shrinking their social capital. The implication is clear: anonymity does not dissolve accountability. It simply shifts responsibility from identity to conduct.

Metrics of misuse add further complexity. Researchers analysing anonymous boards in 2021 found that harmful content surged not when anonymity was available but when moderation collapsed. The visibility of consequences—bans issued, posts removed—mattered more than the visibility of names. This challenges the assumption that anonymity breeds misconduct. Instead, the absence of norms and enforcement does. A well-maintained chain holds; a neglected one snaps.

Our Rotterdam forum user returns here as a motif. Each time they post, they perform a small, deliberate ritual: activate a VPN, check Tor settings, use encrypted messaging, avoid personal anecdotes. These behaviours demonstrate intent rather than malice. Yet their disguise also illustrates the fundamental tension of digital concealment. The more visible the effort to remain invisible, the greater the risk that the disguise itself becomes a marker. Tools protect, but they also attract scrutiny. The chain tightens.

Attempts to strengthen this chain have produced innovations such as onion routing, secure enclaves, and privacy-focused operating systems. Each offers potential. Each also contains gaps. When Apple introduced its Mail Privacy Protection feature in 2021, which masked user IP addresses from tracking pixels, marketing industries criticised the loss of behavioural telemetry. But the measure did not guarantee anonymity; it merely narrowed one avenue of exposure. Similarly, encrypted browsers like Brave reduce fingerprinting but cannot eliminate it. Even privacy coins in the cryptocurrency ecosystem, such as Monero, which obscures transaction paths, face de-anonymisation attempts by forensic analysts working for national agencies. No single layer replaces judgement.

This interplay of capability and constraint raises the central ethical dilemma: does concealment enable free expression or shield wrongdoing? Evidence refuses simplicity. Anonymous whistleblowing platforms run by the International

Consortium of Investigative Journalists have enabled disclosures of global importance, including material used in the Panama Papers investigation in 2016. Yet anonymity has also facilitated coordinated extremist propaganda on fringe forums. The contradiction is unavoidable. But it is instructive. The distinction lies not in the mechanism of concealment but in the economic, political and social structures that shape its use.

What, then, should one expect of these mechanisms? Not perfection. Rather, proportionality. Concealment tools are best understood as negotiation devices—ways of managing exposure in an environment where surveillance scales effortlessly. A pseudonym does not promise invulnerability. Encryption does not eliminate metadata. An anonymity network does not guarantee invisibility. Yet each link, when chosen wisely, expands the margin in which thought and dissent can survive.

As digital infrastructures harden—through biometric enrolment, behavioural analytics, and cross-device identity stitching—the burden on these mechanisms grows heavier. How long can the chain hold? How should societies respond when concealment is framed as suspicious by default? Should the right to be unobservable depend on technical skill, or should it be supported by public norms?

These questions form the horizon of the chapter that follows. They challenge us to decide what kind of digital life we wish to build: one where concealment is feared, or one where it is understood as a necessary counterweight to scrutiny. The chain persists. The tension endures.

Is Anonymity Ethical?

In March 2016, an anonymous source contacted journalists at Süddeutsche Zeitung from an undisclosed location, offering a leak of 11.5 million documents now known as the Panama

Papers. The source never revealed their identity. Yet their decision exposed global tax avoidance schemes, prompted resignations from public officials, and led to investigations across more than seventy jurisdictions. The outcome demonstrated that anonymity can serve democratic accountability when conventional channels remain compromised. But it also raised a more unsettling question: if a nameless individual can reshape global politics, who evaluates the legitimacy of their motives? One act protected the vulnerable. Another could destabilise institutions. This tension forms the ethical spine of digital anonymity.

The paradox sits plainly in the numbers. How can the same structural feature that enabled one of the most significant journalistic revelations of the twenty-first century also be the infrastructure for harassment campaigns that have driven individuals offline? A single tool produces incompatible outcomes. Five words capture the dilemma: anonymity empowers; anonymity endangers. That duality must be dissected rather than romanticised.

Anonymous expression often begins with vulnerability. The whistleblower who contacted Süddeutsche Zeitung described moral outrage rather than personal gain as the catalyst. Show, name, explain, implication: the individual operated outside formal channels because naming themselves carried measurable dangers—detention, retaliation, disappearance. The implication is simple and profound: when systems punish truth-telling, anonymity becomes a civic necessity rather than a personal preference.

Yet, as the same year demonstrated in a different domain, anonymity can corrode public discourse. In 2016, Twitter struggled to contain coordinated harassment campaigns originating from pseudonymous accounts targeting journalists and minority communities. The behaviour was visible: thousands of identical messages delivered within hours. The platform's failure to remove these accounts quickly enough prompted public criticism from Amnesty International. Here anonymity shielded cruelty. Not dissent. It produced no public good. The chain motif from earlier subchapters resurfaces—anonymity is a link, but the morality of the chain depends on what is fastened to it.

The ethical debate hinges on a simple but demanding distinction: anonymity separates identity from action, shifting accountability from who someone is to what someone does. In many contexts, this shift is just. It protects dissidents in Moscow who rely on encrypted channels to criticise state corruption. It safeguards employees in London reporting misconduct within regulatory bodies, relying on anonymous drop boxes approved under UK whistleblowing law. These behaviours demonstrate responsible anonymity—where concealment stabilises institutions by exposing wrongdoing.

A counter-example emerges from 4chan, an American imageboard founded in 2003, which pioneered "post without identity" design. Its anonymity enabled playful creativity, but also provided a staging ground for coordinated abuse, conspiracy dissemination, and harmful pranks. The limitation is clear: a platform designed without accountability mechanisms incubates behaviour that spills into harm. Reconciling these opposites requires attention to context. The platform that enforces norms treats anonymity as a mask worn during meaningful participation. The platform that abdicates norms turns anonymity into a licence.

Cultural norms further complicate the ethical map. Japan's 2channel, created in 1999, has long embraced anonymity as a cultural standard rather than an exception. Users contribute without names, believing ideas should stand apart from social hierarchy. Sociologists analysing 2channel point to a consistent pattern: high-volume anonymous discussion, surprisingly structured self-moderation, and a lower incidence of direct personal harassment compared to Western equivalents. The behaviour is visible—threads self-correct, off-topic comments are ignored rather than attacked, and group norms develop organically. This shows anonymity can coexist with communal responsibility when cultural expectations treat the mask as an equaliser, not a shield for aggression.

The question then arises: does anonymity weaken or refine accountability? When Reddit launched its whistleblowing subreddit r/Whistleblowers in 2020, moderators introduced verification protocols allowing contributors to provide evidence confidentially while remaining publicly anonymous. Trust was measured through documents, not names. Efficiency of investigation was maintained through careful review, not exposure. The visible metric was not identity but verification. The implication is instructive: accountability can be rerouted through process rather than disclosure.

Still, anonymity is not ethically neutral. It changes the distribution of risk. A teacher in Manchester who anonymously reports safeguarding violations protects children. A coordinated troll farm operating from St Petersburg, also shielded by anonymity, destabilises elections. Both rely on the same structural affordances: pseudonyms, untraceable routing, disposable accounts. Ethics therefore cannot be determined by mechanism alone. It is the alignment between motive, context, and consequence that defines whether anonymity is justified.

Threading the motif again, anonymity functions like a lens. It sharpens certain truths and blurs others. It allows individuals to speak without personal cost, yet it removes cues that help communities evaluate credibility, sincerity, and integrity. This tension became visible when the social platform Secret launched in 2014. Promising total anonymity, it quickly filled with defamatory rumours, causing reputational harm to individuals named without evidence. By 2015, the platform had shut down. The lesson was clear: anonymity without guardrails amplifies the loudest voices, not necessarily the wisest.

Yet a limitation remains worth exploring. Some harms associated with anonymity may not originate from anonymity itself but from design flaws—insufficient moderation, poor incentive structures, or lack of community oversight. Wikipedia's pseudonymous system, for example, demonstrates that anonymity can function ethically when linked to transparent edit histories, deliberative processes, and community sanctions. The visible behaviour—reverts, warnings, bans—creates a form of distributed accountability without requiring real names. Reconciling this with more harmful platforms reveals the essential factor: anonymity must coexist with norms that reward evidence, reason, and respect.

Ethical evaluation also demands an awareness of power asymmetry. Anonymity protects vulnerable individuals far more than it protects institutions. When a dissident in Tehran uses Tor to contact an exiled journalist, concealment offsets structural imbalance. When a multinational corporation uses shell accounts to influence policy debates covertly, concealment magnifies power. Same tool. Opposite ethical valence. The implication is that anonymity's moral weight shifts depending on whose interests it serves, and whose risks it mitigates.

Legal frameworks echo this complexity. The European Court of Human Rights has upheld anonymous expression as a vital component of free speech, particularly for journalists and activists. Yet courts across the United States have repeatedly ordered unmaskings in defamation cases, emphasising harm over liberty. These rulings reveal the ethical crossroads: the right to be unknown cannot eclipse the right not to be unjustly injured. Law attempts to balance the two, but the balance remains contested.

Returning to our core motif—the mask—its power depends on how it is worn. A mask can protect identity long enough for truth to surface. A mask can hide malice long enough for wounds to spread. Ethical judgment requires asking not whether anonymity is good or bad, but who benefits, who pays, and who decides.

We reach an unresolved but necessary tension. If anonymity is essential for courage, how much harm are we willing to tolerate for its sake? If accountability is vital for justice, how much exposure are we willing to demand from the vulnerable? And if the digital mask cannot be removed without cost, what standards should guide when it is worn, when it is reinforced, and when it must be lifted?

Balancing Openness and Secrecy

On 28 October 2013, in Geneva, the World Health Organization confronted an unexpected diplomatic storm. Journalists had obtained internal drafts of its pandemic preparedness plans and reported discrepancies between the private assessments and the organisation's cautious public statements. The leak embarrassed officials, but it also revealed a deeper dilemma. Total openness risked triggering panic at a stage when evidence remained inconclusive; total secrecy risked fuelling suspicion at a moment when trust was already brittle. The episode demonstrated that institutions, like individuals, struggle to measure how much to reveal and when. The balance between openness and secrecy has never been simple, and the correct ratio is rarely visible in real time.

One question emerged from that incident and has echoed since: does releasing every detail truly strengthen legitimacy, or does it overload the public with unprocessed uncertainty? Five words offer the puzzle: transparency enlightens; transparency misleads. Both statements hold depending on the context, and both complicate the assumption that more disclosure is always more ethical.

Openness is often framed as a moral default, yet human behaviour shows nuance. A researcher in Manchester may disclose her methodology while withholding personal data that could endanger participants. An activist in Nairobi may livestream a protest but conceal the identities of fellow organisers. These decisions embody layered disclosure: reveal the substance, protect the vulnerable. The motif of the curtain—parted but not fully drawn—captures this better than any slogan.

The idea gains weight when we move from individuals to organisations. Show, name, explain, implication: the Wikimedia Foundation, operating globally since 2003, publishes detailed financial statements and governance decisions. Yet it withholds the IP data of editors to protect them from reprisals. The implication is that ethics lie not in maximal transparency but in the calibration of visibility to purpose. A second example comes from 2018, when the UK Information Commissioner's Office audited WhatsApp after concerns about metadata sharing with Facebook. The company disclosed its encryption protocol but declined to reveal operational details that could compromise security. Here the visible behaviour was selective openness anchored in responsibility rather than convenience.

A credible counterpoint surfaces from the corporate world. Enron, prior to its collapse in 2001, released extensive financial reports filled with disclosures that were technically compliant but engineered to obscure its liabilities. Transparency became camouflage. The limitation is instructive: disclosure without integrity creates an illusion of openness while deepening opacity. Reconciling this with the earlier examples underscores an essential truth: transparency gains ethical force only when aligned with honest intent and practical intelligibility.

Layered disclosure therefore operates across multiple scales. At the personal level, individuals reveal fragments of identity to navigate social life. A student in Glasgow might share her academic achievements on LinkedIn while shielding her political views on private channels. At the organisational level, hospitals publish waiting times but restrict access to patient notes. At the governmental level, intelligence agencies publish oversight reports without disclosing sources. These behaviours measure one principle: openness should illuminate decision-making, not expose people to avoidable harm.

The curtain motif deepens here. When it is drawn too far, exposure paralysis follows. Early open-data enthusiasts in the 2000s believed unfiltered release of government datasets would invigorate democracy. But by 2014, several studies in the EU noted that raw datasets with minimal context created confusion, misinterpretation, and politicised misuse. A dataset on school performance led parents to misjudge institutions based on incomplete indicators. The metric was visible but misleading. This demonstrated that disclosure without explanation can distort understanding rather than advance it.

Yet full secrecy carries its own cost. The Post Office Horizon scandal in the UK, which came to public awareness between 2009 and 2020, showed how institutional opacity can inflict catastrophic injustice. Managers concealed faults in accounting software, leading to wrongful prosecutions of sub-postmasters. The visible behaviour—refusals to disclose technical reports—revealed secrecy weaponised against the powerless. The implication again reinforces the central argument: neither full concealment nor unfiltered transparency offers an ethical default.

Cultural norms shape the balance further. In Sweden, the principle of offentlighetsprincipen—public access to records—has existed since 1766. It reflects a national expectation that transparency is foundational to civic trust. Yet even there, secrecy is permitted in matters of personal data and national security. Meanwhile, in South Korea, strong norms of privacy coexist with state access to communication metadata. Different societies draw the curtain at different lengths, but all maintain the curtain.

Technologists propose solutions to refine this balance. Zero-knowledge proofs, deployed experimentally by companies such as Zcash since 2016, show that it is possible to verify a claim—such as the validity of a transaction—without revealing the underlying data. Privacy-preserving analytics used in medical research allow hospitals to compare patient outcomes across institutions without sharing identifiable information. These methods offer a quieter vision of transparency, one built on verification rather than exposure. Their limitation is technical complexity: they demand expertise and trust in implementation. Yet they point to a future where disclosure is layered by design rather than by instinct.

The counter-example that tempers these hopes comes from facial-recognition deployment in public spaces. Cities such as San Francisco banned police use of facial recognition in 2019 because accuracy disparities across demographic groups made enforcement unpredictable and biased. Even with partial constraints, the technology generated invisible forms of surveillance. These cases show that balancing openness and secrecy is not only about what we disclose, but about what systems infer without consent. Reconciling this complication requires a shift from asking how much individuals should reveal to how much institutions should restrain themselves.

Layered disclosure also extends into interpersonal life. Consider the behaviour visible on encrypted messaging apps such as Signal: people share candid emotions, private decisions, or early creative work within trusted circles, withholding the same material from wider audiences. This controlled sharing strengthens relationships precisely because it is selective. The implication is that secrecy is not antisocial but a precondition for intimacy. If the curtain were always wide open, human connection would thin into performance.

This leads to the collective dimension. Democracies depend on informed citizens, yet they also rely on confidential voting. Journals rely on peer review, yet reviewers remain anonymous. Courts operate openly, yet deliberations by juries remain secret. These contradictions are not flaws; they are structural. Ethical life depends on both visibility and privacy, and on the tension between them.

Threading the curtain motif once more, the question becomes: who decides when it should be drawn, and how far? If decisions remain with individuals alone, institutions may hide wrongdoing. If decisions sit entirely with institutions, individuals lose dignity and autonomy. A shared framework—cultural, legal, and technical—is needed to prevent either extreme from dominating.

We end with an unresolved but necessary challenge. If total transparency can mislead and total secrecy can wound, how should we measure the ethical midpoint? Who calibrates the curtain when interests collide? And in a world where disclosure can be instant yet trust takes years to rebuild, what principles should guide how much we reveal, how much we conceal, and how much we are prepared to let others decide for us?

Chapter 8
Legal Boundaries and Global Perspectives

In December 2015, a court in São Paulo ordered a temporary shutdown of WhatsApp after the company declined to provide decrypted messages sought in a criminal investigation. For forty-eight hours, millions of Brazilians found a familiar tool abruptly inaccessible. The legal order was brief, the public reaction furious, and the underlying tension unmistakable. A judge prioritised investigative reach; citizens perceived an assault on communications privacy; the company insisted it lacked the technical ability to comply. The episode was not an outlier but a harbinger. It revealed how rapidly a legal boundary, once invoked, can expose the cultural values beneath it. One magistrate's interpretation of public interest collided with a population's sense of personal autonomy—and neither side felt unreasonable.

That same year, across the Atlantic, the European Court of Justice struck down the Safe Harbour agreement between the EU and the United States, citing insufficient protections against government access to personal data. Here, unlike in Brazil, the legal decision was celebrated as a principled defence of privacy. Two rulings, issued within months of each other, produced almost opposite public sentiments. Both were grounded in law; both invoked the public good. Their divergence illustrates a theme central to the pages ahead: privacy legislation is never just legal scaffolding. It is a cultural mirror, a political battleground, and a philosophical wager about how societies want to be governed.

Even at this early stage, the motif of the border—a line drawn, contested, re-drawn—emerges. Legal boundaries around personal data are not fixed walls but shifting frontiers shaped by crises, scandals, and technological surprises. The notion that a regulation can simply codify a universal "right" collapses under inspection. Instead, laws expose a deeper question: what does a society fear more, intrusion or uncertainty?

Frameworks for data protection try to answer that question, yet each framework carries the imprint of its birthplace. The EU's General Data Protection Regulation, effective from May 2018, enshrines data minimisation, consent, and purpose limitation—principles reflecting a continent historically scarred by authoritarian surveillance and thus instinctively wary of unchecked information flows. California's Consumer Privacy Act, which entered into force in 2020, takes a market-inflected approach, treating personal data as a form of property that individuals must be able to control, delete, or monetise. Meanwhile, Singapore's Personal Data Protection Act prioritises clarity and efficiency, maintaining tight regulatory oversight while encouraging digital innovation. These policies differ not because legislators failed to agree but because their societies prioritise different balances between risk and opportunity.

Such divergence deepens when examining cultural philosophies of secrecy. Japan's long-standing emphasis on social harmony makes certain forms of personal discretion socially expected, yet it also supports robust systems of administrative data-sharing in sectors such as health insurance. Germany, shaped by memories of the Stasi, legislates fiercely against surveillance, yet maintains centralised registers essential to its welfare state. Neither approach is inconsistent. Each reveals a different instinct about where borders ought to lie: around the individual or around the collective.

This leads directly to the question of state power. Governments have always argued that some degree of information collection is essential for security or order. China's model of governance, formalised most visibly in its national social credit system trials from 2014 onwards, demonstrates how legal frameworks can become instruments of behavioural management. The stated goal was social trust; the effect, critics argue, is deepened surveillance. Contrast this with Norway's tradition of publishing tax records, a practice rooted in egalitarian transparency rather than social control. Both systems reveal personal information. One aims to deter misconduct; the other aims to reinforce civic fairness. The same act—disclosure—means different things depending on who controls the border and for what purpose.

Yet state-sponsored surveillance need not be overt to be powerful. The Snowden disclosures of June 2013 showed that intelligence agencies in the United States and the United Kingdom had constructed vast metadata-collection systems under legal authorities few citizens had read. Statutes intended for targeted monitoring expanded, slowly and quietly, into broad nets. This elasticity—where laws designed to defend national security inch into the domain of everyday communication—illustrates how transparency, once invoked by the state itself, can serve the state rather than its citizens. Borderlines blur; oversight lags; accountability becomes theoretical.

But there is another side to this story. Nations threatened by organised crime, insurgency, or foreign interference often defend surveillance powers as existential tools. Kenya's efforts to use mobile metadata for counter-terrorism after the 2013 Westgate attack illustrate the acute pressures governments face. The debate then becomes less about whether surveillance is permissible and more about who defines its limits, who audits its use, and who safeguards the citizens most vulnerable to misuse.

Against this backdrop, the future of policy appears both urgent and unsettled. Emerging technologies—federated learning, synthetic data, quantum decryption—promise benefits and hazards that current laws cannot fully anticipate. Regulators confront a landscape where innovation outruns legislation, and where a single company's platform decisions can affect billions. To build frameworks that remain relevant, societies may need to shift from rule-heavy systems to principle-based governance: flexible, proportionate, and grounded in shared values rather than rigid compliance checklists. The challenge is formidable. Principles offer adaptability but demand trust; rules provide clarity but risk obsolescence.

The border motif returns here with greater force. The line between personal autonomy and collective welfare, once navigated with paper records and local authorities, is now tested by global platforms, instantaneous data flows, and cross-jurisdictional algorithms. The question is no longer whether nations can protect their citizens' data but whether any static policy can keep pace with rapidly mutating forms of digital exposure.

As we move deeper into the chapter, the stakes will sharpen. Behind every legal clause sits a cultural intuition; behind every regulatory gap lies an ethical gamble. Laws reveal what societies cherish, what they fear, and what they are willing to risk. And as technology shifts the terrain faster than courts can respond, one question stands unresolved: who should draw the next border, and how do we decide whether it ought to hold?

Frameworks for Protection

In October 2016, the Court of Justice of the European Union issued a judgment against the Spanish Data Protection Authority and Google, clarifying the reach of the "right to be forgotten". The ruling required Google to remove links that infringed an individual's privacy, provided the information was no longer relevant to public interest. One man in Madrid, whose decades-old financial troubles continued to surface in search results, gained a degree of relief; the broader outcome pushed digital privacy from a technical footnote into a civic principle. A single case sketched out a boundary: personal data might be public, but its circulation need not be perpetual. The judgment revealed something deeper than legal nuance. It captured a cultural conviction that dignity includes the ability to shed outdated versions of oneself.

This moment also exposed a tension that runs through the global privacy landscape. The legal victory in Luxembourg, celebrated across Europe, would have been unlikely in the United States, where freedom of expression and corporate latitude often take precedence. One dispute, two contrasting instincts. It set the backdrop for a central theme of this subchapter: that frameworks for data protection are not mere technical regimes. They embody divergent moral choices about identity, autonomy, and the role of the state.

Across jurisdictions, a handful of principles recur with striking consistency, yet each takes on a regional accent. Data minimisation, informed consent, purpose limitation, and access rights form the backbone of modern privacy law. These concepts emerged not from ideological consensus but from accumulated crises. The Data Protection Directive of 1995 was shaped by Europe's determination to prevent abuses reminiscent of mid-twentieth-century surveillance. The OECD Privacy Guidelines of 1980 were drafted to support cross-border trade without sacrificing personal rights. Even the Fair Information Practice Principles in the United States—developed in the early 1970s—arose from congressional concern about expanding federal databases. Each framework emerged as a defensive measure, a reaction to a specific historical anxiety.

What these principles do, beyond their formal function, is reveal each society's threshold for discomfort. Data minimisation may look technical, but it carries a cultural message: information should not be collected simply because it can be. Consent suggests that autonomy has legal force. Purpose limitation signals distrust of mission creep. These doctrines show behaviour as much as they prescribe it.

Consider how the GDPR's accountability requirement, enacted in May 2018, reshaped corporate conduct. Firms hired privacy officers, rewrote data flows, and designed dashboards that allowed users to delete stored data. The law changed daily behaviour. Behind each adjustment was an implied value: that individuals should not rely on corporate goodwill but on enforceable commitments.

Yet the frameworks differ where it matters most: their assumptions about the relationship between the citizen, the market, and the state. The GDPR is anchored in the belief that privacy is a fundamental right. California's CCPA operationalises privacy as consumer empowerment. Singapore's PDPA prioritises clarity, predictability, and business confidence. These differences are not accidents but reflections of political culture. In Europe, memories of authoritarianism make individual protection paramount. In California, innovation and market competition dominate public life. In Singapore, order and economic stability guide regulatory posture. Each framework maps a different answer to the same question: who is data for?

Examples make these contrasts vivid. Germany's Federal Data Protection Act, revised in 2017 to align with the GDPR, grants powerful rights of erasure and rectification. These rights reflect a long-standing national commitment to informational self-determination, a term coined by the German Constitutional Court in its 1983 Census Judgment. That decision, prompted by public fears about state tracking, embedded privacy into Germany's constitutional identity. Contrast this with South Korea's Personal Information Protection Act, one of the world's strictest regimes when introduced in 2011 after a series of corporate breaches. The Korean model arose from public outrage at negligent data handling by telecoms providers. One system was born from suspicion of centralised state power; the other from distrust of industry. Both frameworks seek control, but the threat they name differs—and that difference shapes enforcement priorities.

A credible counter-example comes from jurisdictions where privacy laws exist on paper but are weakly enforced. Brazil's LGPD, effective from September 2020, mirrors GDPR principles, yet enforcement remains uneven due to resource constraints and political turbulence. This gap reveals a hard truth: formal frameworks matter little without institutions that commit to them. However, this does not negate the value of the law itself. Even partial enforcement shifts expectations, gives civil society a foothold, and moves organisations toward better practice. The limitation is real; the implication is that cultural change often precedes legal robustness and can, in time, compel it.

The motif of the border surfaces repeatedly. Legal frameworks draw lines—between acceptable use and misuse, between autonomy and oversight, between innovation and restraint. Yet borders shift with public sentiment. The rapid expansion of biometric systems illustrates this. India's Aadhaar, launched in 2009, became the world's largest biometric ID programme. Its architects described it as a tool for welfare delivery; critics saw the risk of mass surveillance. In 2018, India's Supreme Court upheld Aadhaar's constitutionality but restricted its use by private firms. A single system, designed for efficiency, forced the nation to renegotiate the borderline between state benefit and personal privacy. The debate was not only legal; it was moral.

Frameworks also reveal a society's appetite for remedy. The EU's allowance for substantial administrative fines—up to 4 per cent of global turnover—signals that privacy breaches are not minor infractions but significant harms. By contrast, some nations maintain modest penalties, effectively signalling that violations, while undesirable, are tolerable costs. That decision, too, encodes a value. It shows how much a society believes privacy is worth defending.

Yet frameworks alone cannot resolve deeper tensions. Take transparency. Laws often require organisations to provide notices written in plain language. The intention is noble: reduce information asymmetry. The practice often falls short. Lengthy disclosures overwhelm rather than empower. Here, the border motif reappears: a line drawn to strengthen autonomy can blur into administrative formality. The implication is sobering. Legal frameworks can promote rights while inadvertently encouraging complacency, giving the appearance of control without the substance.

Despite their imperfections, these frameworks remain essential scaffolding for modern life. They tame the raw power of data collection and offer tools for redress. They also remind societies that privacy is not a static entitlement but a negotiated settlement. The challenge ahead is how to maintain coherence across jurisdictions whose values diverge. As cross-border data flows accelerate, tensions mount: whose law governs, whose norms prevail, and whose rights matter most when national boundaries become porous?

The tension sharpens as artificial intelligence expands. Predictive analytics, algorithmic profiling, and automated decision-making place pressure on principles drafted for a less complex era. Some regulators, such as the European Commission in its 2021 proposal for an AI Act, seek to categorise risks and impose tiered obligations. Others favour voluntary standards or industry codes. Each strategy, implicit or explicit, asks the same question: can frameworks protect dignity in systems built to infer, categorise, and judge?

We arrive, then, at the unresolved frontier. Legal frameworks can define rights, articulate principles, and constrain abuse. But they cannot alone reconcile cultural values that differ in their views of autonomy, security, and collective welfare. As technologies evolve, the question becomes increasingly urgent: what must the next generation of privacy laws prioritise, and who decides which values deserve legal force?

Divergent Cultural Standards

In February 2020, as COVID-19 cases accelerated in Daegu, South Korea, health authorities pushed phone alerts to millions of citizens. Each notification described an infected person's recent movements with unsettling specificity: a café at 14:05, a bus line, a church, sometimes even a rough age bracket. Restaurants saw business collapse overnight when a location appeared in one of these messages. The system worked. Chains of transmission were traced quickly, and containment improved. Yet when European privacy advocates read the details, many were horrified. The same mechanism that signalled communal care in Seoul looked, from Berlin or Paris, uncomfortably close to public shaming.

This dissonance captures the core puzzle of cultural standards around privacy and security. South Korean citizens, shaped by memories of SARS and MERS, largely accepted intrusive contact tracing as a reasonable trade for collective safety. In much of Europe, where the GDPR had only recently come into force, officials insisted that digital contact tracing apps minimise personal data, avoid centralised storage, and preserve anonymity. Two regions confronted the same virus with data-driven tools and produced strikingly different norms. Neither response was irrational. Each emerged from a different historical memory of risk.

Privacy feels different in Seoul. That five-word observation is not rhetorical. It reflects lived habits: the prevalence of CCTV in public spaces, the routine use of national ID numbers, the expectation that public health may justify disclosure. By contrast, privacy in Vienna is shaped by a long intellectual tradition of individual rights and a dark history of population registries exploited by murderous regimes. The same act—sharing location data—reverberates differently. In one context, it signals solidarity; in another, it triggers alarm.

The motif that will thread through this subchapter is the "social thermostat": the collective sense of how much heat—intrusion, visibility, constraint—a society will tolerate in exchange for security or convenience. That thermostat is calibrated not by universal logic but by culture, trauma, and aspiration.

Consider first the European preference for strong legal privacy guarantees. Show: the European Union's Charter of Fundamental Rights, proclaimed in 2000 and given binding force in 2009, explicitly recognises a right to data protection distinct from a general right to privacy. Name: the GDPR, effective from May 2018, operationalises that right through principles such as data minimisation and consent. Explain: this framework emerged from decades of reflection on state surveillance under fascist and communist regimes, where intimate details compiled in files enabled targeted persecution. The implication: for many Europeans, secrecy about one's movements, beliefs and associations is not a luxury but a bulwark against a historically familiar danger.

Shift the lens to China and the calibration changes dramatically. Show: extensive deployment of networked CCTV, mandated SIM registration, and the integration of disparate datasets—from travel history to financial records—into nationwide systems. Name: pilot versions of the social credit system, tested in several cities after 2014, as well as health code apps that controlled mobility during the pandemic. Explain: official narratives cast these systems as tools to enhance social trust, curb fraud, and coordinate public health. Many citizens, drawing on cultural traditions that emphasise social harmony and respect for authority, view such visibility as tolerable if it delivers safety and stability. Implication: notions of secrecy and exposure are filtered through a collectivist lens, where being known to the state is less disturbing than being insecure in public life.

Neither model is simple. Each carries shadow costs rarely captured in official rhetoric. In Europe, strict privacy norms can hinder rapid data-sharing between agencies, complicating responses to fraud or public health emergencies. In China, expansive surveillance powers risk muting dissent and narrowing the space for genuine pluralism. The social thermostat is calibrated differently, but in both cases the dial can stick.

A third example complicates any neat binary between "West" and "East". Estonia, a small Baltic state, has built one of the world's most sophisticated digital governance systems. Show: its X-Road infrastructure, introduced in the early 2000s, allows secure data exchange between public and private databases. Citizens carry national ID cards enabling access to services from voting to medical records. Name: Estonia's "once only" principle, under which the state may not ask citizens to submit the same information twice. Explain: this architecture reflects both a post-Soviet wariness of centralised data hoarding and a pragmatic desire for efficient, transparent administration. Crucially, Estonian citizens can see who has accessed their records and challenge improper queries. Implication: here, privacy is framed not as secrecy from the state, but as enforceable oversight of it.

The counter-example to this carefully balanced model is a jurisdiction where legal protections exist but cultural expectations are less sharply defined. Brazil's LGPD borrows heavily from the GDPR's language, yet a legacy of clientelism and weak institutional trust complicates implementation. Behaviourally, people may share personal information liberally on social media whilst simultaneously expressing deep suspicion about state data use. The thermostat flickers. It is not set consistently. This gap between formal rights and everyday norms illustrates how culture can undermine, or at least complicate, the impact of legal frameworks.

Religion, too, shapes standards. In parts of the Middle East, notions of honour and modesty may prioritise the concealment of women's images from public platforms, while at the same time extensive state surveillance is justified as a means of preserving order and moral standards. A woman may be fiercely protective of her family's appearance on social media yet live under a regime that monitors political speech closely. Here, secrecy is fragmented: intense around family reputation, thinner around civic liberties.

The social thermostat motif helps make sense of these contradictions. Every society sets a default expectation for what can be seen, by whom, and for what purpose. That default rarely appears in written law; it surfaces in moments of controversy. When the UK's Investigatory Powers Act expanded state access to communications data in 2016, civil liberties groups objected, but broad public mobilisation was limited. Contrast that with the reaction to the Cambridge Analytica revelations in 2018: the idea of political micro-targeting by a private company sparked far more visible outrage. Implication: in Britain, intrusion by commercial actors into the democratic sphere triggered more anxiety than state access justified as counter-terrorism. The thermostat marked different heat thresholds for different intruders.

We can see similar divergences around CCTV. London has long been one of the most heavily monitored cities in Europe, with cameras a familiar part of the urban landscape since the 1990s. Residents might grumble, yet many accept surveillance as a crime-prevention tool. By contrast, the deployment of facial recognition by police—trials began publicly around 2019—provoked sharper resistance, as people sensed a qualitative shift from generic observation to personalised tracking. The same camera becomes ethically different when software alters how it sees. The thermostat responds not to hardware but to perceived intent.

By comparison, high camera density in Singapore elicits limited public contestation. There, a cultural emphasis on cleanliness, order and low crime rates, combined with strong trust in state competence, leads many citizens to accept pervasive monitoring as part of a social contract. The trade-off is rarely framed as a dilemma. It is experienced as normality. Data about citizens is gathered, but the state's record in delivering safety softens perceived risk. This does not erase the potential for misuse; it simply lowers the ambient sense of threat associated with being watched.

The interplay between privacy and collective security is also generational. Younger users in Nairobi or Mumbai might share precise locations with friends via messaging apps whilst being wary of government data collection, especially where corruption or political instability is part of lived history. Their elders, less digitised, may distrust both state and corporate actors equally. Here, secrecy is not a single concept but a patchwork of micro-standards that differ by age, class, and digital literacy.

Then there is the question of global platforms attempting to operate across these divergent climates. A company like WhatsApp faces demands from India's government to trace the "originator" of problematic messages, from European regulators to maintain end-to-end encryption, and from Brazilian courts to cooperate swiftly in criminal investigations. It cannot satisfy all demands simultaneously. Its decisions—where to resist, where to comply, when to threaten withdrawal—implicitly choose one cultural standard over another. The social thermostat, once a national metaphor, becomes a corporate reality. A single service must run at different temperatures in different jurisdictions, and sometimes it overheats.

A tempting impulse arises here: to search for a universal model, a golden mean between collectivist and individualist norms. Yet this search misunderstands the nature of secrecy.

Privacy is not a commodity that can be standardised. It is a relationship—between citizens and state, between neighbours, between users and platforms—embedded in histories of oppression, prosperity, war, and reform. A country that has lived through secret police abuses will calibrate its thermostat differently from one that associates danger primarily with crime or instability. A society with dense kinship networks may view household privacy differently from one built on more atomised living.

The challenge, then, is not to harmonise standards but to develop mutual intelligibility. Cross-border data flows, international law-enforcement cooperation, and multinational services all require some shared grammar of privacy and security. Yet that grammar must leave space for accent. Can the EU's insistence on data subject rights coexist with more paternalistic models of state protection in Asia? Can African Union states, drafting continental data rules, avoid importing frameworks that ignore local communal values? These are not merely technical questions. They are choices about whose fears are acknowledged and whose experiences are taken as normative.

The social thermostat motif returns one final time. As climate scientists remind us, thermostats can be reset—but never without discomfort. The same is true here. Societies can shift their tolerance for surveillance or exposure, often after scandals or crises. The Snowden leaks nudged some Western publics to re-evaluate state power. Terrorist attacks have nudged them back towards security. Pandemics recalibrate expectations of health data sharing. None of these movements settles the matter.

The unresolved question, which leads into later sections of this chapter, is stark. If no universal privacy model fits all, how should we manage systems—technical, legal, commercial—that cross borders by design? Whose thermostat will dominate when data moves faster than law, and how much cultural difference can a shared digital world accommodate before trust itself begins to fracture?

States and State-Sponsored Surveillance

On 6 June 2013, readers of *The Guardian* in London opened the paper to a headline that confirmed what many had long suspected. Documents leaked by Edward Snowden showed that the US National Security Agency, with the cooperation of partners such as GCHQ in Cheltenham, had built systems capable of collecting telephone metadata and accessing data from major technology companies. The programmes had legal authorisation through secret court orders. The scale was vast, the visibility minimal. Governments that publicly championed rule of law and civil liberties were running surveillance architectures whose full contours were known only to a handful of insiders. Trust juddered.

The political response was revealing. In Washington and Westminster, officials insisted the programmes were lawful, proportionate and subject to oversight. They pointed to judicial warrants, parliamentary briefings and strict internal procedures. Civil liberties groups countered that these controls were opaque and often toothless, that the very secrecy of the oversight processes prevented meaningful democratic scrutiny. Through one keyhole—the official narrative—citizens saw targeted monitoring. Through another—the leaked slides—they glimpsed systemic data capture. The same state, two incompatible images, and a central question: who controls the keyhole?

States have always watched. What is new is the ease, speed and granularity with which they can do so, and the variety of legal and cultural stories they tell to justify it. At one end of the spectrum, some governments present themselves as exemplars of openness: publishing budgets, livestreaming parliamentary sessions, releasing open data. At the other, regimes normalise tight informational control, blending censorship with pervasive monitoring. Yet the boundary is not as clear as it appears. The rhetoric of transparency can coexist with, and even disguise, deep surveillance infrastructures. Likewise, even restrictive states sometimes reveal more than expected when it suits strategic aims. The keyhole widens and narrows according to political need.

Start with those who wrap surveillance in the language of security. The United States' USA PATRIOT Act of 2001, rushed through Congress after the 9/11 attacks, dramatically expanded government access to communications records. It enabled "section 215" orders compelling companies to hand over bulk metadata. The UK's Investigatory Powers Act of 2016, sometimes called the "Snoopers' Charter" by critics, consolidated and extended powers to retain communications data and hack devices. The behaviour is concrete: telecoms providers obliged to store logs, intelligence agencies empowered to deploy bulk interception, judicial commissioners asked to approve warrants. The explanation offered is familiar. Faced with diffuse terrorist threats and cyber attacks, states claim they cannot protect citizens with narrow, case-by-case tools. The implication is stark: collective safety, they argue, now requires forms of watching that would once have been politically impossible.

Contrast this with countries that lean heavily on the language of social order. China's networked surveillance system—combining the Great Firewall, real-name registration for SIM cards, extensive CCTV deployment, and emerging uses of facial recognition—operates under legal frameworks such as the National Security Law (2015) and Cybersecurity Law (2016). Officials emphasise stability, anti-corruption and crime prevention. Behaviourally, citizens encounter QR-code health passes, police cameras, and platform moderation tuned to political "guidance". The implication is that good citizenship involves visibility. To be legible to the state is framed as a civic duty.

Real-world examples show how swiftly such visibility can harden into control. During the Hong Kong protests of 2019, demonstrators avoided transit cards and ATM withdrawals near marches, fearing that journey data or financial logs could later be used to identify them. The state did not need to roll out new technologies. It simply reinterpreted existing datasets through a security lens. The keyhole did not change shape; the eye behind it did.

Yet it would be a mistake to treat liberal democracies as straightforward counterpoints. Some nations cultivate an ethos of openness that cuts both ways. Sweden's principle of public access to official documents, enshrined since 1766, allows citizens to examine tax records and administrative decisions. Norway publishes individual tax data, reflecting a belief in financial transparency as a tool of equality. These practices expose citizens to a level of visibility that would feel intrusive elsewhere, but they are widely accepted because they have a clear purpose and long historical pedigree. At the same time, Nordic countries maintain strong data protection regulators and constitutional safeguards against arbitrary surveillance. They show that transparency and restraint can cohabit—if trust in institutions is high and the keyhole points upwards as well as downwards.

A credible counter-example comes from states where "open government" rhetoric masks authoritarian drift. Russia's 2016 "Yarovaya law" package imposed mandatory data retention on communications providers and required decryption assistance on demand. Justified as anti-terror measures, these tools have also been deployed against journalists and opposition figures. Legal frameworks that appear neutral on paper acquire sharp edges in practice. The behaviour tells the story: prosecutions following online posts, arrests after encrypted chats are accessed, media outlets branded "foreign agents" for opaque offences. The limitation of purely legal analysis is clear. Statutes alone do not reveal how power will be used.

To reconcile these patterns, one must look at the alignment—or misalignment—between law, culture and oversight. Where independent courts, free media, and active civil society organisations can contest surveillance powers, the keyhole faces resistance. Judicial rulings in Germany and the Netherlands have curtailed data-retention laws when they were judged disproportionate. The European Court of Human Rights has repeatedly insisted that secret surveillance regimes require clear, accessible legal bases and effective remedies. The visible behaviour here includes governments forced to amend statutes, intelligence agencies required to narrow their programmes, and parliaments pressed to hold hearings. The implication: even within security-conscious states, surveillance can be fenced in if countervailing institutions are strong.

Yet oversight bodies can also be captured or sidelined. In some jurisdictions, "independent" regulators depend on the executive for budgets, appointments or access to classified material. Parliamentary committees receive heavily filtered briefings. Courts defer to national security claims. The formal presence of checks obscures their weakness. The keyhole exists, but it looks only where it is pointed.

The technological shift towards data fusion magnifies these dynamics. It is no longer just about intercepting phone calls or reading emails. States increasingly tap commercial databases, location logs, and social media feeds. Legal frameworks often lag behind. A police force in a European city might use a commercially developed predictive policing tool trained on historical arrest records, producing hotspot maps that reinforce existing biases. A migration agency elsewhere might screen asylum-seekers' phones, scraping communications and browsing histories to "verify" stories. These practices may be authorised under general powers rather than explicit surveillance statutes, allowing them to grow in the shadows of legal ambiguity. The behaviour is granular—every swipe, every check-in, every contact becomes a potential signal. The implication is unsettling: the line between security policy and everyday administration starts to blur.

Consider, too, the export of surveillance tools. Companies headquartered in democratic states have sold deep-packet inspection equipment, facial recognition systems and spyware to regimes with poor human rights records. The Pegasus spyware scandal, which came to light in 2021, showed how sophisticated tools intended for counter-terrorism could be used against journalists, lawyers and political opponents in multiple countries. Here, the state is not always the original designer but the eager client. Legal frameworks in exporting states often lack teeth to prevent such sales, or enforcement is tepid. The keyhole widens far beyond national borders.

Of course, not all state use of data is malign. Public health campaigns depend on epidemiological surveillance. Tax authorities need financial data to investigate fraud. Intelligence services have disrupted genuine plots using intercepted communications. A pandemic response team in Wellington or Copenhagen that tracks anonymised mobility trends to calibrate lockdowns might do so with high transparency and tight retention limits. Citizens see the benefits in lower mortality and shorter restrictions. The same technologies, repurposed without consent, could easily support more intrusive projects. The ethics hinge less on the mere presence of surveillance and more on clarity of purpose, proportionality, and the possibility of refusal.

The recurring motif of the keyhole helps hold these threads together. States insist they peer through it only when necessary, with steady hands and clear rules. Citizens suspect that once the mechanism exists, the temptation to look more often, at more people, for more reasons will prove irresistible. History supports their caution. Emergency powers introduced after crises—wars, terrorist attacks, pandemics—have a habit of becoming permanent. Data collected for one reason rarely stays in one silo.

This brings us to a final tension. Societies expect protection from genuine threats, whether from violent extremists, foreign adversaries or transnational crime. They also expect to live without constant fear of scrutiny. Legal frameworks sit uneasily between these expectations, pulled towards expansion by security agencies and towards restraint by civil libertarians. Some states err towards tight control, others towards openness, but none can escape the basic trade-off.

The unresolved question is therefore not whether states will watch, but under what conditions, at what scale, and with what recourse for those who object. Who should decide where the keyhole points, how wide it opens, and when it must be closed—even if only for a while—to preserve the very freedoms surveillance claims to defend?

Future Directions in Policy

On a grey morning in April 2021, officials gathered in Brussels to present the European Commission's proposal for an Artificial Intelligence Act. Cameras recorded the usual choreography of speeches and handshakes. Behind them sat a dense, 108-page legal draft that attempted to map every conceivable risk category, from children's toys to biometric surveillance. Outside those rooms, engineers were deploying new machine-learning models every week. The mismatch already felt stark. A carefully negotiated legal text moved at the speed of committees; data-driven systems moved at the speed of code.

The paradox was hard to ignore. How can rules crafted over years govern technologies that evolve over months? That question now haunts privacy and surveillance policy from Ottawa to Nairobi. Legislators reach for detailed prescriptions, only to discover that their effort risks obsolescence before the ink dries. Companies plead for clarity, even as some exploit ambiguity. Citizens hear the language of "innovation" and "trust", yet watch scandals recur with numbing regularity. The problem is not a shortage of law. It is a shortage of frameworks capable of bending without breaking.

As we look ahead, policy must act less like a locked gate and more like a compass. Gates block or admit; compasses orient. The challenge is to design legal instruments that keep their bearings in a hyper-transparent world—binding enough to constrain abuse, flexible enough to remain meaningful when the next generation of systems arrives.

The first step in that direction is to acknowledge the limits of the consent-and-notice model that underpinned many earlier privacy laws. Show: by 2018, when the GDPR took effect, European internet users were already drowning in cookie banners. Name: these banners nominally operationalised "informed consent". Explain: in practice, most people clicked "accept" as quickly as possible, driven by impatience rather than genuine understanding. Implication: a framework designed to protect autonomy ended up dulling it, turning consent into a reflex rather than a choice. As AI systems infer intimate traits from behaviour that individuals never "gave" in any meaningful sense, clinging to old rituals of clicking and scrolling will not suffice.

The move towards principle-based, risk-sensitive policy is an attempt to repair that mismatch. The proposed EU AI Act, Canada's Artificial Intelligence and Data Act (first tabled in 2022), and guidance from regulators in Singapore and the UK all revolve around a similar idea: treat some uses of data as intrinsically higher risk and demand more of them—more documentation, more testing, more transparency to regulators, and in some cases outright bans. Instead of regulating every algorithmic detail, these frameworks ask a different set of questions. What is this system for? Who does it affect? How severe are the harms if it fails or is abused?

The compass motif matters here. Instead of trying to sketch every path, lawmakers attempt to point everyone—

developers, executives, auditors, courts—towards orienting principles: necessity, proportionality, fairness, contestability. These principles gain meaning through concrete behaviour. A hospital deploying a diagnostic model must document how it tested for bias across patient groups. A bank using automated credit scoring must provide reasons a person can understand and challenge. Regulators, in turn, must publish what they expect as evidence. Law becomes less a checklist and more an accountability narrative.

Yet principle-based frameworks carry their own risks. One credible counter-example is the way "risk-based" language has occasionally been used by powerful actors to justify opaque practices. A platform might label its recommender system "low risk" because it does not directly affect legal rights, ignoring evidence that it shapes political discourse and mental health. A government agency might classify bulk data analysis as "proportionate" under a generous reading of national security needs. When principles lack teeth, they can become new banners under which old habits persist. Reconciling this requires more than eloquent charters. It demands institutions capable of arguing back.

That, in turn, points to a second direction: strengthening the machinery of oversight rather than merely elaborating the text of rules. Show: data protection authorities in countries such as Ireland, France and the Netherlands have, since 2018, imposed significant fines and ordered changes to behavioural advertising practices. Name: France's CNIL sanctioning Google and Facebook for unlawful cookie practices in 2021; the Dutch regulator pushing municipalities to abandon invasive welfare fraud algorithms. Explain: these interventions illustrate that enforcement, not drafting finesse, often determines whether hyper-transparency is constrained. Implication: future policy must invest at least as much in regulators' independence, technical capacity and budgets as in drafting fresh statutes.

A different model of oversight is emerging through impact assessments and external audits. Canada's federal government has required privacy impact assessments for many digital projects; New Zealand has experimented with algorithmic impact assessment frameworks; the city of Amsterdam has piloted public registries of automated decision systems. The visible behaviours here are modest but telling: project teams documenting reasoning before deployment, civil servants consulting affected communities, citizens gaining a window—however small—into systems that used to be entirely opaque. These practices hint at a way forward where transparency is not just about data leaving citizens but about scrutiny entering institutions.

Future-focused policy will also have to grapple with infrastructural questions that earlier privacy debates side-stepped. One concerns the underlying business models of hyper-transparent platforms. Personalisation, behavioural advertising, attention-tracking: all incentivise the extraction of ever more data and the construction of detailed profiles. Tighter rules on consent help, but they do not alter the core logic. Some scholars and policymakers have therefore floated structural ideas—data trusts, public digital infrastructures, limits on surveillance advertising—as ways to change the incentive landscape itself. A data trust, for instance, would separate the role of data custodian from the entities that wish to analyse or monetise that data, creating fiduciary duties similar to those that bind lawyers or doctors.

Another infrastructural frontier lies in technical standards. Cryptographic techniques such as differential privacy, homomorphic encryption, and secure multi-party computation, once confined to specialist circles, now appear in policy discussions. Show: Apple's use of differential privacy in parts of iOS analytics; Google's early experiments with federated learning to keep certain forms of training data on devices. Explain: these techniques promise to extract useful aggregate insights while reducing exposure of individual records. Implication: if regulators begin to treat such privacy-preserving designs as expected rather than exceptional, technical architecture itself becomes a policy tool. The compass, in this case, points developers towards certain design patterns rather than simply forbidding bad outcomes after the fact.

Of course, there are limits. Privacy-preserving methods can still be misconfigured; anonymised datasets can sometimes be re-identified when combined with other sources; open technical standards can ossify if not revisited. And global uptake is uneven. Large corporations in wealthy countries can afford cutting-edge protections. Small firms and governments with limited budgets may lag. This is the structural inequality that future policy must confront: without attention to capacity-building, hyper-transparency will continue to weigh heaviest on those with the fewest resources to resist it.

International coordination is the third, and perhaps thorniest, frontier. Data ignores borders; law does not. The Schrems II judgment of July 2020 invalidated the EU–US Privacy Shield arrangement, forcing companies to scramble for alternative transfer mechanisms. That ruling highlighted a structural problem: divergent national approaches to surveillance and redress make it hard to guarantee consistent protection for cross-border data. The answer is unlikely to be a single global privacy treaty. It is more plausible to envisage an incremental mesh of adequacy decisions, regional frameworks and sector-specific agreements on issues such as health data, financial messaging, and law-enforcement cooperation.

Here again, the compass image helps. Rather than searching for identical rules, nations might commit to shared minimums: independent oversight, effective remedies, clear purpose limitation for surveillance, and non-discrimination. Above that floor, local cultures and political systems will continue to diverge. The risk is that rhetoric about shared values masks deep substantive gaps. The opportunity is that some convergence—on children's rights, on biometric controls, on limits for social scoring—could give individuals meaningful guarantees even when their data moves abroad.

A fourth direction involves participation. Earlier privacy frameworks largely imagined citizens as data subjects—objects of regulation and notice. Policy now has to recognise them as stakeholders and, in some cases, co-governors. Cities consulting residents before deploying facial recognition in public spaces; unions negotiating algorithmic monitoring clauses in workplace agreements; patient groups shaping governance of medical data platforms: these examples signal a subtle shift. The legal questions move from "What may a controller do?" to "Who gets a say, and when?" Hyper-transparency without shared governance risks deepening cynicism. People will accept some watching if they help decide where the cameras point.

One credible limitation of participatory approaches is speed. Crises do not wait for consultation. Governments facing a fast-moving cyber attack or pandemic need immediate levers, not months of citizen assemblies. Reconciling this tension may require layered regimes: emergency powers with strict sunset clauses and post-hoc review, alongside more deliberative processes for enduring systems. This, too, is a design choice. It must be made in law, not improvised in panic.

All of these directions—principle-based regulation, empowered oversight, infrastructural redesign, international coordination, participation—share a common insight: hyper-transparency cannot simply be restrained piecemeal. It must be re-anchored. Policy that treats each scandal, each leak, each new AI model as an isolated problem will always arrive late. Policy that starts from a clear compass—respect for human dignity, meaningful control, non-exploitation, contestability—stands a better chance of coping with whatever arrives next.

Yet a stubborn question remains. Will societies commit to that compass when doing so constrains profitable surveillance, convenient shortcuts, or powerful security narratives? Or will hyper-transparency continue to expand in small, almost imperceptible increments, each justified as an exception, until secrecy becomes a privilege rather than a right? The legal choices of the coming decade will not fully determine the answer—but they will narrow, or widen, the paths we are able to take.

Chapter 9
Freedom vs Security

The first camera went up before dawn. Workers in reflective jackets fixed it to a lamppost overlooking a busy square, its lens angled to capture every face crossing the morning rush. By midday the local council explained that it was part of a pilot—an automated facial recognition trial to strengthen "community safety". A few residents shrugged, relieved at the idea of fewer muggings. Others hesitated, sensing that something more delicate had shifted. Not long ago, a camera watched for suspicious behaviour. Now it watched for suspicious people. The square looked unchanged, yet its moral temperature felt altered, as though every passer-by had quietly stepped into a different social contract.

Moments like this unfold across the world with remarkable consistency. A new threat emerges—terrorism, organised crime, a missing child—and the demand for tools to detect danger intensifies. In that heightened atmosphere, technologies that once seemed extreme become almost comforting. A nation that, on Monday, rejected universal biometric scanning may, by Friday, insist that it is the only responsible course. When fear swells, liberty narrows. Yet the certainty gained often proves fragile. If everyone becomes legible to the state, does the public truly become safer, or merely more exposed?

This chapter explores that shifting frontier where protection and intrusion meet, a frontier that has never been stable and perhaps never will be. Security once depended on guards, borders, and locks. Today it relies on data: fingerprints stored in vast databases, travel histories analysed before boarding a plane, social media posts sifted for early signals of radicalisation. Each mechanism promises vigilance without friction, and sometimes it delivers. But each also recasts citizens as potential risks to be pre-emptively assessed. Security acquires a double edge: its logic intends to shield, yet its methods can wound the very freedoms they claim to defend.

Historical memory sharpens this tension. More than a century ago, during the First World War, governments across Europe introduced sweeping censorship and surveillance measures to protect national stability. Prison sentences were imposed for private letters deemed subversive. Newspapers were filtered. Public assemblies shrank. Many of those powers were later repealed, but the precedent endured. Even in democratic societies, extraordinary measures introduced during crises rarely disappear without residue. The past reminds us that the language of danger is powerful enough to redraw moral boundaries faster than constitutions can restrain them.

What distinguishes the present moment is scale. Data-driven surveillance collapses the distance between "suspect" and "citizen". It no longer requires targeted warrants or resource-intensive monitoring. Instead, automated systems scan crowds by default, read behavioural patterns by default, monitor communications by default. Tension arises not merely from what the state may do, but from what it can do silently, continuously, and at negligible cost. When the threshold for intrusion falls, so does the barrier that protects personal autonomy. The camera fixed before dawn was just one device, but it symbolised an expanding category of technologies that turn public life into measurable, searchable evidence.

Sceptics of surveillance often emphasise the moral cost: liberty is diminished when people move through cities aware that they are being scored, indexed, or categorised. But there is also a psychological cost. Under sustained observation, behaviour becomes defensive, cautious, strategic. People avoid gatherings or protests that might draw algorithmic scrutiny. Ordinary acts—lingering near a restricted building, photographing a bridge, visiting a foreign news site—gain new connotations. Security may succeed in removing external threats only to create internal ones: anxiety, mistrust, a subtle withdrawal from civic participation.

Yet advocates of security are not reckless. They point to moments where surveillance has saved lives: identifying child traffickers, intervening in violent attacks, tracing fugitives who exploit anonymity. These are real successes, and any honest assessment must acknowledge them. The problem is not the existence of security measures but the calibration of them. The metaphorical scales do not stay balanced through goodwill alone. Societies must deliberately decide how much scrutiny they will tolerate, and under what conditions. Some will prioritise personal sovereignty; others will prioritise collective resilience. The answer is not universal, but the choice always involves a trade-off, even when governments present it as costless.

Public perception plays a decisive role in that trade-off. During moments of acute threat, consent to monitoring expands rapidly. After the 2015 Paris attacks, France declared a state of emergency that broadened police powers and authorised digital surveillance far beyond prior norms. The public accepted it as a necessary shield. Only years later did many citizens reflect on the long-term implications of those temporary measures. Crises distort moral reasoning; urgency narrows the field of vision. What feels essential under pressure may feel excessive in hindsight. This volatility places enormous responsibility on lawmakers to resist opportunistic overreach and on citizens to question what they are being asked to surrender.

That volatility also underscores a deeper truth: freedom and security do not exist in perfect opposition. They coexist uneasily, requiring continuous effort to keep one from overwhelming the other. Surveillance that is entirely unbounded corrodes democracy. Freedom that is entirely unguarded exposes people to catastrophic harm. The space between these extremes is where political imagination must work hardest. Oversight committees, judicial review, independent audits, transparency reports—these are not bureaucratic niceties but structural counterweights designed to prevent security from swallowing liberty whole.

Crucially, the debate cannot be left to officials alone. Surveillance technologies do not merely regulate public life; they shape the expectations of future generations. Children growing up in societies where cameras track their movements may accept monitoring as natural. Adults who adapt their speech online for fear of misinterpretation may internalise a quieter, more compliant civic identity. If freedom is slowly diluted, not through overt repression but through ambient oversight, would we recognise when it had thinned too far? Or would we adjust until the memory of richer freedom faded?

This chapter invites the reader to dwell in that uneasy space. Not to reject security, but to scrutinise the stories told in its name. Not to romanticise liberty, but to recognise the social conditions it requires: trust, accountability, and the possibility of dissent without fear. The camera installed at dawn captured more than faces; it revealed a question that societies will confront repeatedly in the coming decade. How much protection do we demand, and how much visibility are we willing to endure to receive it?

The lines between freedom and security are neither fixed nor symmetrical. They bend according to culture, crisis, and conviction. The pressing task is to determine who gets to bend them, and how far, before the balance breaks.

Defining Security in the Data Age

In May 2019, the Metropolitan Police deployed live facial recognition at Stratford, East London, positioning two cameras above the station entrance as commuters pressed through the morning crowd. Officers explained that the system would scan thousands of faces per hour, comparing them against a narrow watch list of suspects. By mid-afternoon, the trial produced one confirmed match and several false alerts. That single success carried political weight; the false alerts carried human cost. Commuters described a subtle change in atmosphere, a sense that walking through a public space now meant participating in an involuntary experiment. One woman stopped beneath the camera, looked up, and asked an officer a pointed question: *What exactly counts as security now?*

Her question lingers because it exposes a paradox. Security increasingly depends on data-rich scrutiny: cameras that capture gait and micro-expressions, immigration gates that analyse fingerprints within seconds, airport systems that rate risk using behavioural metrics. Yet every new mechanism that promises to protect the public also requires deeper access to the intimate details of their lives. The line between safeguarding and surveillance, once policed by clear constraints, has become porous. It is no longer obvious when a security measure effectively prevents harm, and when it merely shifts the burden of risk onto personal liberty.

The modern security apparatus is built on the premise that visibility protects. Biometric systems measure identity rather than trust; watch lists compare probabilities rather than intentions. Authorities often justify these tools by referring to outcomes—arrests prevented, threats intercepted—while critics point to the quiet expansion of state power. The struggle lies in determining which effects truly enhance public safety and which simply widen the state's field of vision. That tension returns us to the question raised in Stratford: how do we define security when its mechanisms transform the very nature of public life?

Consider automated facial recognition, now tested or deployed in dozens of cities worldwide. It offers a clear narrative: identify a known threat early, intervene quickly, and prevent violence. Show. In 2020, the New York Police

Department's use of the technology helped locate a suspected kidnapper within hours, a case documented in public court records. Name. The technical promise is straightforward: increased identification speed allows authorities to respond before harm escalates. Explain. Yet the implications reach further. When the same system misidentifies innocent individuals—a pattern noted in independent audits, including the U.S. National Institute of Standards and Technology assessment (NIST, 2019)—security loses moral legitimacy. Implication. Citizens cannot reasonably trust a system that may mistake them for someone else, particularly when the mistake is invisible until force is applied. Trust becomes measurable through avoidance: individuals walk different routes, avoid festivals, or lower their gaze as they pass through monitored areas.

A second example shows the widening scope of data-led security. In January 2022, Singapore's Immigration and Checkpoints Authority expanded biometric processing at Changi Airport, replacing boarding passes with fingerprint, iris, and facial scans. Name, place, date. The system reduced queue times dramatically—visible progress measured in minutes saved per traveller—and was heralded as a model of efficiency. Show. However, the same dataset can support retrospective tracking of a traveller's movement, enabling law enforcement to map behaviour long after the journey. Explain. That dual use highlights a structural dilemma: data collected for convenience may reinforce the architecture of surveillance. Implication. The passenger who moves swiftly through the terminal may later be reconstructed as a pattern, a trace, an entity whose movements can be queried without their knowledge.

There are credible counter-examples. Some nations deliberately restrict the use of biometric systems in public spaces. In 2021, the European Parliament endorsed a moratorium on real-time facial recognition in the EU's public areas. Name and date. Legislators argued that indiscriminate scans violated fundamental rights, and several member states supported the principal claim: mass surveillance does not align with democratic norms. This stands as a reminder that surveillance is not an inevitable direction but a political choice shaped by legal and cultural commitments. Yet even here, the limitation is partial. Europe continues to use biometric databases for border control, visas, and law enforcement operations; the restriction applies mainly to real-time public-space scanning. Reconciling the commitment to rights with the appetite for efficient policing illustrates the difficulty of defining security consistently. The EU seeks restraint in the street while expanding precision at the border. The boundary shifts depending on the perceived locus of risk.

Across these examples runs a recurring motif: the gaze. Not a human gaze, with its fallibility and context, but an automated one—continuous, unblinking, and profoundly scalable. The gaze measures and categorises with the assumption that more information equals better protection. But more information also means more exposure. The gaze rarely blinks.

The shift towards data-driven security transforms everyday behaviour. Risk is no longer assessed through visible suspicion; it is inferred from metadata, travel records, financial transactions, social media connections. Some police departments now review public social profiles during background checks for firearm licences or employment screening. Show. The name comes next: in 2020, the Boston Police Department acknowledged using software to monitor social media posts for "threat indicators". Explain. While intended to detect early signs of violence, the system led to disproportionate monitoring of minority communities, as revealed by the ACLU of Massachusetts. Implication. Data-driven policing amplifies existing social biases unless carefully designed and rigorously overseen.

The same mechanism unfolds in private-sector security. Employers increasingly survey digital footprints to measure "character" or "cultural fit." Insurance companies explore telematics data to determine premiums. Universities review applicant behaviour online. Each practice reshapes the definition of safety within its domain. Safety becomes a function of predictability: the individual whose data reveals no anomalies is considered low risk; the one with ambiguous metrics becomes suspect. The consequence is a flattening of human complexity. Individuals become profiles; profiles become decisions; decisions become gates that open or close without explanation.

The core ethical challenge is that security relies on anticipation. It seeks to prevent harm before it occurs, which means collecting more data, scanning more behaviour, forecasting more futures. But anticipation is also where liberty narrows. When your movements are interpreted as signals, your silence as intention, your associations as probabilities, you are no longer simply a person—you are a calculated risk. The boundary between you and your data blurs, and the state's view of you becomes a metric that may be difficult to correct.

Some commentators argue that data-led security promotes fairness: algorithms, they suggest, judge without prejudice. But empirical evidence complicates this claim. Studies by NIST (2019) and academic reviews such as Buolamwini and Gebru (2018) show that accuracy rates vary significantly across demographic groups. Show and name. The implication is clear: a system designed to enhance safety may inadvertently deepen inequality. If certain groups are more likely to be misidentified or flagged, they bear a disproportionate burden of scrutiny. Bias becomes measurable through error rates. These are not abstract injustices but concrete harms recorded in official complaints, court filings, and public inquiries.

One might counter that security requires decisive action. That waiting for perfect systems risks lives. There is truth here: states do bear responsibility for protecting citizens from credible threats. But urgency must not erase nuance. The question is not whether security matters—of course it does—but whether the methods used to achieve it preserve the freedoms they claim to safeguard. A society that commits to total visibility in the name of protection risks constructing a brittle form of security: one that insulates against immediate threats while eroding the civic trust on which long-term stability depends.

The gaze appears again. It expands in airports, train stations, football stadiums, shopping centres. It moves into schools, where attendance may be tracked by cameras; into hospitals, where patient movements are logged to prevent loss or harm; into workplaces, where performance metrics blur with surveillance tools. Every extension asks the same implicit question: does security require watching more, or watching better?

As this subchapter closes, we return to the commuter who paused in Stratford. She was not opposed to safety. Her protest was quieter, more personal. She resisted the idea that security is something done *to* people rather than something built *with* them. That distinction matters. It invites a final, unresolved question: if data-led security continues to expand, who decides the limits of visibility, and what happens when those limits blur beyond recognition?

The Scales of Freedom

On 31 October 2001, less than seven weeks after the attacks on New York and Washington, the United States Congress passed the PATRIOT Act in a single day of votes. At the Capitol, staff worked through stacks of draft pages still warm from the printer, while surveillance provisions—many previously rejected—were reinstated with overwhelming bipartisan support. The mood was unmistakable: fear quickened legislative consent. By nightfall, federal agencies had gained expanded powers to conduct searches, monitor communications, and access personal records with reduced oversight. The political outcome was clear. The human outcome was quieter, measured in the gradual normalisation of practices once considered exceptional. A single day reset the scale on which freedom and security were weighed.

Such moments test democracies because they reveal how quickly rights can contract when safety feels fragile. The temptation is understandable. When danger strikes without warning, surveillance promises foresight. Monitoring appears rational; restraint feels reckless. Yet as the Capitol's hurried drafting showed, the language of safety can slide seamlessly into the architecture of control. The scale tilts before anyone notices the weight shifting.

History provides no shortage of precedents. In 1793, during the French Revolution's Reign of Terror, the Committee of Public Safety authorised widespread surveillance of "suspicious persons", a category so elastic it stretched to include neighbours who failed to display sufficient enthusiasm. The logic was identical: uncertainty magnified suspicion, and suspicion justified scrutiny. The pattern is instructive for a data-saturated century. Fear compresses judgment. It shortens the distance between liberty and intrusion.

The motif recurs: a weight placed on the scale—sometimes gently, sometimes with force—until the balance tips.

In assessing this pattern, it helps to follow the structure of evidence. Show first. In June 2013, documents leaked by Edward Snowden revealed the extent of digital surveillance conducted by the U.S. National Security Agency and its partners. The disclosures named specific programmes—PRISM, XKeyscore, Tempora—and documented collection at a scale few had imagined. Name. The explanation that followed from governments was consistent: such systems were necessary to detect terrorism, disrupt networks, and protect citizens. Explain. Yet the implications were stark. Entire populations found themselves monitored as potential risks, not specific suspects. Millions of people unknowingly became part of a security dragnet. Implication. The promise of safety had reweighted the scale.

Europe offers its own examples, revealing how democratic states wrestle with similar pressures. In the United Kingdom, the 2016 Investigatory Powers Act expanded the ability of authorities to retain internet connection records for up to twelve months. Name and date. The measure was defended as essential to national security, but civil liberties groups argued that mass retention violated proportionality. Show. The act triggered multiple legal challenges, including rulings by the Court of Justice of the European Union, which held certain elements incompatible with fundamental rights. Explain. The implication is that even mature democracies struggle to reconcile surveillance ambitions with constitutional commitments. Freedom resists confinement, yet security continually attempts to encircle it.

A credible counter-example appears in post-apartheid South Africa. After 1994, lawmakers intentionally limited state surveillance powers, influenced by the memory of intrusive monitoring under the previous regime. Name. The landmark Regulation of Interception of Communications and Provision of Communication-Related Information Act (2002) required judicial authorisation for most forms of interception. Show. Yet limits remain: critics argue that metadata collection persists with insufficient transparency, and oversight bodies lack resources. Limitation. The reconciliation is straightforward: principled restraint must be matched with robust enforcement. Without both, even well-designed safeguards erode.

The question persists. How do societies measure the right amount of freedom to surrender in pursuit of safety?

To understand what is at stake, consider visible behaviour. Residents begin to change how they move through space when surveillance intensifies. Footfall data from London's King's Cross, collected during controversial facial recognition trials in 2016–18, showed subtle shifts in walking patterns. Some pedestrians slowed to avoid cameras; others diverted through side streets. Behaviour adjusted in anticipation of unseen evaluation—a metric that recorded the psychological cost of monitoring before any formal rights were touched. The scale tipped again.

This behavioural lens helps to expose the mechanics of compromise. When a surveillance measure enters public space—be it a CCTV network, drone patrol, or automated licence plate reader—it defines risk through visibility. People become legible. Legibility, in turn, becomes vulnerability. Germany's history demonstrates how this can change public culture. During the Stasi era in East Berlin, estimated at its height in 1989, one informant existed for every sixty-three citizens (figures from the Stasi Records Agency). Name. The sheer density of monitoring reshaped social norms; silence became a defensive habit. After reunification, Germany adopted some of the world's strictest data protection rules precisely because memory had recalibrated the national scale. Freedom required intentional protection.

The motif of weight returns. Each historical episode shows how surveillance accumulates like sediment. Small additions add up until the freedom side of the scale lifts almost imperceptibly.

Contemporary debates repeat older patterns but with faster tools. Predictive policing systems recommend patrol routes based on algorithmic risk scores. Airline passengers pass through biometric corridors that track their movements from entrance to departure gate. Schools adopt behaviour-monitoring software to detect early signs of harm. All justified by security. All expanding the state's interpretive reach. Show, name, explain. The implication is cumulative: risk is no longer defined by action but by *probability*. And when probability governs suspicion, freedom becomes fragile.

Consider a second named example. In October 2020, during the COVID-19 pandemic, South Korea's government used credit card logs, CCTV footage, and mobile location data to trace infection vectors. The measure proved effective at suppressing outbreaks. Outcome: transmission clusters were quickly isolated. Yet the same system exposed intensely personal details: movements, social habits, even private relationships. Public debate ignited when contact-tracing reports inadvertently revealed the location of certain nightclubs, leading to social stigma. Here lies the duality. Surveillance prevented harm; it also risked collateral intrusion. The scale could not hold both values without strain.

Such cases illustrate the hinge of the argument: safety is essential, but not absolute. The measure of a society is not how quickly it reacts to danger but how carefully it preserves liberty while reacting. Democracies falter when they assume that rights surrendered can always be restored later. History suggests otherwise. Powers once granted expand; oversight once weakened rarely strengthens without crisis.

The public's shifting tolerance complicates the picture. When threats feel distant, people defend rights vigorously. When threats feel close, they accept intrusions without hesitation. After the 2005 London bombings, polling by Ipsos MORI recorded a sharp increase in support for expanded CCTV coverage and data retention. Name. Yet within two years, the same surveys revealed rising discomfort with the permanence of those measures. Emotion moved the scale as much as law.

This fluidity matters because it demonstrates that freedom is not a fixed asset. It is a negotiation, affected by fear, memory, and trust. Trust especially. When citizens believe that security measures serve their protection rather than their control, they are more willing to consent. When trust falters, even benign systems become suspect. Trust is measured in oversight committees, judicial checks, and the credibility of public communication. Without these, freedom steadily erodes.

A recurring question threads through these examples like a counter-melody: *How far is too far?* It is quiet but persistent, surfacing whenever surveillance grows faster than the explanations that justify it. The question returns whenever the state collects more than citizens expect, or retains data longer than originally promised, or applies tools more broadly than stated in policy documents. The weight shifts; the scale trembles.

The paradox is that freedom and security are not opposites. They depend on each other. A society that protects rights builds trust, which stabilises public life. A society that maintains security enables rights to be exercised without fear. But the balance is delicate. Tilt too far toward security and freedom becomes ceremonial. Tilt too far toward unbounded freedom and security becomes brittle.

Historical precedents leave us with a final tension. If fear drives the expansion of surveillance, what restores equilibrium? Is it judicial intervention, public protest, legislative reform, or collective fatigue? Each answer carries consequences. Each implies a different kind of oversight. Each depends on a population that recognises when the scale has shifted too heavily.

And so the unresolved question stands, pressing with increasing urgency: when the next crisis arrives—and history assures us it will—how will we measure the weight placed on freedom, and who will notice if the balance tips beyond return?

Public Acceptability

In March 2020, Singapore's Ministry of Health stood before cameras and introduced TraceTogether, a smartphone app that would log proximity encounters using Bluetooth. The promise was specific: faster contact tracing, fewer lockdowns, more targeted quarantines. Within weeks, millions of residents had downloaded it, and queues formed later that year to collect the physical tokens. The same city that prided itself on order now embraced a system that made everyday proximity legible to the state. At press conferences, officials spoke of solidarity and civic duty. The prevailing emotion in many households was simpler: fear of infection. Fear changes what people accept.

This shift was not uniquely Singaporean. Across continents, COVID-19 contact-tracing apps, emergency location tracking, and expanded data-sharing enjoyed a degree of public support that would have been almost unthinkable months earlier. The central paradox is stark. The very populations that, under normal conditions, resist intrusions into their private lives can, under strain, demand tools that scrutinise them more closely. Public acceptability is not a stable line on a graph. It behaves more like a tide, rising and receding with each perceived threat.

To understand this volatility, we need to look carefully at how opinion moves, who shapes it, and how quickly temporary concessions become durable norms. Public acceptability is not decided in abstract charters; it is forged in headlines, briefings, family conversations, and the quiet calculations people make about risk when the environment feels hostile. It has a temperature. It can be raised.

Historically, crises have been potent accelerants. Show. After the 7 July 2005 bombings in London, support for additional CCTV cameras and expanded powers for the security services surged in the United Kingdom. Name. The explanation was clear at the time: people wanted reassurance that the state could spot danger earlier, intervene faster, and prevent repeats. Explain. The implication, noticed only later, was that surveillance infrastructure installed as an emergency precaution soon blended into the urban landscape. Cameras that might once have symbolised a trade-off became just part of the city's furniture, their presence rarely questioned in everyday life.

The same pattern appeared, decades earlier, with the United States' PATRIOT Act in 2001. Polling at the time suggested broad public backing for expanded surveillance and data-sharing between agencies. The justification felt almost self-evident in the aftermath of 9/11; any measure that might avert another attack was framed as necessary. Yet as the immediate shock faded, criticism grew. Civil liberties organisations, journalists and some lawmakers began to ask whether powers rushed through under emotional pressure would ever be scaled back. Public acceptability, once high, started to crack in the face of concrete stories about misuse, secrecy and mission creep.

These episodes reveal an important dynamic: people often accept surveillance when its benefits are vivid and its harms seem abstract. A bombed train, a crowded hospital ward, a highly publicised kidnapping—these are specific, visceral events. By comparison, the loss of privacy feels diffuse, deferred and uncertain. It appears as a risk, not a reality. The trade-off therefore leans towards immediate safety. Only later, when examples of overreach surface—journalists targeted, protesters tracked, minority communities disproportionately scrutinised—does the balance of feeling begin to shift.

A second dynamic concerns *who* is perceived to be watched. When surveillance is framed as something that targets "others"—foreign terrorists, hardened criminals, undocumented migrants—public resistance tends to soften. The majority do not expect to be affected. They see themselves on the safe side of the lens. This is not simple selfishness; it reflects a cognitive pattern. People discount risks that feel remote from their own lives. Yet as digital systems become more pervasive, the boundary between target and bystander dissolves. Location data swept up for one purpose is later re-analysed for another. Social media monitoring intended for extremist content drifts into assessing protest movements. Over time, more people discover that they have been standing under the gaze all along.

Public acceptability therefore rests heavily on perceived control. When citizens feel they can understand, question and influence the scope of surveillance, they are more inclined to tolerate certain measures. Behaviour demonstrates this. Cities that hold public consultations before deploying facial recognition often encounter resistance but also gain legitimacy for modified, constrained deployments. By contrast, when technologies appear suddenly, without transparent debate, the reaction is sharper. People feel tricked. Trust cools. The temperature drops.

South Korea's experience with COVID-19 contact tracing illustrates both sides of this equation. Aggressive use of credit card logs, CCTV footage and phone location data was widely credited with helping to contain outbreaks. Many residents praised the responsiveness of the Korea Disease Control and Prevention Agency. Yet when detailed movement histories were published in ways that allowed identities to be inferred—especially during outbreaks linked to sensitive venues—public concern rose. Individuals were outed, livelihoods damaged. A system widely accepted in its early phase began to encounter criticism over the handling of stigma and the breadth of disclosure. The same data practices that had felt protective now looked, for some, like exposure.

A credible counter-example comes from Germany's handling of its national contact-tracing app launched in 2020. Authorities opted for a decentralised design that stored most data on devices rather than central servers, and they consulted publicly with privacy experts before rollout. Adoption was imperfect; not everyone downloaded or used the app consistently. There were technical limitations and periods of lukewarm engagement. Yet the app never triggered the same level of privacy backlash as some centralised models elsewhere. The lesson is not that decentralisation solves all problems, but that visible privacy safeguards can stabilise public acceptability even under pressure. Trust is not guaranteed; it is built through design choices and communication.

Throughout these cases, a motif appears: the dial. Governments, companies and citizens constantly adjust a dial that controls how much transparency they are prepared to live with. During crises, the dial often turns towards more visibility. Once the immediate danger recedes, some settings snap back; others stay quietly elevated. The difficulty is that the dial is rarely in a single pair of hands. Politicians, security agencies, platform providers, local authorities and international bodies each maintain their own controls. Public opinion becomes the aggregate of many small nudges rather than the result of a single, clear decision.

This fragmentation is visible in debates over social media monitoring. When police in various countries began to use software to scan public posts for signals of unrest or gang activity, many citizens initially shrugged. After all, the content was "public". Over time, however, stories emerged of environmental activists, student organisers, and minority communities being monitored, catalogued and placed on watch lists. The behavioural response was subtle but significant. Some users closed their accounts, others set stricter privacy settings, still others shifted politically sensitive conversations to encrypted messaging apps. Acceptance had not disappeared, but it had become more conditional. The dial turned slightly back.

The role of media framing cannot be overstated. When newspapers and broadcasters present surveillance technologies primarily as crime-fighting tools or health safeguards, the emotional emphasis lies on protection. When investigative reporting exposes misuse or disproportionate impact, the narrative shifts towards rights and abuses. Public acceptability oscillates with these stories. A facial recognition system that appears in the news associated with catching a violent offender draws one reaction; the same system, linked to wrongful arrests of innocent citizens, draws another. People update their stance based on narratives as much as on technical detail.

This malleability raises a pressing question about the quality of public debate. If acceptance can be moved by fear-driven headlines as easily as by sober evidence, democratic oversight is at risk. Informed compromise requires time, context, and the presence of dissenting voices. Yet crises compress time, strip away nuance, and reward confident, decisive rhetoric. The actors who argue for caution are easily cast as naïve, or worse, indifferent to harm. Under such conditions, the dial tends to turn towards greater transparency because that direction feels more concrete: you can point to new cameras, new apps, new databases and say, "We are doing something."

One might ask whether there are contexts where public acceptability of surveillance has genuinely decreased over the long term. The fallout from the Snowden revelations suggests that this can happen. In several countries, legal challenges, corporate promises of stronger encryption, and civic advocacy did manage to push governments and firms towards more constrained practices. Yet even in this case, the picture is mixed. Some programmes were curtailed or rebranded; others shifted deeper into classified terrain. Public attention moved on. The dial did not return neatly to its previous setting.

The complexity deepens when we consider uneven acceptability within a single society. Marginalised communities often experience surveillance not as a temporary response to crisis but as a constant feature of daily life. Stop-and-search practices, predictive policing tools, and immigration enforcement regimes create a baseline of observation that shapes attitudes towards new measures. What appears to the majority as a modest sacrifice of privacy may be experienced by minorities as an additional weight on an already heavy scale. Public acceptability is rarely uniform; it is stratified by race, class, geography and history.

This fragmentation places a special burden on institutions charged with gauging opinion—parliaments, regulators, ethics councils—to avoid mistaking loud majorities for consensus. Holding town-hall meetings in affluent districts while collecting cursory online responses from poorer ones produces a false picture of comfort. Designing systems based on that picture can deepen distrust. Behaviour becomes a diagnostic: protests, legal challenges, non-compliance, and quiet workarounds indicate that acceptability has been overestimated.

The dial motif returns one final time. A society that aspires to manage hyper-transparency responsibly must decide how that dial is set, who has permission to adjust it, and what kind of evidence is required before it moves. Quick polls taken in the aftermath of shocking events are poor instruments for this. Deliberative forums, transparent impact assessments, and independent research provide richer guidance, but they demand patience and political will.

The unresolved question is simple to ask and hard to answer: when the next crisis presses governments to collect more data, will public acceptability be shaped mainly by fear and speed, or by informed, contested, and genuinely representative debate—and how would we recognise the difference while we are still in the middle of deciding?

Constructive Boundaries

On 5 February 2020, in a courtroom in The Hague, the District Court of the Netherlands struck down the government's SyRI system, a data-matching tool built to detect welfare fraud. The room was almost silent when the judgment was read. A machine that combined housing records, benefit histories and neighbourhood classifications had promised efficiency. Instead, judges ruled that its opacity and scale violated the right to privacy under the European Convention on Human Rights. The decision was more than a legal defeat; it was a public declaration that even in a digital age saturated with risk, safeguards must bite. A line had been drawn. Others watched closely to see where the next line might fall.

This moment offers an early truth about constructive boundaries. They emerge not from grand philosophical arguments alone but from real conflicts between institutional ambition and civic restraint. Show the behaviour, name the actor, explain the tension, trace the implication. The Dutch ruling did all four. It made visible the machinery of data profiling, identified the state agency driving it, clarified how asymmetry of power can hollow out fairness, and signalled to other countries that structural oversight is neither ornamental nor optional. The ruling serves as a quiet motif running through this discussion: a reminder that boundaries are built not once but repeatedly, each time a system threatens to overreach.

Constructive boundaries begin with the basic proposition that public safety and personal secrecy need not be adversaries. They can co-exist through mechanisms that measure, constrain and scrutinise government and corporate access to data. Independent oversight committees, judicial authorisation, algorithmic audits and codes of practice all serve the same essential function: to temper the surveillance instinct with accountability. When these mechanisms work, they cool the temperature of public fear and institutional appetite at the same time. When they fail, the dial turns unchecked.

Consider the example of the United Kingdom's Investigatory Powers Commissioner's Office (IPCO), established in 2017. IPCO reviews the deployment of interception warrants, bulk powers and intrusive techniques across the intelligence community. Its inspectors visit agencies, examine logs, interview officers and publish annual reports detailing compliance. The measures are concrete. They involve site visits, document sampling and retrospective case analysis. IPCO's existence reflects a cultural judgment: that the state's extraordinary powers require extraordinary scrutiny. The implication is direct. Without persistent, external review, the risk of drift towards excessive surveillance increases, and public trust erodes.

A second example comes from France. The Commission nationale de l'informatique et des libertés (CNIL), created in 1978, remains one of Europe's most assertive data-protection bodies. It conducts audits of public-sector databases, issues sanctions against unlawful data practices and publishes guidance on emerging technologies. A CNIL inspection is not symbolic; it involves examining system logs, interviewing data controllers and requiring corrective action within specified timeframes. This is behaviour, not abstraction. And the cultural value it enshrines is unmistakable: vigilance is a civic duty, not a technical formality. The implication radiates outward. When a regulator acts with teeth, institutions adjust their internal culture accordingly. Boundaries become part of organisational reflex rather than external imposition.

There are limitations, and they are serious. A credible counter-example is the struggle faced by several countries to establish meaningful oversight of facial recognition deployments. Even where committees exist, their mandates may be narrow, their access restricted or their findings non-binding. In 2019, before the UK's Court of Appeal intervened, South Wales Police deployed live facial recognition at large events and shopping centres using broad watchlists and limited transparency. The policing bodies overseeing the trial lacked the capacity and clarity to subject the technology to rigorous scrutiny. Yet this limitation does not invalidate the broader claim; instead, it demonstrates that boundaries without authority function as decoration. The reconciliation lies in reform: strengthening mandates, widening access to materials, and insisting on public reporting that compels institutions to justify their choices.

Constructive boundaries also rely on visible rules for data minimisation, retention and proportionality. These are not ethereal principles; they can be measured. A system that logs location data for seven years signals a different institutional temperament from one that deletes logs after 30 days. A programme that limits analyst access to tightly defined roles demonstrates a form of restraint absent in systems where any authorised user can browse widely. These details reveal cultural values more reliably than rhetoric ever could. They show whether a society prizes controlled transparency or convenient omniscience.

There are further examples that strengthen this point. In Canada, the collapse of Toronto's proposed Sidewalk Labs smart-city project in 2020 highlighted the power of public scrutiny and independent review. Civil society groups, privacy experts and municipal officials questioned the scale of data collection planned for the waterfront development. The debate centred on concrete matters: who would control the datasets, how they would be anonymised, which actors could access them, and what governance model would prevent function creep. When Sidewalk Labs withdrew, it did so in a political environment shaped by constructive boundaries—boundaries articulated through public hearings, expert analysis and institutional pushback. The implication is plain. Healthy societies do not rely on trust alone; they embed friction into systems that could otherwise expand unchecked.

Threaded through all these cases is the motif of the line. A line judged, a line reviewed, a line defended. Sometimes the line is drawn by courts; sometimes by legislatures, regulators or civic campaigns. The form changes, but the function remains steady: to halt drift, to question assumptions, to ensure that the machinery designed to protect does not quietly switch into a machinery designed to control.

Yet constructive boundaries must account for a different reality too. Surveillance tools evolve faster than institutional norms. Machine-learning systems that infer emotion from facial expressions, predictive-policing algorithms that flag "high-risk" individuals and mass-data pipelines that combine health, financial and mobility information were not anticipated when many oversight regimes were written. This mismatch between technological tempo and legislative caution creates gaps. In those gaps, systems can operate with minimal scrutiny until scandal forces review. The implication is uncomfortable but unavoidable. Vigilance must be continuous because the ground under it shifts.

Two named examples illustrate this gap. First, in the United States, the Privacy and Civil Liberties Oversight Board (PCLOB), created in 2007, has produced detailed reports on surveillance programmes such as Section 702, examining their legal basis and recommending reforms. Yet PCLOB's authority depends on access to classified material, which is sometimes delayed or restricted. Its work shows the importance of independent audits but also reveals how fragile such arrangements can be. Second, in the UK, the deployment of the Gangs Matrix by the Metropolitan Police raised concerns in 2018 when the Information Commissioner's Office found serious data-protection breaches. The ICO demanded reforms, including purging outdated entries and introducing clearer criteria for inclusion. These actions show boundary-setting in practice. They also show how easily systems can metastasise without periodic, evidence-based challenge.

Constructive boundaries therefore require more than technical controls. They require civic education, political will and institutional humility. A society that understands how surveillance works—and why oversight matters—is better positioned to hold power accountable. This understanding is expressed through behaviour: public consultations that attract genuine participation, parliamentary committees that interrogate evidence rather than rubber-stamp proposals, journalists who request documents and publish findings, and citizens who treat privacy not as a niche concern but as a shared resource. These actions assign weight to privacy in the scales of democratic life.

But constructive boundaries cannot be static. They must evolve as threats and tools evolve. Oversight committees need training in technical methods; auditors must understand machine-learning models; judges must grapple with probabilistic risk scores. Regulation that cannot adapt becomes hollow. The implication is stark: societies must commit to building institutions capable of learning. Without that commitment, the gap between the ambition of surveillance systems and the competence of oversight widens dangerously.

One question lingers beneath all these discussions: who decides when a boundary has been crossed? States, companies and citizens rarely agree. A government may argue that a new data-fusion platform enhances national resilience. A corporation may claim that behavioural analytics improve safety or efficiency. Civil society may warn that both claims conceal latent risks. Constructive boundaries require a forum where these competing interpretations collide. They also require the courage to refuse easy answers. The presence of an oversight committee is meaningless if its recommendations can be ignored. The presence of an audit is insufficient if its results remain confidential. Boundaries must be enforceable, not merely aspirational.

The line motif returns one final time. A society that manages to keep that line brightly lit—visible, contested, regularly redrawn—protects both its freedoms and its safety. But the line dims when vigilance fades. Laws grow out of date. Committees fall silent. Investigations stall. The balance of security and privacy depends on how sharply that line is etched into institutional memory and public expectation.

The unresolved tension is this. When the next data system promises to predict threats with greater accuracy, or to streamline policing, or to detect contagion sooner, who will have the authority—and the patience—to measure its claims, examine its logs, question its reach and decide whether the line must shift?

Chapter 10
Resistance and Adaptation

On a grey afternoon in October 2019, a crowd gathered outside London's King's Cross station, not to board trains but to demand answers. It had just emerged that private developers in the surrounding area, working with local authorities, had installed facial-recognition cameras without public notice. Commuters who had assumed they were simply passing through a transport hub learned instead that their faces had been scanned, compared, assessed. The protest was modest in size but fierce in tone. Cardboard signs competed with phone screens, and chants rose against the wind. What mattered was not the number of people in the square but the sentiment animating them: a quiet refusal to accept that transparency must always flow in one direction. This was resistance in a minor key—ordinary individuals asserting that visibility should never be compulsory.

Moments like this recur around the world. They flare up in city centres, on university campuses, in online forums where digital petitions gather thousands of signatures in a day. They remind us that the story of surveillance is never only about technology; it is also about civic appetite, public patience and the instinct to push back. People resist for different reasons. Some do so out of principle, others because a particular intrusion unsettles them, and others still because they sense that a subtle shift in power has occurred. What unites these disparate impulses is a belief that privacy is not a relic but a right—one that must be refreshed, defended and, when weakened, rebuilt.

Yet resistance alone cannot chart a hopeful path. Adaptation must accompany it, not as a capitulation but as a creative strategy. For every protestor holding a banner, there is someone arranging a workshop on secure messaging or teaching neighbours how to use an anonymising browser. For every legal campaign challenging an intrusive system, there is an engineer designing a tool that shrinks the footprint of personal data. These countercurrents complicate the dominant narrative of inevitable transparency. They suggest that even in a world saturated with capture—of images, movements, preferences—there remains space for agency. People can build their own forms of shelter.

Grassroots activism shows how quickly that agency can spread. It rarely begins with grand organisations or wealthy sponsors but with small groups responding to a specific threat. A leaked contract, a sudden rollout of public-space biometrics, an opaque change to a platform's terms of service—these triggers mobilise those who would otherwise remain bystanders. The tools they use are varied: coordinated social-media campaigns, encryption meet-ups in borrowed community halls, collaborative mapping of surveillance infrastructure, public-comment submissions that force regulators to take notice. These are not the dramatic episodes that dominate political histories; they are the modest interventions that prevent overreach before it calcifies.

But resistance is not solely defensive. Many of the most meaningful forms of adaptation arise from technical innovation. Privacy engineers, researchers and open-source communities have developed tools that change the texture of everyday digital life. Browsers that strip metadata, networks that avoid centralised data collection, messaging platforms that leave no archive—each offers a glimpse of a future where secrecy and connection need not be opposites. Technology has often been accused of eroding privacy; the counter-movement demonstrates that it can also restore it. These tools do more than hide; they recalibrate the relationship between individuals and systems, narrowing the amount of information one must surrender simply to participate.

The rise of civic movements strengthens this recalibration. Organisations dedicated to data rights transform scattered concerns into coherent political agendas. Some of these groups work at the local level, monitoring municipal deployments of surveillance technology or educating residents about their digital rights. Others operate across borders, linking policy debates in Brussels to activism in Nairobi or São Paulo. Their presence highlights a critical truth: privacy is not a matter merely of personal preference but of public architecture. When advocacy groups challenge unlawful data retention or expose harmful algorithmic practices, they reshape the environment in which everyone lives, not just the digitally attentive.

Throughout all these developments, a recurring motif emerges: that resistance and adaptation are two halves of the same civic instinct. One protests against pressures that narrow autonomy; the other builds structures that widen it. To resist is to say no. To adapt is to imagine yes. Both are necessary to prevent a world in which hyper-transparency hardens into resignation. The tension between these modes keeps society flexible, responsive and, crucially, disputatious. That friction is not a failing—it is a sign of democratic health.

As we look ahead, the chapter asks the reader to consider their own place in this unfolding landscape. Surveillance will not retreat by itself. Nor will privacy reconstitute itself automatically in the face of new technologies. The shape of the digital world is being influenced daily by those who choose to act: citizens who write to their representatives, technologists who commit code that reduces data exposure, parents who question the surveillance built into educational platforms, community groups who challenge the normalisation of biometric access systems. None of these actions alone redraws the map. Together, they shift its contours.

The introduction closes by turning that quiet, persistent motif back towards the reader. Resistance and adaptation are not distant phenomena but living practices. They belong not only to campaigners or coders but to anyone who recognises that privacy is the scaffolding of autonomy. To participate—to speak, question, assemble, design—is to ensure that the future is not merely something endured but something shaped.

Grassroots Activism

On a warm June evening in 2013, hundreds gathered outside Berlin's Brandenburg Gate carrying homemade placards and paper masks bearing the face of Edward Snowden. The protests followed revelations published that month about the scale of US and allied intelligence surveillance. Crowds spilled across Pariser Platz, chanting into the twilight as bicycles clattered past and tourists looked on, unsure whether they had stumbled into a cultural festival or a constitutional reckoning. The gathering achieved no immediate legal reform, yet it marked something subtler: people who rarely considered surveillance suddenly felt implicated. Ordinary citizens, not seasoned campaigners, occupied a public square to insist that privacy deserved a defence.

This moment continues to echo because its core insight endures: meaningful resistance often begins far from formal institutions. It grows in streets, cafés, encrypted chat groups and neighbourhood halls. It thrives when individuals discover that the erosion of privacy is not simply a policy issue but a democratic concern. One quiet motif runs through these movements—the notion of a shared threshold. A small intrusion that one person might ignore becomes intolerable when a community recognises its cumulative effect. This threshold animates protests, petitions and workshops that teach people how to protect what bureaucracies and corporations steadily expose.

Grassroots activism starts with visibility. When London's Metropolitan Police tested live facial-recognition vans in Shoreditch in February 2020, observers documented police conduct, recorded the cameras' placement and mapped the radius of scanning. The outcome was modest: heightened scrutiny, media coverage, and a subsequent review. Yet this example shows how a single act—recording a surveillance deployment—can expose the distance between official assurances and lived experience. It demonstrates that the first task of resistance is often to witness. Without concrete evidence, public concern remains abstract; with documentation, it becomes political.

The pattern is not unique to Europe. After the 2014 Umbrella Movement in Hong Kong, activists trained volunteers to use secure messaging, manage metadata and avoid device tracking. These workshops were hardly glamorous. They took place in cramped community centres and borrowed university rooms, with whiteboards scrawled with threat models and layers of encryption. But they illustrate how knowledge functions as infrastructure. Teaching someone to switch to an end-to-end encrypted app or disable a default location tracker is a mundane act, yet it alters the balance of informational power. It shifts the threshold slightly back in favour of the citizen.

A contrasting example is Estonia's well-known e-governance model, launched nationally in 2001. Its digital identity system is widely praised for convenience and security, and residents have strong trust in its infrastructure. This appears at first to run counter to arguments for activism: if a system is well-designed and enjoys popular confidence, why resist? The limitation becomes apparent when considering export attempts. When similar identity frameworks were proposed in countries without Estonia's culture of transparency and distributed oversight, grassroots scepticism intensified. The counter-example clarifies a central point: activism adjusts to context. It is not opposition for its own sake. It is a demand that surveillance or data collection be grounded in accountability and cultural legitimacy rather than borrowed models.

Tools have become the backbone of this citizen-led ecosystem. Digital petitions, hosted on platforms such as Change.org or parliamentary websites, offer measurable markers of sentiment. A petition with 100,000 signatures triggers a debate in the UK House of Commons; the number itself becomes a political gesture. Encryption workshops provide another tangible practice. They translate concerns about surveillance into specific behaviours: installing Tor, securing Wi-Fi, adopting password managers, or learning the difference between metadata and content. These actions are visible, replicable, and empowering. They keep the motif of the shared threshold alive by marking the point at which people refuse passive acceptance.

Yet activism is not without friction. Movements sometimes fracture over priorities or strategies. The 2017 debate in France over mandatory device backdoors exemplified this. Privacy advocates argued that weakening encryption endangered journalists and dissidents; security proponents insisted that the tools hindered counter-terrorism efforts. Public opinion split. Many sympathised with the need for safety, even while distrusting state overreach. This tension highlights a limitation: activism can illuminate trade-offs but cannot resolve all of them. Its power lies in forcing questions into the open, not in guaranteeing consensus.

To reconcile the limitation, activists often pair critique with construction. They help design alternatives rather than merely opposing proposals. In 2021, when several US cities debated bans on facial recognition, local coalitions did more than protest; they drafted model ordinances informed by expert input. These texts defined narrow exceptions, required independent audits, and set retention limits. The implication is profound: activism can mature into governance. It can produce frameworks that bridge aspirations for safety with protection of civil liberties.

The shared threshold motif reappears when crises strike. Fear reshapes the boundary between acceptable surveillance and perceived overreach. After the March 2016 Brussels attacks,

Belgian public support for expanded monitoring surged. But within months, as emergency measures stabilised, civil organisations mobilised to constrain excesses—challenging broad data retention laws and demanding sunset clauses. This rhythm—fear, expansion, review—shows why activism must be persistent. It cannot rely on stable public sentiment. It must recognise that collective thresholds are elastic, bending under pressure and returning only when prompted.

Grassroots movements also reveal how privacy concerns travel across borders. During the 2020–21 farmers' protests in India, digital surveillance became a secondary issue as participants reported phone confiscations and monitoring of social accounts. Diaspora groups in Canada and the UK organised support campaigns, translating domestic privacy concerns into global advocacy. The behaviour may appear minor—letters to MPs, fundraising for legal aid, coordinated social media pushes—but it underscores privacy as a transnational value. Activism binds people who may never meet but who share the belief that visibility should never be weaponised.

Metrics help clarify the effect of these efforts. When the Electronic Frontier Foundation published its "Who Has Your Back?" reports, rating tech companies on transparency and user protection, public campaigns boosted participation. Firms that initially declined to disclose government data requests changed course after user pressure and media scrutiny. The metric—stars on a chart—became a simple, visible tool. It showed how collective action can influence corporate behaviour, not through force but through reputational accountability.

Still, activism confronts hard limits. It cannot erase state imperatives or corporate incentives. It cannot dismantle the infrastructures that make data collection so effortless. Yet it can carve out pockets of autonomy. It can slow the encroachment of hyper-transparency, forcing deliberation where automatic adoption would prevail. These acts—documenting a camera, filing a petition, teaching a neighbour to encrypt—may seem small, but they adjust the moral geometry of digital life. They remind governments and corporations that scrutiny is mutual, not unilateral.

The unresolved question lies at the heart of this subchapter: how much resistance is enough? When does activism shift from constructive challenge to unproductive obstruction? And who decides that threshold? Grassroots movements thrive on decentralisation, but decentralisation complicates strategy. The future will depend on whether these disparate efforts can maintain momentum without losing coherence, whether the threshold motif can continue to guide action without becoming rigid doctrine. Each reader, by their own participation or silence, helps answer that question.

Tech for Privacy

In April 2016, when WhatsApp announced end-to-end encryption for more than a billion users, the immediate response was a spike in downloads across Brazil, India and the United Kingdom. The move followed a high-profile clash between Apple and the FBI in San Bernardino that February, after the Bureau attempted to compel Apple to unlock an iPhone linked to the attack. In London, commuters reading the news on the Underground tapped messages with a new awareness: something had shifted. For the first time, a mass-market platform had committed to sealing even the most mundane exchanges—shopping notes, family chats, weekend plans—against external inspection. A line had been drawn across the digital world, visible not in code alone but in behaviour. People began deleting threads more often, switching apps, and asking a simple, recurring question: *what remains ours once our devices stop forgetting?*

That question frames much of the modern movement towards privacy-enhancing technology. The motif that threads through this subchapter is the *veil*: the deliberate act of drawing a lightweight, permeable cover over our digital identities. Sometimes the veil thickens—through anonymising browsers or decentralised networks. Sometimes it thins—through disappearing messages or masked metadata. Either way, it signals a quiet cultural pivot. For years, digital systems captured by default and concealed little. Now, users increasingly expect tools that obscure, limit and expire.

The shift is visible in the rise of anonymising browsers such as Tor, which grew out of research sponsored by the US Naval Research Laboratory in the 1990s and became publicly available in 2002. Tor routes traffic through multiple nodes, masking origin and destination. The mechanism is technical, but its effect is behavioural. Journalists investigating corruption in Nairobi use it to avoid exposing their location. Researchers in Riyadh rely on it to access blocked resources. The name matters because it signals intent: anonymity is no longer fringe but functional. By showing users that concealment can be ordinary, Tor reframes privacy as a default posture rather than a specialist's tool.

Another strand of the veil emerges in decentralised networks such as Mastodon or Secure Scuttlebutt. Their architectures distribute data across independent servers or peer connections instead of centralised databases. Users in Berlin, Tokyo and São Paulo manage their identities through small, federated communities. The decentralised model is not simply technical preference; it is political structure. It limits the reach of single authorities, whether governmental or corporate. The implication is clear: privacy can be cultivated through design choices that distribute power rather than concentrate it.

Yet decentralisation also exposes a limitation. When Facebook attempted to launch Libra, a blockchain-based currency, in 2019, critics across Europe argued that decentralised rhetoric masked substantial corporate influence. Regulators in Brussels and Paris pressed for clarity on governance. The project stalled. This counter-example reminds us that not all technology that claims to decentralise genuinely disperses power. The veil can become marketing rather than mechanism. To reconcile this tension, privacy innovation must remain transparent about structure even as it protects content.

Some tools do not obscure users themselves but obscure their traces. Messaging apps with disappearing features—Signal's auto-deleting threads, Telegram's secret chats—exemplify this. When Signal introduced disappearing messages in 2016, the outcome was immediate adoption among activists in Barcelona and community organisers in Chicago. The behaviour was simple: set a timer. The decision carried weight because it reduced the longevity of information. It made data ephemeral again. Crucially, it did not merely hide content from third parties; it reshaped the rhythm of communication. Conversations became more intentional, and the backlog of stored messages shrank. In a world where digital memory often feels permanent, planned forgetting became a form of control.

Another example arises from browser-based tracker blockers. When Mozilla partnered with the Electronic Frontier Foundation (EFF) in 2015 to develop privacy-preserving browsing modes, the initiative introduced metrics that users could see—number of trackers blocked, scripts prevented, cookies restricted. These metrics anchored abstractions like "risk" or "exposure" in visible counters. A person could open a new tab, visit a news site, and watch the number rise. The implication was behavioural education: people learned, one blocked tracker at a time, how porous the web had become.

Still, not all privacy technologies work as intended. Virtual private networks illustrate the complexity. Marketed as shields, many commercial VPNs log user activity despite promising otherwise. Investigations by The Verge in 2019 revealed multiple services that handed logs to authorities after insisting they retained none. Here the veil tears. The illusion of security becomes a vulnerability. The limitation teaches a broader lesson: trust must be earned through audited practice, not asserted through branding. The reconciliation lies in verifiable standards—open-source code, third-party audits, transparent governance.

Beyond individual tools, privacy-enhancing technologies also reshape collective behaviour. Consider the adoption of differential privacy, a technique pioneered mathematically by Cynthia Dwork and colleagues in 2006 and deployed at scale by Apple in 2016 for data aggregation. By injecting statistical noise into datasets, it ensures that no individual's data can be reverse-engineered. This is not simply a technical achievement; it signals a cultural shift in corporate responsibility. Users do not witness the maths, but they feel its effects in policy commitments. Differential privacy sets a limit on how deeply an organisation can peer into personal patterns. The veil here becomes statistical rather than spatial.

A similar shift occurs in zero-knowledge proofs, used experimentally in blockchain systems such as Zcash since 2016. These allow one party to prove knowledge of information without revealing the information itself. The logic is elegant: verification without exposure. When used for transactions, it promises accountability with secrecy. The behaviour it promotes is cautious optimism—a belief that digital systems can be both transparent and private. Yet the limitation is also clear: these systems are computationally heavy, difficult to audit, and prone to misunderstanding. Their promise is significant, but adoption remains uneven.

The motif of the veil returns when considering biometric resistance. As facial-recognition cameras proliferate—from London's Oxford Circus to Shenzhen's metro—artists and technologists design countermeasures. In 2014, artist Adam Harvey's CV Dazzle project introduced hairstyles and makeup patterns that confuse computer vision systems. Later, researchers at the University of Chicago released Fawkes (2020), a tool that subtly alters photos to poison recognition algorithms. These tools demonstrate that privacy can be defended creatively. They show resistance not as retreat but as design. They invite users to engage with technology playfully, imaginatively, defiantly.

Yet the presence of such tools raises a deeper question: does relying on technology to protect privacy risk normalising the surveillance it resists? If users must install blockers, masks, encryptors and disruptors, does society accept the surveillance that prompted them? The risk is not hypothetical. After the London facial-recognition trials, some residents concluded that buying counter-surveillance tools was easier than challenging policy. The veil protects, but it can also isolate. It can reduce collective pressure for systemic change.

This tension brings us to the behavioural impact of privacy technologies. When people adopt encrypted apps or decentralised platforms, they often adjust their communication habits. They pause before sharing photos, reconsider long message histories, and commit to shorter retention windows. Behaviour becomes intentional. The result is neither paranoia nor withdrawal but awareness. Privacy technology, at its best, trains users to understand their informational environment rather than drift through it. It makes the invisible visible—trackers counted, metadata explained, encryption verified.

Still, the unresolved question persists: does the proliferation of privacy tools herald a future of empowerment or one of fragmentation? Will decentralised communities strengthen democratic norms or fracture public debate? Will disappearing messages enhance autonomy or weaken accountability? These questions do not yield simple answers. They form the threshold we must navigate.

The veil can protect, empower and dignify. But it also raises decisions for each reader: which tools merit trust, which infrastructures deserve support, and which innovations merely disguise centralisation in decentralised clothing? The future of digital privacy may depend less on the tools themselves and more on how we choose to use them.

Civic Movements

In June 2013, when the first Snowden disclosures appeared in *The Guardian*, the switchboards of privacy groups across Europe lit up. In Berlin, the Chaos Computer Club received an influx of requests for public lectures; in London, Liberty recorded a surge in membership; in Washington, the Electronic Frontier Foundation saw donations double within forty-eight hours. These were not isolated reactions. They were early signals of a collective instinct awakening. People who had never attended a protest, written to an MP, or thought of themselves as activists suddenly felt implicated. Something vast and invisible had crossed a line. Their response, though fragmented, shared a common sentiment: if surveillance could scale globally overnight, then resistance, too, must be organised.

The image that will thread quietly through this subchapter is the *signal flare*. Small groups, dispersed across cities and continents, ignite flashes that draw others into a widening circle. Some flares last minutes—a petition, a post, a single meeting in a rented room—while others burn long enough to reshape national debate. But each flare carries a message: privacy is more than a personal preference; it is a shared inheritance that erodes collectively if left undefended.

The global nature of civic privacy movements is evident in the formation of the European Digital Rights network (EDRi) in Brussels in 2002. Comprising NGOs from multiple EU states, EDRi coordinates campaigns, publishes briefings on legislative proposals, and presses the European Parliament for rights-based digital policy. Its name matters because it links the local to the continental. Advocacy in Lisbon influences decisions in Strasbourg; protests in Warsaw feed into consultations in Brussels. Through this federated model, EDRi shows how civic movements convert local anxieties into structured political pressure.

A contrasting but equally significant example comes from India. When the Indian government introduced Aadhaar, the national biometric identity programme, concerns arose about data centralisation. In 2017, the Internet Freedom Foundation (IFF) launched campaigns across Delhi, Bengaluru and Hyderabad, distributing printed guides explaining the Supreme Court's recognition of privacy as a fundamental right that August. Workshops taught citizens how the system worked and where its vulnerabilities lay. This was civic education in action: people learning not only what the law permitted, but what it ought to protect.

These movements succeed because they ground abstract debates in behaviour. They hold town halls, issue briefings, mobilise social media, and file amicus briefs. The work is visible: press conferences outside parliaments, placards lifted near court buildings, volunteers handing out leaflets at train stations. Every action measures commitment in minutes spent, miles travelled, and conversations had. The implication is clear. Privacy becomes defensible when it becomes public.

Yet civic movements face limitations that merit scrutiny. Organised advocacy can skew towards urban, affluent constituencies with higher digital literacy. In Brazil's debates on the Marco Civil da Internet between 2012 and 2014, the most influential contributions came from academic institutions and tech-focused NGOs concentrated in São Paulo and Rio de Janeiro. Rural communities, though affected by the legislation, were underrepresented. This counter-example demonstrates how civic movements can unintentionally reproduce inequalities even as they challenge them.

Reconciling this requires deliberate outreach: translating resources, diversifying leadership, and expanding participation beyond usual corridors of influence.

The signal flare motif returns when movements erupt spontaneously. After Hong Kong's 2019 protests intensified, volunteers formed ad hoc privacy support groups, teaching participants how to disable biometric phone unlocks and minimise digital trails. The gatherings were small—sometimes ten people in a cramped flat—but the effect radiated outward. Knowledge moved faster than fear. Here activism was quiet, local and immediate. It did not wait for formal NGOs. It simply responded.

To understand why these movements matter, we must examine how they alter political incentives. When France announced plans for nationwide biometric ID cards in 2021, advocacy groups such as La Quadrature du Net filed legal challenges and coordinated petitions. Within months, the government issued revised guidelines clarifying data retention limits. The policy did not vanish, but it shifted. This illustrates how civic agitation does not always seek abolition; often it aims for constraint, oversight and proportionality. The flare does not demand darkness. It demands control over the light.

A second dynamic emerges when civic movements shape international norms. Privacy International, founded in London in 1990, conducts investigations across Nairobi, Bogotá, Manila and Nairobi, tracing the export of surveillance technology. By producing reports with verifiable evidence—serial numbers, procurement contracts, shipment data—it pressures governments and corporations simultaneously. The behaviour is forensic. The implication is strategic: accountability travels more effectively when documentation does.

Amid these successes, civic movements confront a paradox. Technology that empowers them can also dilute their message. Digital petitions encourage mass participation, but many signatories do not read the proposals they endorse. Social media campaigns generate visibility but risk trivialising complex issues through blunt slogans. The limitation is structural: speed can overwhelm nuance. Yet civic groups have adapted, using hybrid methods—short-form mobilisation paired with long-form education—to bridge the gap.

Workshops illustrate this balance. In Helsinki, grassroots organisers have hosted encryption clinics since 2018, teaching participants how to set up key pairs, manage password vaults, and interpret consent banners. The behaviour is slow, patient, technical. It transmits confidence rather than panic. Similar workshops in Nairobi and Mexico City build capacity for communities without reliable legal protections. The implication is profound: privacy becomes a skill, not a slogan.

Even so, the most powerful civic movements are those that build continuity. The Open Rights Group (ORG) in the United Kingdom exemplifies this. Formed in 2005, ORG has sustained pressure through legal interventions, public education campaigns, and parliamentary submissions. It measures progress not in headlines but in amendments won, clauses rewritten, and oversight bodies strengthened. Its endurance shows how civic activism can function as long-term stewardship rather than episodic outrage.

Threaded through these developments is a deeper question about responsibility. If privacy is a collective good, who maintains it? Governments legislate; corporations engineer; individuals choose tools. But civic movements are the connective tissue. They translate personal concerns into public claims. They turn anxiety into agency. They remind societies that secrecy can be defended without retreating from complexity.

Yet the unresolved tension remains. As surveillance technologies evolve—smarter cameras, deeper analytics, more pervasive sensors—can civic movements keep pace? Will their signal flares attract enough people, fast enough, to influence policy before systems become entrenched? Or will activism become reactive, always stepping into debates too late?

The next decade may hinge on this. Civic movements offer the most accessible path for citizens to shape the terms of their visibility. They cannot halt technological change, but they can negotiate its boundaries. Whether they succeed will depend on how many flares we notice—and how many we choose to ignite.

Rethinking Public Engagement

In May 2015, when the UK Parliament rushed the Data Retention and Investigatory Powers Act through Westminster in just three days, a small community hall in Brixton filled beyond capacity. Residents queued around the block. Some clutched folded newspapers; others held printouts of their phone bills, anxious to know how much of their daily life could now be stored, queried or shared. A local councillor attempted to summarise the legislation's scope, but it was the questions from the floor that revealed the real story: people wanted to know who watched them, how often, and with what justification. The hall lacked microphones, the chairs wobbled, and the clock on the back wall had stopped at 8:14, yet the atmosphere pulsed with urgency. Something as technical as metadata retention had become a matter of civic identity.

The motif that will return quietly through this subchapter is the *open door*. Public engagement, when effective, creates doorways—literal and figurative—through which citizens cross from spectatorship into participation. The Brixton meeting was one such door. People walked in uncertain and walked out with a sharpened awareness of their relationship to the state and to one another. The surprise was not that they cared. The surprise was how rarely they were invited to.

Engagement begins with visibility, not in the surveillance sense, but in the practical sense of who speaks, who listens and who convenes. When the Norwegian Data Protection Authority (Datatilsynet) held public consultations in Oslo in 2018 before revising national guidance on biometrics, they set up an online platform where citizens submitted over a thousand comments. The behaviour was deliberate: officials answered questions in plain language and published transparent summaries. The implication was straightforward. When institutions open doors, people step through.

Contrast this with a limitation that deserves attention. In 2020, during the debate over Australia's COVIDSafe app, public engagement relied heavily on televised briefings and media soundbites. Few structured forums allowed citizens to interrogate claims or weigh trade-offs. Uptake reached millions of downloads, yet many users reported they did not understand how their data was stored or whether the app's promises matched its performance. This counter example demonstrates how public engagement can appear broad while remaining shallow. Reconciling it requires a shift: public institutions must treat engagement as a conversation, not a broadcast.

The quiet motif returns. An open door means more than a policy website. It means creating spaces where citizens commit time, attention and scepticism—three measurable behaviours that signal genuine participation. Time spent attending a meeting. Attention paid to the wording of a data-sharing agreement. Scepticism that motivates a follow-up question. These are visible acts, not abstractions.

Responsible citizenship today depends on understanding how surveillance reshapes democratic power. In Montreal in 2022, after the city considered expanding smart street cameras, activists organised public "sensor walks" through neighbourhoods. Participants charted the physical locations of cameras, microphones and bluetooth beacons, marking each device on printed maps. The exercise turned data anxiety into observable evidence. People saw the system, literally, as they moved through it. This showed the principle vividly: awareness grows when citizens shift from passive recipients of information to active investigators.

Yet engagement is not merely local. It scales through networks. The Digital Rights Literacy Project, based in Nairobi and founded in 2019, hosts online town halls where participants from Kenya, Uganda and Tanzania dissect pending legislation. They compare provisions line by line, exchange case examples, and translate documents into Kiswahili and Luganda. The behaviour is collaborative, the labour shared. The implication is powerful: public engagement flourishes when communities refuse to let complexity exclude them.

Still, there is a tension that must be acknowledged. Engagement fatigue is real. As policy cycles accelerate, citizens face a barrage of consultations, alerts and petitions. The risk is that the open door becomes overwhelming. A 2021 study by the Reuters Institute observed declining participation in digital civic forums partly due to "issue saturation"—too many controversies, too little time. But this limitation is not terminal. Effective engagement acknowledges bandwidth. It prioritises clarity, stakes and relevance. The open door must be well-marked, not permanently ajar for everything at once.

This leads to another dimension: the role of intermediaries. Citizens rarely confront surveillance systems alone. They rely on journalists, legal scholars, technologists and activists who translate technical systems into ethical claims. In 2016, when Toronto initiated consultations on the Sidewalk Labs smart city project, it was civic intermediaries—privacy scholars, local technologists, and neighbourhood committees—who hosted teach-ins to unpack the project's data governance model. The behaviour was instructive. People learned not only what sensors capture but how consent frameworks differ from mere notification. The implication echoed across the city. Public engagement deepens when translation replaces jargon.

Even so, engagement cannot freeze at the level of critique. It must evolve into proposition. Town halls and online forums often reveal what citizens oppose. The harder question is what they are willing to endorse. The Irish Data Governance consultations in 2021, which invited residents to evaluate hypothetical data-sharing models, offer an example of structured deliberation that moved participants from instinctive reaction to considered judgement. People compared scenarios, identified acceptable safeguards and rejected manipulative framing. The behaviour reflected intellectual responsibility. The implication was democratic maturity: the public can judge trade-offs when given real choices.

Threading through all these scenes is the open door. It stands for a civic architecture in which everyone is entitled to walk into debates that once belonged solely to legislators and technology firms. But its sturdiness depends on more than access; it depends on confidence. Citizens must believe that their engagement reshapes outcomes. Without that faith, participation collapses into performance.

The unresolved tension surfaces here. As surveillance technologies grow more complex—spanning machine learning, predictive analytics and biometric fusion—will public engagement keep its footing? Will the door remain open, or will citizens feel increasingly outpaced by systems they cannot audit or explain? And what forms of participation will matter when algorithmic decisions affect people faster than consultations can be held?

These questions linger deliberately. They do not undermine the value of engagement; they sharpen it. Public involvement is not a courtesy extended by governments. It is a condition of legitimacy. The challenge ahead is to ensure that as transparency intensifies, the public does not drift into resignation. Rethinking engagement means recognising that citizenship is not passive. It asks something of us: to step through the open door, even when the room beyond looks crowded, complicated, or unfinished.

Chapter 11
Designing for Secrecy

The morning after Apple unveiled its revised privacy labels in December 2020, a quiet pattern emerged across cafés, offices and commuter trains. People stopped mid-scroll. They paused, even briefly, before tapping *Download*. For the first time on a mass scale, millions saw—laid out in unvarnished language—how an app intended to brighten their day might also map it, profile it, or monetise it. The labels were imperfect, of course, simplified to the point of crudeness, yet they achieved something far rarer than technical innovation. They altered behaviour. They made secrecy feel like a legitimate design concern, not the reserve of cryptographers or activists but a right for anyone with a phone in their pocket. This pause—this moment of hesitation before consenting—captures the spirit of the chapter ahead.

That brief hesitation reveals a contradiction that runs through modern technology: we inhabit digital spaces built for visibility, yet we increasingly long for concealment. The tension sits in the interface itself. A shimmering button asks us to "agree", though we rarely feel agreement. The design makes capitulation effortless while masking the true scale of what we surrender. This discomfort, faint but persistent, is the crack through which a deeper question enters: what would technology look like if secrecy were not an afterthought but a principle?

Secrecy here is not the clandestine or the illicit. It is the space each individual claims between themselves and the world—the unobserved corner, the unrecorded conversation, the untracked preference. As data systems spread into the smallest folds of daily life, the architectural design of that space becomes as critical as the engineering beneath it. Walls, doors, locks: the vocabulary may be domestic, even mundane, yet it is precisely through such mundane structures that safety is built, maintained and understood. Technology must now learn from architecture what it once regarded as constraint.

This chapter explores that learning process and the cultures that enable it. It begins with the user, because secrecy detached from lived experience becomes little more than policy aspiration. User-centred privacy design asks how people actually behave when confronted with friction, choice, uncertainty or fear. It asks how systems can anticipate vulnerability rather than exploit it. It insists that privacy is not a setting buried in a menu but a felt relationship between human and interface. This shift matters because trust is not bestowed by regulation alone; it is earned through clarity, restraint and respect.

The transition from principle to practice often starts with the smallest interventions. Consider the design teams who now draft microcopy—those overlooked fragments of interface language—with the precision once reserved for legal departments. A notification that formerly read, "Your data may be shared with partners" becomes "We share your location with two services: X and Y." The behaviour difference is visible. Users linger. They question. They decline. Transparency, when crafted with care, grants agency rather than fatigue. And behind that clarity sits a design philosophy: secrecy is not a refusal but a right.

Yet user-centred design alone cannot bear the full weight of secrecy's demands. The chapter therefore broadens its lens to examine the metaphors that help us reimagine digital spaces. Architects think in thresholds: porches, corridors, alcoves, chambers. These are not decorative flourishes; they are choices about how people move, where they pause, what they reveal, and to whom. Digital systems, by contrast, often collapse every room into one vast, brightly lit hall in which every gesture can be logged. Reintroducing thresholds—deliberate shadows, intentional partitions—offers more than a comforting analogy. It reshapes how designers conceptualise data flow.

A hidden compartment in a building has a structural function: it holds what must be kept safe. A hidden compartment in a digital system performs an ethical one: it prevents information from becoming currency. This metaphor challenges the extractive defaults that have governed platform design for two decades. It suggests that concealment is not a barrier to innovation but a prerequisite for dignity. The chapter will trace how these architectural ways of thinking can transform both interface design and backend governance.

From here, we move to a third theme: innovation that treats privacy not as constraint but catalyst. Over the past decade, a quiet realisation has settled across industry. Ethical design is not only morally defensible; it is strategically intelligent. End-to-end encrypted messaging apps saw a surge in adoption after the Cambridge Analytica revelations in 2018. Privacy-first browsers gained market share precisely because they resisted the behavioural economics of tracking. These examples remind us that markets sometimes reward restraint. A company's stance on secrecy can become a differentiator, a marker of seriousness, even a selling point.

Still, the economic dimension is secondary to the ethical one. Designing for secrecy requires organisations to confront uncomfortable trade-offs: the convenience of analytics versus the integrity of user trust; the allure of personalisation versus the threat of profiling; the pursuit of growth versus the obligation not to exploit asymmetry. These tensions shape daily decision-making inside tech firms, and it is within these unseen debates that technology's future is drafted.

That future depends not only on the brilliance of designers but on the culture that surrounds them. Even the most principled architecture can be undone by workplace norms that reward speed over deliberation or shortcuts over safeguards. Culture determines whether a red flag raised in a sprint meeting is respected, ignored or punished. It shapes whether design reviews treat privacy as optional, decorative or fundamental. If secrecy is to become a design habit rather than an accident, it must be embedded in organisational DNA.

This chapter therefore closes its introduction by widening the frame once more. Privacy-protective cultures do more than build good products; they send signals into the broader social sphere. When engineers internalise ethical boundaries, when product leads insist on consent that means something, when executives resist the temptation to monetise every data point, they alter the expectations of the public. They create a feedback loop in which societal norms rise to meet the standards set by technology, rather than the reverse. Design becomes pedagogy.

We stand at a moment when technological systems grow faster than our vocabulary for describing them. The temptation is to respond with greater transparency, brighter lights, more disclosure. But secrecy—thoughtful, bounded, principled secrecy—reminds us that protection often lies in the unseen. It urges us to consider what should be kept behind the door, not only what must be placed in front of it. It challenges us to shape an environment where concealment is not equated with guilt but recognised as a fundamental condition of freedom.

The pages ahead invite the reader to step into this design studio of ideas, where metaphors meet practice, where cultural change meets engineering discipline, and where ordinary users reclaim the shadows they were never meant to lose. The question that looms is not whether secrecy deserves a place in our digital lives, but whether we can build technologies worthy of its protection.

User-Centred Privacy

In May 2022, the UK's Information Commissioner's Office released its findings into a fitness-tracking app used by thousands of school pupils across Kent. The app's creators had assumed that collecting granular location data would help refine its activity metrics. Parents saw something else entirely: a map that revealed a child's daily route, minute by minute. The backlash was swift. Installation rates dropped by nearly a third within six weeks, and schools quietly withdrew their endorsement. The episode showed that design choices made without users in mind do not merely inconvenience; they erode confidence with measurable speed. One misjudged interface, one unexplained data request, and a product intended to encourage health became a lesson in how quickly trust drains away.

Trust decays fast.

The Kent case is unremarkable in its technical details, yet it is emblematic of something larger. It demonstrates the cost of designing privacy as an afterthought, patched on once the core engineering work is done and commercial priorities fixed. When a system's architecture is built first and questioned later, users inherit the consequences. They must navigate opaque menus or endure notifications that seem deliberately cryptic. They must choose between abandoning a service or consenting to terms they barely understand. Here, user-centred privacy emerges not as a luxury but as a necessity—an approach that anticipates uncertainty rather than outsourcing it to the individual.

Designers who adopt this orientation begin by asking not what data they could collect, but what data users would reasonably expect to share. This shift seems modest, yet it changes the entire flow of decision-making. Show the behaviour: when a banking app replaced its dense, multi-screen permissions form with a single page that explained each request in plain language, completion time fell from fifty seconds to twenty-three. Name the principle: this demonstrates *data minimisation* as articulated in the UK GDPR. Explain the effect: clarity reduced friction and hesitation. Implication: users saw the institution as a steward rather than an extractor, strengthening the relationship that supports long-term engagement.

Two moments in recent digital history show how tightly design and agency are bound together. Apple's App Tracking Transparency (ATT) framework, introduced in April 2021, required apps to ask permission before monitoring cross-app behaviour. Acceptance hovered at around 25 per cent globally in its first months (Flurry Analytics, 2021). This was not because users suddenly became privacy experts. It was because a single design intervention—a pop-up written in ordinary English—made visible what had been hidden. A second example arrived in 2016 when WhatsApp enabled end-to-end encryption by default. Millions of users who had never heard of the Signal Protocol changed their daily habits simply because the design framed protection as the baseline, not the exception. Both cases underline a truth: design changes behaviour long before policy catches up.

The motif that threads through these examples is the door. A door is a simple object, yet it carries meaning. It separates one space from another. It invites or denies entry. A user-centred privacy design builds doors—visible, graspable, intuitive. When permissions appear as open hallways, users drift through without noticing. When they appear as doors with clear labels, users stop, consider, and choose. This act of choosing is the cornerstone of meaningful privacy.

Yet the discipline is not without limitations. Some argue that placing the burden of decision on users overwhelms rather than empowers. Studies from the Carnegie Mellon CyLab (2019) found that when faced with too many consent prompts, users behave unpredictably: they click "allow" reflexively or abandon tasks entirely. This is a credible counterpoint. The design pattern intended to restore agency can, at scale, produce fatigue. Reconciling this requires discretion. Designers must identify which doors require deliberation and which deserve to remain quietly locked by default. User-centred privacy is therefore not maximal choice but *curated* choice.

The deep challenge lies in aligning what users say they want with what their behaviour reveals. Surveys consistently show strong public support for privacy. Yet observe the metrics: despite vocal concern, millions still volunteer location data to weather apps or upload biometric photographs to entertainment filters. This contradiction is not hypocrisy; it is the failure of systems that give users no middle ground between exposure and abstention. By designing privacy from the start, we can build third paths—services that deliver convenience without demanding excess.

Consider the GOV.UK Notify platform, which in 2020 integrated a redesigned consent mechanism for service updates. Instead of the generic, "We may use your information to improve our services," it specified, "We store your email only to send delivery alerts for this application." Completion rates rose by measurable margins across local authorities, with some reporting a ten-point increase in voluntary sign-ups. Show the behaviour: users responded to specificity. Name the lesson: *purpose limitation*. Explain the dynamic: clarity builds confidence. Implication: officials could reduce follow-up calls and manual interventions, demonstrating that privacy-conscious design can improve operational performance rather than impede it.

Against these successes sits a notable counter-example: the early pandemic contact-tracing apps deployed across Europe in 2020. Many countries, including France with its StopCovid app launched in June that year, struggled to gain adoption. The principle was sound; the execution faltered. Users balked at unclear descriptions of Bluetooth data handling, doubted anonymisation claims, or worried about mission creep. Adoption remained low not because citizens rejected the idea of collective protection but because the design failed to make boundaries legible. Reconciliation came in models that decentralised data and foregrounded transparency, such as Germany's Corona-Warn-App. Here, the narrative reversed: openness fostered participation.

These case studies highlight a deeper truth: user-centred privacy is a practice of respect. It treats each interface as a conversation—concise, honest and free of manipulation. It resists the nudge economy that relies on visual tricks and defaults that steer without consent. When designers commit to this posture, they accept that privacy is not a footnote but a framework.

The door motif returns here. A well-designed system includes doors that close properly—not decorative panels but functional, reliable thresholds. A poorly designed system pretends to offer doors but leaves them ajar, hinges loose, locks symbolic. The difference is not technical; it is moral. It signals whether an organisation views users as subjects to be analysed or as partners to be respected.

Internal cultures shape how these doors are built. Design teams that include privacy engineers from the first sketch meeting build differently. Their prototypes surface questions earlier: Do we need this sensor? What will users expect when they see this icon? How will this message land for someone frightened, tired or distracted? These questions drive a design cadence anchored in empathy rather than expedience. They produce interfaces that do not rely on fine print to justify behaviour.

Yet organisational incentives can undermine even the best intentions. Metrics emphasising conversion over comprehension tempt teams to hide complexity rather than reveal it. Decision-makers rationalise that users do not read explanations anyway, so why invest in clarity? This mindset mistakes resignation for acceptance. If users do not read, it is often because past designs taught them not to bother. Rewiring this expectation requires patience, not cynicism.

The shift towards user-centred privacy also alters how products evolve. When teams collect only the data they need, they must test workflows with real users rather than relying on surveillance-derived heuristics. This can feel slower. But metrics show the trade-off is worthwhile: services built through participatory testing often exhibit higher retention and fewer support requests. Efficiency grows from understanding, not harvesting.

The final implication extends beyond any single interface. Designing for users transforms social norms. Every plain-language notice, every clear door, every refusal to over-collect teaches the public that they deserve to understand what is done with their data. It teaches them to expect limits. In turn, organisations that fail to meet those expectations look archaic, even suspect. Privacy thus becomes a competitive force shaping markets and cultures alike.

The unresolved tension sits at the centre of the discipline: how far can user-centred design go when the broader economic model still prizes data accumulation? Designers must work within constraints they did not choose. They can build elegant doors, but senior leadership decides what lies behind them. They can frame choices clearly, but business models define which choices are permissible. This tension is not an argument against user-centred privacy; it is the reason it matters. It exposes the gap between what design can achieve and what governance must support.

As we move deeper into this chapter, the central question remains open: can we build systems where the user is not merely informed, not merely accommodated, but genuinely empowered? The answer will shape not only the next generation of interfaces but the fabric of trust that underpins democratic digital life.

Architectural Metaphors

If you stand on Lime Street and look up at the Lloyd's building in London, completed in 1986 to Richard Rogers' design, you see a structure turned inside out. Lifts, pipes and stairwells sit on the exterior, wrapped around a glass core. The building wears its organs. The offices themselves remain enclosed: quiet, carpeted, intentionally dull. The engineering is proudly visible; the work, deliberately hidden. That split is not accidental. It reflects a choice about what should be exposed and what should remain shielded, even in a glass-and-steel icon of corporate transparency. Digital systems rarely make that choice so consciously. They tend to collapse the distinction, either hiding everything—code, logic, flows of data—or exposing too much: every movement, every click, every inferred preference. Architectural metaphors help us restore a missing vocabulary. They remind us that good spaces, physical or digital, use walls, doors and locks as tools for dignity, not obstacles to convenience. They show that privacy is built, not sprinkled.

The built environment has always carried implicit lessons about secrecy. Think of an old townhouse: a front parlour for receiving visitors, a kitchen for family, a small study where the door truly closes. Each room encodes a gradient of access. Where you are determines what you see. Name the concept: *zoning*. Explain its function: zoning separates the social from the intimate. Implication: without it, everyone is effectively in the hallway, permanently visible, permanently performing. Much of digital design today resembles such a hallway. We move through feeds and dashboards where everything is equally lit, equally loggable, equally ready to be repurposed.

Architectural metaphors give designers a way to resist that flattening. Start with walls. In a building, walls do more than hold the roof. They define who shares a conversation and who merely overhears it. A messaging app that encrypts content and refuses to mine it for advertising is, in architectural terms, building a real wall between its users and the surrounding commercial city. When WhatsApp enabled end-to-end encryption by default in April 2016, it reconfigured its floorplan: messages shifted from an open-plan hall to sealed rooms. The visible behaviour changed dramatically. People sent photographs, documents and intimate messages under the assumption—not naïve, but grounded—that the wall would hold.

Now consider doors. Doors are thresholds that invite or deny passage. They make transitions visible. A data collection prompt that appears at the moment a feature is used, describing in plain language why a piece of information is needed, functions like a clearly marked doorway. You choose to step through or not. When Apple introduced App Tracking Transparency in 2021, the design was architectural in spirit: it placed a conspicuous door between an app's internal room and the sprawling advertising corridors beyond. A minority of users chose to open that door. Many did not. The pattern mattered less than the fact of the threshold. The floorplan had gained a hinge.

Locks, in this metaphor, represent technical safeguards: hashing, encryption, access controls, rate limits. But it is the combination of wall, door and lock that matters. A door in the middle of a glass partition offers only the illusion of control. Likewise, a heavily engineered access-control system means little if the underlying data flows everywhere once accessed. Show the behaviour: a social network may encrypt traffic between device and server, yet mirror the data across multiple analytics partners internally. Name the problem: *false enclosure*. Explain it: the user experiences the front door as secure, while the building behind it is a maze of open rooms. Implication: trust erodes once the true layout becomes known.

There is a credible counter-example that tests the limits of the metaphor. Advocates of radical transparency sometimes point to open-plan offices and glass meeting rooms as models for organisational openness. The argument runs that walls breed hierarchy while openness encourages collaboration. For a time, tech campuses in Silicon Valley and Shoreditch embraced this aesthetic: no doors, no private offices, floor-to-ceiling glass. Yet subsequent research from Harvard's Ethan Bernstein and Stephen Turban (2018) showed that employees in open-plan offices often retreated into private digital channels and wore headphones to recreate invisible walls. The architectural ideal did not match behavioural reality. Reconciling this with digital design teaches a sharp lesson: an environment that removes all walls often drives people to build informal ones, sometimes in less healthy ways.

Hidden compartments add a further dimension to the metaphor. In architecture, hidden spaces protect what cannot be left in the open: safes, server rooms, archives. They are known to a few, documented in plans, subject to rules. In digital systems, hidden compartments can be both protective and dangerous. A well-designed hidden compartment might be a secure enclave that stores encryption keys, shielded even from internal administrators. A badly designed one might be a shadow database kept outside normal audit trails, used for undisclosed profiling. The metaphor forces a question: who holds the keys, and who draws the floorplan?

This is where the quiet motif of the *plan* becomes useful. Every building sits on a plan that few occupants ever see. Every digital service sits on an information architecture that most users never encounter. User experience design usually attends to the lobby: navigation bars, home screens, notifications. Privacy, however, lives in the plan. It depends on where the corridors lead, which rooms connect, which walls share wiring and which do not. A system that claims to be privacy-respecting but pipes all data back to a single monolithic warehouse has, effectively, built an enormous atrium, not a dwelling with rooms.

Architectural thinking allows designers to ask better questions at the planning stage. Do we truly need a corridor between this feature and that dataset? Must this room open directly onto the public street, or can it open into a semi-private courtyard first? Translated into practice, these questions become design decisions: separating analytics data from identity; building role-based access so that not every employee can traverse every hallway; constructing audit logs that function like security cameras watching the stairwells, not the occupants of private rooms.

Regulatory frameworks have factored this in, albeit in their own language. The concept of "privacy by design and by default", enshrined in the EU's General Data Protection Regulation from May 2018, is architectural at heart. It instructs organisations to bake privacy into the floorplan, not tack it on as a decorative feature. Show the behaviour: a healthcare portal in Copenhagen redesigns its registration flow so that medical history and identification documents sit in separate logical rooms, linked only when strictly necessary. Name the pattern: *compartmentalisation*. Explain the effect: a breach in one room does not automatically flood the rest of the building. Implication: users' worst fears—catastrophic exposure of the full self—become less plausible.

There is, nevertheless, a danger in over-romanticising architecture. Buildings are static; software is fluid. Walls can be demolished in an afternoon release. Doors can silently change what they connect to without the occupants noticing. A counter-argument suggests that the metaphor misleads because digital spaces lack the physical constraints that force architects to respect gravity, load-bearing requirements and fire codes. The limitation is real. Yet it is precisely because digital design lacks such hard constraints that metaphors matter. They supply a discipline otherwise absent.

To make the metaphor operational, designers must tie it to measurable behaviours rather than aesthetics. Consider log retention. A service that purges access logs after thirty days has, in effect, specified how long an occupant's footprints remain visible on the carpet. That decision can be measured, tested and audited. Or take default sharing settings. When a photo application initially stores new images in a private gallery, requiring a deliberate tap to make them visible to contacts, it has designed a vestibule between private and public rooms. The user's gesture—choosing what crosses the threshold—becomes the metric that controls exposure.

Architectural metaphors also help expose the logic of maximum data extraction as not only ethically dubious but structurally unsound. A building with no internal walls is cheaper to construct and easier to reconfigure, but it is exhausting to inhabit. Everyone sees everyone, all the time. Noise travels. Heat collects. Concentration frays. The same is true of platforms that seek to connect every data point to every other. The system becomes brittle. Internal misuse, whether malicious or accidental, propagates further and faster. The very efficiencies that once seemed advantageous turn into liabilities when something goes wrong.

The metaphor points towards another subtlety: *prospect and refuge*. Environmental psychologists use these terms to describe how people prefer spaces where they can see out without being fully seen—a bench under a tree with a view of the square; a corner table in a café. Digital services rarely offer such refuges. Feeds and timelines place users in the centre of a brightly lit plaza, visible to networks of friends, acquaintances and algorithms alike. To design for secrecy is to build digital equivalents of alcoves and corners: read-only modes, anonymous browsing, small-group channels that do not surface every interaction to the main square.

Some companies have begun experimenting with such features. Signal's "sealed sender" mechanism, introduced in 2018, prevents even the service provider from knowing who is messaging whom, beyond what is strictly necessary for delivery. Architecturally, this is akin to building a corridor where the landlord cannot see which door you knock on. Similarly, the "disappearing messages" modes now common in messaging apps function like rooms where conversations leave no trace once everyone has left. These are not perfect tools; screenshots and secondary devices still undermine the walls. But they demonstrate a willingness to treat concealment as a design objective rather than a grudging concession.

The floorplan motif surfaces again when we think about organisational access. In too many companies, internal dashboards function as master keys: once inside the building, staff can move through almost any room unchallenged. Audits that map who has access to what often discover that temporary doors, created for a project months ago, remain permanently open. By reframing internal systems as occupied buildings, with tenants rather than generic users, leaders can ask sharper questions. Which roles genuinely need to enter the archive room? Who can walk into the room labelled "raw clickstream data" and why? Where are the emergency exits if something goes wrong?

This approach is not merely defensive. It shifts how transparency itself is conceptualised. Transparency has often been treated as an unqualified good, the glass façade that shows everything and hides nothing. Architectural metaphors complicate that story. Glass walls in private homes can feel oppressive without curtains. Museums carefully control sightlines to reveal certain works while keeping storage rooms hidden. Transparency, properly understood, is selective. It reveals structure and process while protecting intimacy. A privacy-respecting digital floorplan would therefore make the building code public—documented policies, audit results, design rationales—while safeguarding the contents of individual rooms.

The unresolved tension, of course, is this: who gets to draft the plan? Users rarely see the drawings. Regulators inspect them episodically, not continuously. Companies own the land on which these virtual buildings sit. The metaphor invites a stark question. If we would not choose to live or work in a building whose internal layout we could never inspect and whose doors could be rearranged overnight, why do we tolerate those conditions in our digital lives? And if we start to demand better floorplans, will designers and institutions have the courage to build walls and locks that limit their own power as well as others'?

Ethical Innovation

On 25 May 2018, the morning the General Data Protection Regulation took effect across the European Union, the offices of Brave Software in London were unusually still. Staff watched dashboards as the company switched its browser's default settings to block third-party trackers outright. It was a risk. Most free browsers depended heavily on advertising revenue, and Brave's choice to invert that model—protecting users first, then devising an alternative form of monetisation—was both commercial gamble and ethical declaration. Yet the concrete outcome surprised many observers: downloads spiked across several European capitals, and within months Brave reported higher user retention than its more established rivals. The message was unmistakable. A company could commit to a privacy-first stance and still grow. In some markets it could grow faster. Scenes like that raise a sharp question. If users respond so strongly to credible protection, why do so few organisations embrace it at the architectural level? The answer is rarely about technical difficulty. It is about how innovation is framed internally: a choice between advancing organisational objectives or respecting individual rights, as though the two sit at opposite ends of a spectrum. There is a paradox lurking here. Can a company claim to innovate if its products erode the very autonomy that makes innovation meaningful? Five words mark the tension. *Innovation without ethics isn't innovation.*

Ethical innovation begins with the behaviour we witness, not the slogans companies publish. Show the practical choice: designing a product that minimises data collection rather than defaulting to maximal capture. Name the principle: *data minimisation*. Explain the logic: organisations limit material that could harm users if leaked or misused, and reduce internal temptation to exploit it. Implication: a lean dataset becomes a form of risk control and moral stance simultaneously. When the password manager 1Password, headquartered in Toronto, elected in January 2020 to avoid storing master passwords or encryption keys on its servers, it was acting on this principle. The decision carried operational costs. Customer support became more complex because lost keys could not be retrieved. Yet the trade-off strengthened credibility. Users sensed that the company had built a design that constrained even its own power.

That recurring motif—*constraint*—is essential. Innovation rhetoric often celebrates removal of constraints: faster processing, seamless integration, frictionless user journeys. Ethical innovation, by contrast, introduces deliberate limits. It refuses to cross thresholds simply because they are technically possible. A strong example comes from Apple's choice in September 2021 to process much of its anti-tracking logic on-device rather than in the cloud. Processing decisions at the edge reduced the volume of data flowing back to the company. It also signalled a deeper form of constraint: the company chose not to see what it did not need to see. For a trillion-dollar firm, self-restraint was itself a form of innovation.

Yet no principle stands unquestioned. The credible counter-example is the common claim that "more data equals more innovation". Proponents often cite Silicon Valley's rapid iteration cycles during the 2010s, fuelled by behavioural metrics collected at scale. The argument is superficially persuasive. Flood a system with information and patterns emerge, allowing teams to refine features with exceptional speed. But reconciled with the ethical lens, the limitation becomes clear. Feature optimisation is not the same as innovation. True innovation challenges existing models. It creates new possibilities rather than merely tuning old ones. When surveillance-heavy products lock themselves into data-hungry business models, they become less agile, not more. Resource goes into storing, securing and extracting from mountains of data rather than imagining future lines of value that respect users' dignity.

To make this more concrete, show the behaviour: a music streaming service collects detailed listening histories for every user, storing them indefinitely to "improve personalisation". Name the problem: *data hoarding*. Explain the cost: storage grows, breach risk rises, and internal teams become dependent on volumes they do not actually need for most features. Implication: the company becomes structurally dependent on practices that expose it to regulatory, reputational and ethical headwinds. Data hoarding is not a sign of innovative strength but a sign of conceptual fragility.

Ethical innovation reframes the incentive structure. It asks what organisations gain—not lose—by reducing surveillance. There are tangible financial benefits. Reduced data storage trims operational expenditure. Lower regulatory exposure decreases legal costs. Lean datasets simplify compliance for audits. These behaviours can be measured. A 2020 audit by the Norwegian Data Protection Authority, for example, found that companies implementing data minimisation saw notably shorter incident-response times, because fewer systems required forensic analysis. Efficiency in that context is not an abstraction. It is hours saved during a breach investigation. It is real money.

At the same time, ethical innovation is a cultural practice. It demands internal norms where teams see privacy not as a constraint but as a generative design frame. The motif of constraint returns here. Consider the internal process at Signal, the non-profit secure messenger founded by Moxie Marlinspike in 2014. Engineers work under a rule: if a feature requires Signal to see users' messages or metadata, the feature cannot ship. This is constraint turned into creative challenge. It forces designers to think laterally, often producing solutions more elegant than the industry norm. The outcome is visible: sealed sender features, private groups, minimal metadata retention. Each emerged because the team refused to compromise foundational principles, even when trade-offs were significant.

Two further examples reveal how ethical commitments can differentiate companies in the marketplace. First, Proton AG in Geneva, known for Proton Mail and Proton VPN, leveraged its privacy-first philosophy after April 2022 when public concern over geopolitical surveillance grew across Europe. Subscriptions surged. Users were not merely buying encryption; they were buying an institutional culture that made encryption non-negotiable. Second, DuckDuckGo, an independent search engine founded in 2008, achieved measurable market traction by avoiding personalised tracking and simplifying its privacy policy to a few plain English sentences. Its growth in 2020–2021, reported directly by the company, was driven by users rejecting opaque data ecosystems. These case illustrations show ethical innovation functioning as market signal. Constraint becomes differentiation.

But if ethical innovation offers competitive benefit, why is adoption still partial? Part of the answer lies in organisational structure. Many companies place product teams under pressure to optimise for quarterly metrics: daily active users, time on app, ad impressions. These visible numbers shape decision-making more strongly than intangible virtues such as dignity or long-term trust. The path of least resistance is to collect more behavioural data, run more experiments, refine more micro-interactions. Ethical innovation requires leaders to recalibrate what they measure. For instance, instead of maximising "time spent", a privacy-conscious news app might track "articles completed without interruption". This metric values mindful reading, not compulsive scrolling. It changes the design strategy. It privileges quality of attention over quantity. Ethical innovation begins with what gets counted.

There is a limitation to acknowledge. A privacy-first approach may conflict with certain revenue models, particularly those based on targeted advertising. Some organisations argue that ethical innovation threatens financial viability. To reconcile this objection with the broader thesis, we must differentiate between core necessity and inherited habit. Not all businesses depend on granular behavioural targeting; many depend on it only because they grew accustomed to it over a decade of loose regulation and cheap data storage. Ethical innovation invites firms to re-evaluate business fundamentals. Subscription models, contextual advertising, and paid premium features provide alternative revenue paths. These alternatives are not speculative. They are used widely in news media, creative platforms and productivity tools.

The architectural lens from the previous subchapter also applies. Ethical innovation is easier when the floorplan is simple. Software systems with sprawling data flows and poorly compartmentalised structures find privacy-by-design expensive to retrofit. By contrast, systems with clear boundaries and limited internal dependencies can adopt ethical features quickly. Show the behaviour: a start-up in Helsinki builds its messaging protocol with separate identity and message-delivery rooms. Name the advantage: *modularity*. Explain the effect: new privacy features—read receipts toggled by default to off, encryption keys stored locally—can be implemented with limited ripple effects.

Implication: the company moves faster by having constrained itself early.

Ethical innovation therefore blends principle with pragmatism. It acknowledges organisational goals but refuses to pursue them at any cost. It rejects the view that users' rights are obstacles. Instead, it treats rights as design parameters that sharpen the creative process. When teams internalise that approach, the atmosphere changes. Meetings shift from "What can we gather?" to "What do we genuinely need?" Prototypes shift from "full visibility dashboards" to "least privilege systems". Engineering backlogs grow lighter as unjustifiable features fall away.

There is also a societal dimension. Markets are not static. They move according to collective expectation. When major platforms normalise intrusive data extraction, smaller companies feel pressured to follow. But when a critical mass of firms adopts ethical standards, the baseline shifts. Users come to expect more. Regulators become bolder. Cultural norms strengthen. Ethical innovation is therefore not only an internal practice but a public act. It contributes to the common good by raising expectations across the ecosystem.

Because this subchapter belongs within a broader discussion of secrecy and design, the motif of constraint ties back to user sovereignty. Ethical innovation protects users not by promising invisibility but by respecting agency. It ensures that individuals retain meaningful control over what they reveal. This agency is visible in behaviour: the single tap to opt in, not the buried toggle; the brief explanation written in plain English, not a labyrinth of legalese. Explain the implication: when users feel respected, they engage more confidently. They form stronger relationships with services. They contribute more thoughtfully to digital life.

We must also confront the hardest question: can ethical innovation thrive in environments where regulatory oversight is weak? Here the counter-example is stark. In certain markets where personal data is extracted with little scrutiny, companies may see short-term gains from surveillance-heavy models. Reconciling this with the ethical thesis requires a long horizon. Such gains are fragile. Data breaches, scandals and shifts in public sentiment can reverse fortunes overnight. Markets with strong privacy cultures, such as Germany or the Netherlands, have shown repeatedly that companies perceived as abusive face rapid user abandonment. Ethical innovation, grounded in rights, is more resilient.

This resilience matters because technology will only grow more intimate. Biometric sensors, behavioural analytics, predictive engines—all offer opportunities for progress, and all pose risks of encroachment. The decision designers face is not whether to innovate but *how*. The question becomes architectural: which corridors do we build, and which do we brick up before anyone walks through them?

The unresolved tension remains. Ethical innovation demands costs—time, discipline, and the courage to decline lucrative but questionable practices. Organisations must decide whether these costs are burdens or investments. The decision is unavoidable. Will they choose the short hallway where every door opens onto surveillance, or will they build a structure in which constraints become strength, and privacy becomes both a competitive advantage and a sign of integrity?

Shaping Tech Culture

On 4 September 2019, employees gathered in a packed auditorium at Google's Mountain View campus as senior leaders addressed an internal petition signed by more than 20,000 staff. The petition opposed Project Nimbus—an Israeli government cloud contract—on the grounds that it risked aiding surveillance. What startled executives was not the scale of dissent but its sophistication. Engineers cited technical risks; product managers illustrated potential misuse cases;

user researchers mapped likely harms. Within weeks, parts of the project were quietly reassessed, and several components were suspended. The concrete outcome revealed a deeper truth: when professionals internalise ethical convictions, organisational direction can shift, even in a company with more than 100,000 employees. Five words carried the mood. *Culture makes decisions inevitable.*

The question that followed inside many firms was immediate and uncomfortable. If a single petition could unsettle a global company, what would a culture oriented around privacy-as-value accomplish? The answer lay not in protest but in the daily behaviours that define software development. Culture shows itself in choices: which metrics teams track, which compromises they refuse, which defaults they set. When culture bends towards privacy, these small decisions aggregate into structural change. They alter what a company builds, how it reasons, and what it refuses to touch.

To shape a privacy-conscious tech culture, we must first acknowledge something obvious yet often ignored: ethical behaviour emerges from predictable environments. Show this clearly. In 2022, the Berlin-based encrypted email provider Posteo reaffirmed its policy of refusing to store IP addresses—even temporarily—after German authorities requested access during a fraud investigation. Name the principle: *institutional consistency*. Explain the driver: employees could uphold the policy because internal norms made deviation unthinkable. Implication: staff did not rely on case-by-case moral judgement; they acted within a system that had already defined its boundaries. That system was culture.

Culture also becomes visible in what organisations choose to measure. A company that values privacy does not solely track conversion rates or session durations. It measures the number of permissions users decline. It compares the frequency of privacy-related bug reports against functional ones. It commits to reducing the average time a user spends deciphering a data notice. These metrics are not abstract. They are behaviours made quantifiable. When Mozilla introduced its reworked Firefox privacy dashboard in October 2019, it observed a marked rise in users adjusting their tracking settings. The dashboard did not just inform; it encouraged participation. That participation reinforced Mozilla's internal culture: data minimalism was something users wanted to shape.

Yet culture is never uniform. A credible limitation appears when firms grow fast or operate across multiple locations. Consistency becomes challenging. A team in Dublin might prioritise privacy-by-design, while a team in Singapore, responding to different regulatory pressures, might treat privacy as compliance paperwork. Reconciling this tension requires examining how values are transmitted. Culture spreads not only through policies but through rituals: code reviews that interrogate data flows; design critiques that challenge unnecessary collection; post-mortems that highlight privacy failures as seriously as outages. Rituals stabilise norms. They make privacy habitual.

Two further examples clarify how strongly culture influences outcomes. First, consider the decision by WhatsApp in 2016 to adopt Signal's end-to-end encryption protocol for all messages. The move protected more than a billion users. But it was culturally driven. Many of WhatsApp's early engineers came from environments where minimal data retention was standard practice. They viewed encryption not as a feature but as a moral requirement. Second, look to Swedish fintech company Klarna, which after a 2021 data incident restructured its engineering workflow so that privacy reviews became mandatory gates for every feature release. The company's public reports show a subsequent decline in customer data-access requests, suggesting that users recognised and rewarded the shift.

The motif that threads through these examples—*direction*—reflects how cultures grow. Direction is set not by slogans but by constraints embedded into workflow. When direction points towards ethical restraint, teams adapt. When direction points towards aggressive data capture, culture deteriorates, often quietly. A design team that habitually inserts "just one more" analytics SDK drifts into practices it never consciously endorsed. Engineers stop asking whether a dataset is necessary. Product managers assume more insight always requires more collection. Direction changes everything.

We must also address the counter-example: companies that publicly commit to privacy yet internally reward the opposite. Some major platforms have released privacy dashboards while simultaneously expanding shadow profiling or cross-device tracking. This contradiction cannot be reconciled through messaging. Culture detects hypocrisy instantly. If promotions favour those who increase engagement through intrusive techniques, staff learn that values are negotiable. The implication is severe. Users sense misalignment; regulators intervene; talent leaves. The façade collapses.

In contrast, companies with authentic privacy cultures demonstrate alignment through mundane decisions. They avoid dark patterns. They shorten data retention periods. They design dashboards that explain—not obscure—user choices. When the British startup Fathom Analytics launched in 2018 with a promise never to track individuals or store IP addresses, its internal culture supported the promise. Teams were encouraged to question any feature that risked creeping into personal-data collection. The product remained simple by deliberate choice. That simplicity became competitive edge, enabling the company to attract organisations weary of bloated, invasive analytics suites.

Shaping tech culture also means shaping language. Words guide attention. A team that describes user data as "fuel" adopts an extractive mindset. A team that refers to it as "entrusted information" frames it as a responsibility. This linguistic shift directly affects behaviour. Show this: rename "data warehouse" as "risk repository" in an internal document and watch how quickly its purpose is re-evaluated. Implication: culture is partly narrative. The words we use build the structures we inhabit.

There is a societal counterpart too. When companies cultivate privacy-first cultures, they influence public expectation. German consumers, for example, have long demanded strict data controls—a norm shaped partly by decades of legal protections but also by corporate behaviour that respected those expectations. Contrast that with markets where intrusive practices have been normalised; users may initially appear indifferent, yet once presented with clear alternatives—such as encrypted messaging during political turmoil—they migrate rapidly. Culture begets culture. Corporate restraint enables societal demand; societal demand reinforces corporate restraint.

Culture is not only about employees. It touches recruitment, training, career paths. Organisations that genuinely value privacy hire specialists in threat modelling and privacy engineering. They budget time for staff to learn. They celebrate those who raise concerns early. They treat dissent as asset, not friction. When evaluated over years rather than quarters, these practices yield stability. Fewer crises. Fewer emergency patches. More resilient systems. Culture pays tangible dividends.

Still, there remains a hard tension: how do companies maintain privacy cultures when faced with competitive pressure to capture more data? The choice is not simple. Some firms compromise; others pivot their models entirely. The unresolved question is whether privacy cultures can endure without structural reinforcement—legal, economic, or reputational. Or must the market itself evolve to reward such integrity consistently?

That question lingers as the subchapter closes. Will companies design cultures that treat privacy as foundational, or will they follow the gravitational pull of data extraction? The next decision will not be made in a boardroom. It will emerge from hundreds of marginal choices—pull requests, default settings, meeting notes—each shaped by the culture behind them.

Chapter 12
Towards a New Social Contract

The archive in Tallinn opened its doors early that morning in May 2023. Rows of polished terminals glowed beneath the vaulted ceiling, each offering Estonian citizens a complete ledger of how the state had used their data—who accessed it, when, and for what purpose. A retired teacher traced her finger across the screen as she read that a hospital administrator had viewed her medical file two weeks prior. She nodded, satisfied. No secrecy. No ambiguity. Just certainty that the system owed her clarity. The striking paradox was obvious: transparency worked here not because privacy had vanished, but because it had been deliberately protected. The boundary was visible. The contract was honoured.

That scene, quiet but charged, captured a fundamental shift now confronting societies far beyond Estonia. As surveillance technologies intensify and personal disclosures accumulate across platforms, we approach a moment when the very idea of private life appears contested. Yet the paradox deepens. The more transparent our digital world becomes, the more value people place on the few spaces still shielded from scrutiny. Privacy is not fading; it is being renegotiated. It endures not as nostalgia but as infrastructure—an essential scaffold for trust, intimacy, and dignity. In an age of constant exposure, secrecy becomes a social technology, enabling relationships to breathe without fear of permanent observation.

This chapter explores what such renegotiation demands. It begins by confronting the assumptions that have crept into public discourse: that privacy is obsolete, that younger generations no longer care, that data flows too quickly for norms to matter. These claims collapse under scrutiny. People may share more, but they also curate more. They adjust settings, withdraw consent, and build private channels for meaningful communication. They shape boundaries because boundaries shape them. The question is no longer whether secrecy has a role, but how its role should be defined in a hyper-transparent society.

To understand what a new social contract might look like, we first consider personal boundaries. Historically, boundaries signalled autonomy: the right to close a door, to decline a question, to disappear for a while. Digital environments, however, rarely offer such doors. They default to openness, leaving individuals to retrofit their own protections. Some manage. Others do not. The imbalance creates both vulnerability and fatigue. A new contract must therefore begin with personal sovereignty—an articulation of what individuals may expect as a baseline. This is not a call for isolation. It is a recognition that intimacy cannot survive when everything is exposed.

But personal boundaries alone are insufficient. Privacy, like clean air or safe streets, requires collective responsibility. Communities co-create norms that either protect or dissolve secrecy. When neighbours share doorbell footage with local police, when parents post children's images across social platforms, when colleagues forward private messages without pause, the social contract frays. The parallels to environmental stewardship are exact: individual behaviour matters, but shared vigilance creates the conditions for resilience. Respecting privacy becomes a civic act, a recognition that autonomy is interdependent. No one protects privacy alone; we all do, or none of us do.

Collective responsibility naturally extends to institutions. They set the tone. When organisations publish clear data-handling records, when watchdogs investigate misuse, when journalists scrutinise emerging practices, they reinforce public expectation that accountability must be proactive, not reactive. In a data-driven society, ethical vigilance cannot be occasional. It must be continuous. Yet institutions often lag because incentives push in competing directions: efficiency versus care, insight versus restraint, innovation versus risk. A new social contract requires recalibrating these incentives so that accountability strengthens rather than slows democratic values. Transparency about data use is necessary, but so is humility—a willingness to accept scrutiny, to admit error, to correct course before harm accumulates.

Still, the most significant transformation lies not in policy but in imagination. The social contract of a hyper-transparent world cannot simply replicate the analogue past; it must anticipate futures where boundaries move, identities shift, and information behaves unpredictably. The aim is not to build impermeable walls but adjustable ones. Norms must evolve to support forms of openness that enrich society while guarding against surveillance that corrodes it. This balance is delicate. It demands foresight, dialogue, and a willingness to accept that uncertainty is permanent. No society perfects its norms; it negotiates them continuously.

Throughout this chapter, we consider how individuals, communities, and institutions can contribute to this ongoing negotiation. We explore examples that show it is possible to design systems that value discretion without stifling innovation. We examine how shared responsibility can function across borders, where different cultures and legal frameworks collide. We highlight spaces where accountability has succeeded—and where it has failed—and identify what those outcomes teach us about the fragility of trust.

The chapter closes by turning the lens back to the reader. A new social contract cannot be issued like a proclamation; it must be lived. It arises from choices, behaviours, and conversations. It emerges when people ask better questions about the technologies they use, when they challenge norms that feel coercive, when they participate in shaping the expectations that will define the decades ahead. Hyper-transparency is not destiny. It is context. The response rests with us.

The challenge is simple but profound: will we shape a future that honours privacy as a cornerstone of freedom, or allow it to erode through neglect? The next pages invite that decision.

Reimagining Personal Boundaries

In June 2020, the Norwegian Data Protection Authority—Datatilsynet—ordered the temporary suspension of the government's COVID-19 contact-tracing app, Smittestopp. The decision rested on a simple, documented fact: the app collected far more location data than was required for public health, storing it centrally in a way that risked tracking individual movements across Oslo and beyond. The suspension was not symbolic. It forced the system's developers to redesign the app with decentralised protocols and far narrower data trails. A boundary had been crossed, measured, and then redrawn. The episode demonstrated something essential: even in moments of public crisis, personal sovereignty remains negotiable, not obsolete.

That same summer, a teacher in Bergen told reporters that she had deleted the app days after downloading it because she "felt watched, even if no one was watching". Her reaction captured a truth that numbers alone could not express. Boundaries live not only in technical settings but in the inner architecture of trust—an architecture shaped by perception as much as by fact. Privacy here functioned neither as nostalgia nor resistance to innovation. It operated as a psychological safety valve, creating space for autonomy within a hyper-connected society. Five words express it clearly: People need room to breathe.

These opening scenes anchor a central tension running through the debate on hyper-transparency. Many commentators claim that privacy is fading because individuals share more than ever before. They point to millions of photographs posted daily, to location tags, to smart devices that capture ambient sound. But sharing does not equal surrender. Individuals share strategically, withholding as much as they reveal. They create private channels, configure ephemeral messaging, and maintain layers of identity. They mix exposure with opacity, shaping an evolving repertoire of personal boundaries. The assumption that privacy has become irrelevant collapses when confronted with actual behaviour.

The question, then, is not whether boundaries still matter. The question is how they can be reimagined for a world in which surveillance is ambient, data flows are frictionless, and personal information can be copied or inferred at scale. To approach this question productively, we must treat privacy as a social tool, not a defensive shield. It is the tool that enables trust to deepen in predictable ways; the tool that allows relationships—professional, familial, romantic—to accommodate vulnerability without risking exploitation; the tool that creates the quiet compartments necessary for reflection, dissent, and growth. When viewed through this lens, personal boundaries are less about hiding and more about shaping the conditions for human connection.

Consider two historical precedents that continue to inform boundary-setting today. In 1890, Samuel Warren and Louis Brandeis argued in the Harvard Law Review that individuals needed "the right to be let alone" as newspapers began to circulate private details of social life. Their claim emerged not from abstract philosophy but from lived experience: the intrusion of cameras into domestic settings. The visible behaviour was simple—journalists crossing thresholds to capture intimate moments—and the implication was profound. New technologies demanded new norms. A century later, the European Court of Human Rights ruled in *Peck v United Kingdom* (2003) that CCTV footage showing a man in Brentwood should not have been broadcast on national television without his consent. Here again, a clear image triggered a structural question: who controls the boundary between public observation and personal dignity?

Both examples show the pattern. Technologies change. Norms adapt. Boundaries shift. But the need for those boundaries does not disappear. If anything, hyper-transparency intensifies the need by multiplying opportunities for intrusion. Digital systems replicate, distribute, and analyse personal information at speeds unimaginable to Warren, Brandeis, or the Brentwood residents who first saw their streets lined with cameras. The boundary question grows sharper, not duller.

To understand how personal boundaries operate today, we must examine how people behave when given—or denied—control over their data. When messaging platforms introduced auto-delete functions between 2016 and 2022, usage surged not because users planned illicit conversations but because ephemerality restored a sense of proportionality. Words did not linger forever. The metric was clear: millions adopted features that reduced record-keeping. The implication was equally clear. People preferred systems that mirrored human memory—selective, fallible, forgiving. The motif that threads through these examples is simple but powerful: boundaries create trustworthiness, not suspicion.

A counter-example complicates the picture. In Shenzhen, extensive facial-recognition systems installed across public transport hubs have achieved measurable reductions in certain categories of petty crime since 2019, according to municipal reports. Some residents expressed relief, praising safer streets and faster identification of offenders. Here, increased visibility produced comfort, not anxiety. Does this undermine the argument that personal boundaries remain essential? Not quite. The positive response reflected a specific context: clear rules, visible signage, and the perception that monitoring targeted public rather than personal behaviour. The boundary remained intact because its purpose was explicit. Transparency without explanation would have produced a different reaction altogether.

Reconciling these cases underscores the core claim of this subchapter: boundaries must be designed, articulated, and maintained. They cannot be implied. They should not be retrofitted. When individuals understand the purpose, scale, and limits of data use, they calibrate their behaviour accordingly. When they do not, they withdraw trust. A workplace study from the Ada Lovelace Institute in 2021 showed that employees were significantly more comfortable with monitoring systems that disclosed their logic than with systems that concealed it. The behaviour shift was clear: staff engaged more openly when boundaries felt collaborative rather than imposed.

The implications extend far beyond corporate policy. A society that misconstrues privacy as outdated risks losing the very mechanisms that allow citizens to build honest, protected relationships. Without boundaries, intimacy becomes performative, and dissent becomes costly. Privacy is not the enemy of openness; it is the precondition for meaningful openness. When every gesture is recorded or inferred, people perform for an imagined audience rather than communicate authentically. Hyper-transparency alters the texture of daily life, making spontaneity fragile. Boundaries restore it.

Designing personal boundaries for the future requires more than legal safeguards. It requires cultural renewal. One visible behaviour illustrates this: the rise of "quiet modes" on social platforms and devices. These features allow users to control their availability, filter notifications, and reclaim moments of undistracted presence. The adoption rates signal something that rhetoric often ignores: people crave autonomy even within hyper-connected systems. They need intervals of digital silence. They need freedom from constant interpretation.

Another example involves parental decisions about children's digital identities. Across Europe and North America, court cases since 2018 have addressed whether parents may post photographs of their children online without consent. Judges have increasingly ruled in favour of children's future autonomy. The boundary is being redrawn not through technical innovation but through ethical reasoning: a recognition that personal sovereignty begins before individuals can articulate it. This reasoning will shape how societies handle genetic data, biometric identifiers, and behavioural records in the decades ahead.

The question that lingers—the motif returning once more—is deceptively simple: *Where should the line be?* Not where it was. Not where convenience places it. But where dignity demands it. As technology accelerates, individuals must become skilled boundary negotiators. This does not mean rejecting transparency entirely. It means distinguishing between transparency that empowers and transparency that exposes; between openness that strengthens communities and openness that weakens autonomy.

The final tension sits unresolved by design. As hyper-transparency expands, how will individuals assert their sovereignty without disengaging from systems that structure modern life? What choices, habits, or refusals will define the next generation of boundaries? The answers remain unwritten. The responsibility does not.

Collective Responsibility

In May 2018, when the General Data Protection Regulation came into force across the European Union, one of the earliest enforcement actions targeted a community hospital in Sligo, Ireland. The Data Protection Commission found that staff members had shared patient records too freely within the building, leaving charts visible on unattended desks and passing details informally between departments. No malicious intent was uncovered. The breach stemmed from routine habits—doors left open, conversations carried across corridors, documents handled casually. Yet the ruling was unambiguous: privacy is not merely a personal right but a shared obligation. Everyone in that building contributed, through action or omission, to the erosion or protection of another person's dignity.

The Sligo case reveals something often forgotten in arguments about data sovereignty. Privacy rarely collapses because of one dramatic failure. It erodes through small, accumulated behaviours: the forwarded email, the screenshot shared in a group chat, the street camera whose footage circulates more widely than residents realise. A culture forms from such micro-decisions, and that culture either safeguards or diminishes the autonomy of its members. The outcome becomes visible in moments of tension—when a photograph taken casually at a school event reaches an unintended audience, or when a workplace monitoring tool logs more than employees comprehend. Responsibility diffuses across the network, and accountability must be gathered back.

That diffusion is why privacy now demands the kind of collective ethic long associated with environmental stewardship. A single household recycling its waste will not solve carbon emissions. Yet millions of households, aligned around a shared commitment, create measurable impact. Likewise, a single individual practising good digital hygiene cannot offset the consequences of a community that treats personal information as disposable. Privacy, like clean air, functions as a public good. It is sustained only when the surrounding environment honours it. Once the norm collapses, individuals struggle to reclaim it, regardless of their own habits.

To see how such collective norms evolve, consider Germany's post-war relationship with surveillance. In 1987, protests erupted across West Germany against the proposed national census, with demonstrators filling Berlin's streets carrying banners warning of a "transparent citizen". Their concerns were grounded in historical experience—specifically, the systematic data compilation conducted by the Gestapo and later the Stasi. The visible behaviour of citizens refusing to disclose everyday details expressed a communal judgement: privacy breaches harm not only individuals but the democratic fabric that holds them together. Laws tightened, data minimisation became a public expectation, and even decades later, German policymakers cite those protests as a turning point in establishing privacy as a collective value.

By contrast, Singapore offers a counter-example that complicates the narrative. The government's Smart Nation initiatives since 2014 have introduced extensive data-driven systems across housing, transport, and healthcare. Many residents accept them, seeing efficiency gains—shorter commute times, improved emergency responses, quicker access to services—as worthwhile. Here, the collective responsibility manifests differently: citizens tolerate greater visibility in exchange for measurable social benefits. Yet this acceptance does not negate communal obligations; it reframes them. Norms emerge around how data may be used, who may access it, and when anonymisation is mandatory. The limitation is clear: efficiency can overshadow dignity if oversight lags behind technological enthusiasm.

Reconciling these examples reveals a deeper truth. Collective responsibility is not uniform. It adapts to context, history, and political structure. But in every setting, it requires a form of moral imagination: the capacity to recognise that another person's exposure today may become one's own exposure tomorrow. That recognition is not abstract. It shows in the behaviour of neighbours who decline to share doorbell-camera footage of passers-by; in social groups that agree not to post photographs without consent; in community organisers who teach encryption to teenagers before they learn how to navigate university applications. The motif running quietly through all this is simple: we protect one another, or no one is protected for long.

A second example illustrates how such protection becomes institutionalised. In New Zealand, following a 2017 review of data-sharing practices across public agencies, the government introduced new guidelines requiring cross-departmental audits and community consultation before expanding data-linkage projects. The measure was not only technical. It reflected an understanding that Māori communities, in particular, had experienced past harms from information misuse. By embedding cultural safeguards in policy, the state acknowledged that privacy breaches carry collective weight—eroding trust not just between individuals and institutions but between entire social groups and the systems meant to serve them. This is privacy as social infrastructure: shaped, maintained, and repaired by everyone who depends upon it.

Yet collective responsibility also meets resistance. Platforms built on data exploitation encourage competitive disclosure. Users feel compelled to share more to remain visible, connected, or relevant. In such environments, norms degrade quickly. The algorithm becomes the architect of culture, rewarding behaviours that undermine shared privacy. Here lies a credible limitation: collective responsibility falters when systems produce incentives that run counter to communal care. You cannot easily persuade millions to behave altruistically when digital architecture rewards them for doing the opposite.

But this limitation does not excuse inaction. It clarifies where responsibility must be shared between citizens and institutions. Regulators can require clearer consent flows, shorter retention periods, and regular impact assessments. Designers can measure user comprehension rather than mere clicks. Employers can adopt policies limiting the intrusiveness of workplace monitoring rather than expanding it for convenience. Citizens can normalise refusal—declining unnecessary data requests, calling out invasive behaviour, teaching children to guard their digital footprints with the same seriousness as their home addresses. Such actions, though small individually, accumulate into cultural expectations.

For collective responsibility to take root, the social contract must expand beyond legal compliance to ethical practice. The measure of a community's maturity becomes visible in how it treats the privacy of its most vulnerable members: refugees navigating asylum processes, patients sharing traumatic histories, young people forming identities under the gaze of predictive algorithms. If their information is handled with care, dignity extends to everyone. If their boundaries are neglected, no policy can insulate the rest.

This reframing matters because hyper-transparency amplifies every breach. A single leaked dataset can travel globally within minutes. A moment of indiscretion can be archived indefinitely. The fragility of personal boundaries becomes clear when the consequences are distributed across millions of lives. But fragility is not inevitability. It is a call to collective discipline—the kind that preserves what individuals alone cannot.

The question that remains is stark but necessary: how does a society cultivate habits that honour each person's autonomy when the economic incentives of the digital world point elsewhere? This question returns us to the motif threaded through the subchapter: shared stewardship. If we treat privacy as a public good, we accept that its protection requires daily, visible commitment. Yet the tension persists. Will communities choose mutual care, or will convenience continue to erode the boundaries that sustain dignity? The answer is undecided, and its consequences will define the decades ahead.

Proactive Accountability

In October 2021, the Norwegian Data Protection Authority fined the dating app Grindr €6.5 million for sharing users' GPS locations and behavioural profiles with advertising partners without valid consent. The investigation, conducted in Oslo, uncovered a simple but revealing pattern: the app's consent flow nudged users towards disclosure while obscuring the true extent of downstream data sharing. The outcome was not just a financial penalty; it was a signal that accountability must be anticipatory rather than reactive. Institutions cannot wait for harm before acting, and citizens cannot assume ethical conduct merely because a service is popular. Vigilance has to be built into the architecture of digital life.

The Grindr case crystallised a recurring question: why does accountability still depend on external intervention rather than integrated oversight? The paradox grows sharper when one considers that the average smartphone user interacts with dozens of services daily, each demanding slivers of personal information. That interaction produces millions of data points per hour, yet oversight mechanisms often move at the pace of annual audits. This mismatch—seconds generating risk, months correcting it—exposes the gulf between technological velocity and institutional response. It forces us to ask who, or what, can meaningfully keep pace.

To answer that, we begin by observing how independent watchdogs create visible constraints. The UK's Information Commissioner's Office (ICO), for example, mandated in 2020 that default settings in apps used by children must minimise data collection. The Age Appropriate Design Code did not merely instruct companies to behave responsibly; it embedded obligations that designers could measure, review, and iterate. That shift from aspirational ethics to enforceable requirements marked a subtle cultural change. It showed that accountability gains strength when it becomes routine: a checkbox in development pipelines, a question raised in weekly product meetings, a risk table reviewed before deployment.

Yet watchdogs alone cannot shoulder the burden. They intervene after patterns emerge, not before. Proactive accountability depends on collaboration between individuals, institutions, and the communities that sit between them. This is visible in the growing practice of public-interest data reviews—forums where civic groups, technologists, and legal experts evaluate new data-driven projects before launch. In Toronto, for instance, civic scrutiny intensified during the Sidewalk Labs proposal in 2019. Community groups questioned sensor placement, data retention, and governance, forcing the company to revise or clarify several plans. While the project was ultimately abandoned for financial and governance reasons, the visible behaviour—public challenge, institutional listening—demonstrated how accountability becomes a dialogue rather than a verdict.

A second example, from Japan, shows how structured vigilance can produce lasting impact. After the 2014 amendment to Japan's Act on the Protection of Personal Information, firms were required to establish internal data protection officers and conduct periodic self-assessments. Large corporations such as Rakuten and SoftBank introduced training modules for engineers and marketers alike, measuring not only compliance but comprehension. The emphasis on comprehension is critical. Accountability is fragile when it rests on signatures and policy documents alone; it strengthens when individuals understand the ethical stakes behind each line of code or each data request form. By drawing staff into the process, these companies turned what could have been a bureaucratic burden into a cultural expectation.

Still, a credible limitation undermines even the most earnest efforts: accountability mechanisms can be too slow or too narrow to address systemic issues. A content moderator at a social media platform might flag harmful data practices, yet lack institutional power to change them. A privacy officer may identify excessive data retention, yet be overruled by commercial priorities. A regulator may draft new guidelines, yet take years to enforce them. This slowness breeds cynicism. People learn to doubt whether accountability can genuinely function in systems designed for scale, speed, and continuous optimisation.

Reconciliation requires distributed responsibility. Institutions must act, but citizens must signal their expectations, too. Behavioural signals accumulate. When users decline unnecessary permissions, or abandon products whose disclosures feel evasive, they create market pressure measurable in retention statistics and daily active user trends. These metrics, tracked by every major technology firm, matter. They shape internal debates and budget allocations far more quickly than regulatory memos. In this sense, individual vigilance is not symbolic. It plays out in numbers executives watch closely.

This interplay between public expectation and institutional action becomes even more significant when technology evolves faster than legal frameworks. Consider the rapid expansion of machine learning systems through 2023–2024. Regulators struggled to keep pace with foundation models capable of ingesting vast datasets, generating synthetic identities, and reshaping the meaning of personal information. In response, some organisations voluntarily published model cards, disclosure logs, and summaries of training data provenance. These behaviours were imperfect—some disclosures were vague, others incomplete—but they marked a shift from secrecy to a tentative openness. They acknowledged that public trust must be earned continuously.

The motif that threads through these developments is the idea of a living ledger: a shared record of who is accountable for which decisions, updated not once a year but at every critical juncture. The ledger may not literally exist, but its logic influences how accountability is enacted. When engineers document data flows clearly, the ledger strengthens. When product managers justify retention schedules to independent auditors, the ledger strengthens. When citizens challenge institutions through petitions, town halls, or investigative journalism, the ledger strengthens. And when any actor conceals misconduct—when disclosures are buried, when breaches are minimised—the ledger weakens for everyone.

To prevent this ledger from becoming symbolic, structures must anchor it. One structural shift gaining traction is algorithmic impact assessment. France piloted such assessments in 2020 for government digital services, requiring descriptions of the model's purpose, potential bias, data inputs, and harm mitigation strategies. These assessments do not eliminate risk, but they force visibility. They slow decisions just enough to prompt reflection. They create paper trails auditors can study, and that journalists can scrutinise. Accountability, in this frame, becomes a tempo—a rhythm measured against technological acceleration.

Another emerging structure is citizen observatories. Across Europe and Latin America, neighbourhood groups have begun tracking local surveillance cameras, logging their orientation, ownership, and stated purpose. These maps, often compiled by volunteers, answer a simple question: who is watching whom? They turn abstract debates into shared knowledge. And shared knowledge, unlike secrecy, cultivates informed consent. It enables residents to challenge intrusive installations, or to demand that authorities justify their presence. The implication is clear: accountability spreads outward when information flows inward.

Yet vigilance brings its own tension. Citizens may fatigue under the weight of continuous oversight. Institutions may become defensive, interpreting scrutiny as hostility. Platforms may flood users with disclosure notices, overwhelming them into indifference. The risk is that accountability becomes performative—a flurry of documents, dashboards, and public statements masking practices that remain opaque. The challenge, then, is not simply maintaining vigilance but doing so meaningfully, without diluting its force.

That challenge leads us toward the unresolved question at the heart of proactive accountability: how do we sustain ethical discipline when technology outpaces our collective attention? The answer remains open. A society can choose structures that measure, disclose, and correct. Institutions can choose openness over convenience. Individuals can choose curiosity over resignation. But whether these choices align, consistently and at scale, is uncertain. The next decade will test how committed we truly are to the ledger we claim to keep.

The Next Chapter

On 6 June 2013, readers of *The Guardian* in London opened the paper to discover that a young contractor named Edward Snowden had revealed extensive surveillance programmes operated by the United States' National Security Agency. Within days, the disclosures ricocheted through parliaments, newsrooms, and dining rooms across continents. Emergency debates were convened in Westminster; experts argued over encryption on late-night television; governments issued carefully worded denials and partial admissions. And yet, as the shock settled into habit, most of those same readers continued to accept new terms and conditions, download new apps, and feed new systems with data that would have astonished intelligence agencies a generation earlier. That choice is never neutral.

The Snowden moment marked a cultural threshold. It stripped away the comfort of ignorance and made it harder to treat digital surveillance as a distant rumour. People knew, with dates and documents, that a global infrastructure of watching and recording existed not just for criminals or extremists but for everyone caught in its vast dragnet. Yet the social contract that governed this infrastructure remained largely implicit. No major referendum was held on whether such systems should exist. No global assembly convened to redraw the boundaries between secrecy and exposure. The line shifted, silently.

This subchapter is written in that afterglow. A decade on, with new forms of hyper-transparency woven into work, intimacy, and governance, the question is no longer whether surveillance happens but how we, as citizens, professionals, and neighbours, respond to it. The next chapter is not merely chronological; it is moral. It asks what we are prepared to normalise and what we are willing to resist. Above all, it asks whether we see privacy as an awkward relic or as a living condition for freedom.

To understand what is at stake, begin not with institutions but with a familiar scene. A parent sits at a kitchen table late at night, hovering over the settings on their child's first smartphone. Location tracking: on or off? Photo backup: automatic or manual? Social media: private account or public profile? None of these choices existed for previous generations at that age. Now they are routine. Yet behind each toggle lies an unspoken curriculum about autonomy, vulnerability, and trust. When the parent allows a messaging app to scan the address book "to help you find friends", they are making a decision not only for their child but for every contact listed there. Casual settings, shared consequences.

Here the motif of the line returns. Each small configuration draws a line in the sand: who may see what, under which conditions, and for how long. The cumulative effect of millions of such lines becomes culture. When we default to "share", we push the line outward; when we default to "ask first", we pull it back. The next chapter of hyper-transparency will be written less by a single global treaty than by these ordinary acts of drawing and redrawing boundaries.

Major legal efforts show how those individual lines can be backed by collective resolve. The European Union's General Data Protection Regulation (GDPR), which came into force in

May 2018, did more than introduce new compliance forms in Brussels. It codified a principle that individuals ought to know who processes their data, for what purpose, and with which safeguards. It required organisations to explain, in accessible language, how information would be used. At its best, GDPR embodies the idea that privacy rights are not granted at the whim of companies but recognised as pre-existing claims grounded in dignity.

Yet GDPR also exposes a limitation. Many users now confront longer pop-ups, more consent banners, and denser privacy notices than before. Some click "accept all" simply to move on with their tasks. The form of accountability has improved; the substance of informed choice remains uncertain. This tension reminds us that no regulation can, by itself, make a disengaged public suddenly attentive. The law can set minimum standards for protection; only culture can sustain active scrutiny. The next chapter demands both.

Alongside law, we see technical counter-movements which show how design choices can rotate the system towards privacy rather than away from it. The Signal Foundation, established in California in 2018, offers one example. By building an encrypted messaging service where metadata is minimised and no advertising business model exists, it demonstrates that large-scale communication need not depend on behavioural profiling. Users cannot buy premium visibility or targeting. In an environment accustomed to extraction, this is a radical design decision. It signals that alternative futures are not abstract manifestos but functioning software that millions use every day.

Still, encrypted messaging is not a universal solution. A secure channel can protect dissidents and journalists; it can also assist organised crime. A system that retains minimal logs protects activists from retaliation; it can also frustrate legitimate investigations. The same cryptographic strength that preserves one person's safety may impede another's search for justice. Recognising this does not weaken the case for strong encryption; it forces us to consider the broader ecology of safeguards, oversight, and due process. The line we draw around secrecy must be thick enough to protect the vulnerable yet porous enough to accommodate public interest in specific, constrained circumstances.

The challenge grows sharper as predictive systems mature. Employers run background checks that trawl through social media posts; landlords examine credit scores generated from behavioural traces; border agencies assess risk profiles using opaque algorithms. In such contexts, privacy is no longer only about who reads our messages but about who labels us and on what basis. Here, transparency must apply not only to individuals but to institutions. What data did they use? How accurate is the model? Who audits its outcomes? The next chapter in hyper-transparency will turn, at least in part, on whether we demand visibility into the systems that judge us.

Historical experience warns what happens when we do not. The United States' USA PATRIOT Act of 2001, passed swiftly after the September attacks, greatly expanded surveillance powers with limited debate. Many provisions were justified as temporary, emergency measures; several persisted for years. In each renewal cycle, legislators were reminded of the same fear: what if rolling back powers exposed the country to avoidable harm? That fear is not irrational. Yet it demonstrates how easily extraordinary measures become ordinary once they root themselves in bureaucratic routines and security narratives. Reversing them later requires not only evidence that they are ineffective but courage to accept residual risk.

Contrast this with episodes where societies chose restraint even under pressure. Following the fall of the Berlin Wall in 1989, Germany confronted the legacy of the Stasi, whose files had mapped relationships and opinions with obsessive detail. Civil society groups demanded access to personal records, not as a form of voyeurism but as a precondition for accountability and healing. The decision to open archives while curbing new forms of mass surveillance reflected a collective judgment: some kinds of knowledge, once amassed, are too dangerous to trust to any state. The line, again, was drawn publicly rather than silently.

The environmental analogy introduced earlier offers a helpful lens. For years, pollution was treated as a regrettable but acceptable by-product of economic growth. Over time, scientific evidence, activist pressure, and visible degradation shifted that framing. Clean air and water are now widely recognised as shared goods that require shared investment and shared restraint. Privacy sits in a similar position today. It has often been treated as a personal preference—something one can trade for convenience or entertainment. Yet the more we understand about data's role in shaping opportunities, reputations, and power, the harder it becomes to pretend that the consequences fall only on the individual who clicks "agree".

If privacy is a common resource, then the next chapter demands stewardship rather than mere self-defence. Stewardship has a particular rhythm. It requires continuous, modest actions rather than a single heroic gesture. A product team that rejects an intrusive feature and documents why performs stewardship. A school that teaches students how to read a privacy policy with scepticism performs stewardship. A journalist who interrogates the data practices behind a popular app, rather than only reviewing its interface, performs stewardship. Each example grounds the abstract language of responsibility in visible practice.

At the same time, we must confront a counter-example that challenges easy optimism: many people, understandably, feel too overwhelmed or exhausted to engage. They may suspect that their efforts are trivial compared to the scale of corporate and state infrastructures around them. They may have more immediate worries—income, housing, health—than the fate of their browsing history. Dismissing this as apathy misses the point. It is precisely why institutional duty cannot be reduced to consumer choice. The next chapter cannot rely on the most informed and energetic among us alone. It must embed protections that work even when individuals are distracted, stressed, or misled.

This brings us to the quiet but decisive motif that has threaded through these pages: the threshold of refusal. Every society has moments when it decides what it will not normalise. Public executions. Child labour. Leaded petrol. These norms did not change overnight, nor did they change by accident. They shifted because enough people refused to accept the previous baseline. Hyper-transparency presents its own set of thresholds. Will we accept ubiquitous facial recognition in schools? Mandatory social media checks for employment? Real-time emotion tracking in workplaces? Each contested deployment marks a point where a community can say "no further" and mean it.

The next chapter, then, is less a destination than a series of tests. When a government proposes a new "smart" policing tool, will citizens ask to see the evidence for its accuracy and fairness? When a platform offers frictionless login through pervasive tracking, will organisations and individuals seek alternatives that respect boundaries? When designers and engineers gather to sketch new products, will someone in the room ask, early and insistently, what secrets people should be allowed to keep? These are not rhetorical questions. They are diagnostic.

Throughout this book, privacy has appeared as shield, currency, burden, and privilege. Here, at the edge of the narrative, it takes on one more role: promise. The promise that every person is more than the sum of their data points. The promise that we are entitled to grow, err, and reimagine ourselves without every misstep frozen on a server. The promise that intimacy still depends on chosen revelation rather than compulsory exhibition. Whether that promise holds will depend less on the ingenuity of future technologies than on the stubbornness of future publics.

The systems that surround you will continue to evolve. Sensors will shrink. Algorithms will deepen. New justifications for data collection will emerge, persuasive and polished. Against that, the question this subchapter leaves you with is disarmingly simple: when you encounter the next request for your information, the next novel form of watching, what line will you draw, and with whom?

About the Author

Kaia Solander is a technology researcher and social observer driven by a curiosity to understand how rapidly evolving digital systems reshape human emotions and rights. Growing up in a region where open discussion of political issues was once discouraged, she developed an appreciation for privacy's power to safeguard personal autonomy. Through field experiences and work in community-focused projects, she has seen first-hand how surveillance can subtly influence individual choices. Writing for a wide range of readers, her approach is informed by a commitment to personal dignity and collective well-being. Kaia draws upon a fascination for the medieval tradition of guarded correspondence, finding parallels in today's encrypted messaging and data-hungry platforms. Above all, she seeks to empower people to ask probing questions about transparency, technology, and how to protect the deeper layers of who we are in an age of precarious openness.

www.ingramcontent.com/pod-product-compliance
Lightning Source LLC
Chambersburg PA
CBHW031337230926
51848CB00002B/276
9789374592076